"Dr. Kenneth Mathews is a superb student of the Holy Scriptures who always teaches the Bible with a view toward its proclamation. In this lively exposition, he shows us that Leviticus, though neglected today in many pulpits, is not only theologically seminal but also eminently preachable. A great contribution to this series!"

**Timothy George**, Dean of Beeson Divinity School, Samford University; Senior Editor, *Christianity Today*

"Ken Mathews is a respected scholar and a faithful expositor. Both of these competencies are reflected in this work on Leviticus. Mathews brings to life the marvelous truths of a book that intimidates and therefore causes far too many to ignore it. This is a welcomed addition to this outstanding series. Read it and be blessed. Use it and bless your people."

**Daniel L. Akin**, President, Southeastern Baptist Theological Seminary, Wake Forest, North Carolina

"An illuminating treatment! Kenneth A. Mathews is among the few scholars who know how to discuss the legal texts of the Old Testament with appreciated aliveness, and that aliveness is vividly evident in his treating of the *holiness* theme in Leviticus. His new commentary illumines the text for preaching the gospel against the backdrop of Old Testament rituals and hopes. An excellent study!"

**James Earl Massey**, Dean Emeritus and Distinguished Professor-at-Large, Anderson University School of Theology

"Dr. Mathews shows something of what Jesus meant when he said of Moses, 'He wrote of me' (John 5:46). He demonstrates that Leviticus is a book that foreshadows the riches of Christ the fulfiller. The preacher will find much help in this commentary for the task of showing that Leviticus is not to be dismissed as dull, legal prescription for ancient Israel, but is arresting, interesting, and relevant to Christian living."

**Graeme Goldsworthy**, Visiting Lecturer in Hermeneutics, Moore Theological College, Sydney, Australia; author of *Preaching the Whole Bible as Christian Scripture* and *Gospel-Centered Hermeneutics*

# LEVITICUS

# PREACHING THE WORD
## Edited by R. Kent Hughes

((( PREACHING *the* WORD )))

# LEVITICUS

## HOLY GOD, HOLY PEOPLE

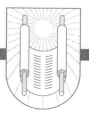

## KENNETH A. MATHEWS

R. Kent Hughes
*Series Editor*

**:: CROSSWAY**®

WHEATON, ILLINOIS

*Leviticus*

Copyright © 2009 by Kenneth A. Mathews

Published by Crossway Books
        1300 Crescent Street
        Wheaton, Illinois 60187

Cover design: Jon McGrath, Simplicated Studio

Cover image: Adam Greene, Illustrator

First printing, ESV edition, 2019

Printed in the United States of America

Hardcover ISBN: 978-1-4335-6574-
ePub ISBN: 978-1-4335-6577-9
PDF ISBN: 978-1-4335-6575-5
Mobipocket ISBN: 978-1-4335-6576-2

---

**Library of Congress Cataloging-in-Publication Data**

Mathews, K. A.
   Leviticus : holy God, holy people / Kenneth A. Mathews; R. Kent Hughes, general editor.
   p. cm.
   Includes bibliographical references and index.
   ISBN-13: 978-1-4335-0628-4 (hc)
   1. Bible. O.T. Leviticus—Commentaries. 2. Bible. O.T. Leviticus— Relation to the New Testament. 3. Bible. N.T.—Relation to Leviticus. 4. Christian life—Biblical teaching. I. Hughes, R. Kent. II. Title.
BS1255.53.M38    009
222'.1307—dc22                  2008051194

---

Crossway is a publishing ministry of Good News Publishers.

| VP | | 34 | 33 | 32 | 31 | 30 | 29 | 28 | 27 | 26 | 25 | 24 |
|----|----|----|----|----|----|----|----|----|----|----|----|----|
| 14 | 13 | 12 | 11 | 10 | 9 | 8 | 7 | 6 | 5 | 4 | 3 | 2 |

*To my pastors*

*C. E. Colton (1959–1975), who modeled humility*
*W. A. Criswell (1980–1989), who exhibited perseverance*
*Charles T. Carter (1989–1997), who displayed wisdom*
*Danny Wood (1997–present), who shows courage*

*You shall love your neighbor as yourself: I am the L<small>ORD</small>.*

LEVITICUS 19:18

# Contents

# A Word to Those Who
# Preach the Word

There are times when I am preaching that I have especially sensed the pleasure of God. I usually become aware of it through the unnatural silence. The ever-present coughing ceases, and the pews stop creaking, bringing an almost physical quiet to the sanctuary—through which my words sail like arrows. I experience a heightened eloquence, so that the cadence and volume of my voice intensify the truth I am preaching.

There is nothing quite like it—the Holy Spirit filling one's sails, the sense of his pleasure, and the awareness that something is happening among one's hearers. This experience is, of course, not unique, for thousands of preachers have similar experiences, even greater ones.

What has happened when this takes place? How do we account for this sense of his smile? The answer for me has come from the ancient rhetorical categories of *logos*, *ethos*, and *pathos*.

The first reason for his smile is the *logos*—in terms of preaching, God's Word. This means that as we stand before God's people to proclaim his Word, we have done our homework. We have exegeted the passage, mined the significance of its words in their context, and applied sound hermeneutical principles in interpreting the text so that we understand what its words meant to its hearers. And it means that we have labored long until we can express in a sentence what the theme of the text is—so that our outline springs from the text. Then our preparation will be such that as we preach, we will not be preaching our own thoughts about God's Word, but God's actual Word, his *logos*. This is fundamental to pleasing him in preaching.

The second element in knowing God's smile in preaching is *ethos*—what you are as a person. There is a danger endemic to preaching, which is having your hands and heart cauterized by holy things. Phillips Brooks illustrated it by the analogy of a train conductor who comes to believe that he has been to the places he announces because of his long and loud heralding of them. And that is why Brooks insisted that preaching must be "the bringing of truth through personality." Though we can never *perfectly* embody the truth we preach, we must be subject to it, long for it, and make it as much a part of our ethos as possible. As the Puritan William Ames said, "Next to the Scriptures, nothing makes a sermon more to pierce, than when it comes out of the inward affection of the heart without any affectation." When a preacher's *ethos* backs up his *logos*, there will be the pleasure of God.

Last, there is *pathos*—personal passion and conviction. David Hume, the Scottish philosopher and skeptic, was once challenged as he was seen going to hear George Whitefield preach: "I thought you do not believe in the gospel." Hume replied, "I don't, but *he does*." Just so! When a preacher believes what he preaches, there will be passion. And this belief and requisite passion will know the smile of God.

The pleasure of God is a matter of *logos* (the Word), *ethos* (what you are), and *pathos* (your passion). As you *preach the Word* may you experience his smile—the Holy Spirit in your sails!

R. Kent Hughes
Wheaton, Illinois

# Preface and Acknowledgments

I owe a debt of gratitude to Dr. R. Kent Hughes, general editor of the Preaching the Word series, for the invitation to contribute this volume. It is a reflection of Dr. Hughes's ministry as pastor-scholar that he asked a divinity school professor to write sermons on the book of Leviticus. Old Testament scholars are apt to fragment the Bible, treating the Old Testament as an independent witness unrelated to the message of the New Testament's gospel. Pastors know instinctively that this is wrongheaded. Through the experience of preaching week in and week out, they recognize the holistic witness of the Old and New Testaments to Jesus as Lord and Savior.

Yet, accepting that the Old Testament is interpreted and presented as Christian Scripture does not come easily. What precisely is the relationship between the Testaments has been a long-standing challenge in the history of the church. The polarity in approach to the challenge is telling. The pendulum swings in the direction of description instead of proclamation when the Hebrew Scriptures are considered solely the history of the development of Israel's religion. This is the sin of the modern interpreter. Jesus becomes an add-on, much like updating a computer system by adding a memory card. The opposite view formerly dominated the church, a sin of excess. It read in every verse some hidden allusion to Jesus, ignoring the unique witness of the Old Testament Scriptures. The unintended consequence was relegating them to the old folks' home, making them entertainingly antiquarian and effectively obsolete for Christians. The challenge for me was to navigate between these interpretive Scylla and Charybdis when preaching the less than popular book of Leviticus.

I say less than popular because clergy in general, and certainly the laity, aren't sure what to do with the Old Testament, especially books like Leviticus. One clergyman in a mainline denominational body bemoaned with regard to Leviticus the "simplistic and proof-texting approach to the Bible" evidenced by many who hope to "explain away" Leviticus's teaching. He remarks, "Then I realised what the problem might be. The book of Leviticus only appears once in the Revised Common Lectionary [an ecumenical lectionary], and then only a short truncated reading from Chapter 19 so they can refer to verse 18 ["love your neighbor as yourself"]. You see, Leviticus has never been read in their congregations let alone preached. No wonder they can't fit their Old Testament together!"[1] Lest we think evangelicals do a superior job, one of our leading New Testament scholars who also is a pastor comments on the paucity of whole-Bible preaching when he says, "Our pastors turn into moralists rather like Dear Abby who give advice on how to live a happy life week after week."[2] If it is not moralizing of the Old Testament, some pulpits are satisfied with an allegorizing through "free association" of words or a descriptive history of Israel's religion that is then abandoned for the "real story" of the New Testament.

This problem is compounded by the literary nature of Leviticus. It is prejudged as a catalog of laws when in fact it is a narrative, part of an extensive story that spans creation in Genesis to the final message of Moses to the people of God in the book of Deuteronomy. There are, of course, embedded in the story line of Leviticus many laws regarding the proper relationship between the Lord and his redeemed people. The word *laws*, however, brings to mind the modern concept of lawmaking and law-observing that is misleading. This bridge too must be crossed. Another false assumption about Leviticus is that the book is primarily for preachers and ministers, not for laypeople. Actually, little is specifically addressed to the clergy (chapters 21–22), with the majority intended for the people of Israel.

I find, however, that despite these challenges, parishioners have an appreciation for the book of Leviticus when the minister gives them a chance. The problem might reside more with preachers than with laypeople's refusal to grasp the theological significance of the book for their Christian lives. Christians read the laws with spiritual sensitivity that transcends theological training. When they read books like Leviticus, their Christian intuition tells them they should not imitate everything found in the laws. The most obvious is the sacrificial regulations. On the other hand, when they read the laws, they "hear" the voice of God (John 10:27) and know with the same measure of conviction that there is something to be gained. How the continuity and discontinuity between the Old Testament life of Israel and the New Testament Christian's experience works out exactly is what discourages clergy and laity.

My approach to the problem of preaching Leviticus as Christian Scripture is acknowledging what the Lord implied (Luke 24:27, 44; cf. John 1:45; Acts 26:22; 28:23) and what the history of the church has explained. What holds the Bible together is the common proposition "Thus says the LORD." It is a coherent proclamation declared by God's prophets and apostles that contains the same essential theological message. Jesus Christ is the core, and from his gospel emanates the whole of the Bible's proclamation—the Old Testament anticipates him, and the New Testament culminates in him. You as the reader must judge if the sermons in this book honor the individuality of Leviticus's testimony *and* its role in the chorus of testimonies resounding in the whole of the Bible.

I was aided in writing this book by others. Ted Griffin, senior editor at Crossway Books, and others on the able staff there were a delight to work with and made improvements in the manuscript. I acknowledge with appreciation the encouragement of my colleagues at Beeson Divinity School who considered the task an important one. Also, I thank my students in several doctor of ministry seminars who agreed with me that "if a person can preach from Leviticus effectively, a person can preach from anywhere in the Bible!" Also, because this book is dedicated to the pastors who have been my chief spiritual shepherds, I want to acknowledge the one who represents the whole —my home pastor, Dr. C. E. Colton, former pastor of Royal Haven Baptist Church, Dallas, Texas. It was my blessing to have had a pastor who modeled for me the two most important features of a pastor. He was a compassionate spiritual guide and a consistent biblical preacher. Finally, I want to acknowledge the two most important persons in my life who have contributed largely to my life as a minister—my mother, Margaret Mathews, who at ninety years of age is still going strong as a Bible teacher in the church of my youth, and my wife, Dea Grayce Mathews, who has modeled for me the spiritual gifts of encouragement and sacrificial love.

Kenneth A. Mathews
January 20, 2009

# 1

# Hearing from God before Seeing God

## LEVITICUS 1:1

GOD HAS SPOKEN that we might believe, and that believing we might see.

Our image-driven culture in the West operates as the Chinese proverb recommends: "Hearing about something a hundred times is not as good as seeing it once."[1] We often say, "I'll believe it when I see it." We typically give priority to seeing over hearing. Home video cameras and surveillance cameras have caught events serendipitously and broadcasted them as part of our "reality" culture. Perhaps we are caught off guard by the Bible's picture of God who speaks before he shows himself. At creation God spoke the worlds into existence, and at Sinai the Lord created the nation Israel by his commanding word (Genesis 1; Exodus 20). The New Testament tells us that faith comes by hearing, and this hearing fosters belief in those things not seen (Romans 10:14–17; Hebrews 11:1). Jesus commended those who had heard and believed in his resurrection, though they had not seen him. "Jesus said to [Thomas], 'Have you believed because you have seen me? Blessed are those who have not seen and yet have believed'" (John 20:29).

## When God Speaks

Leviticus begins in the same manner, giving priority to the word of the Lord (1:1). The book continues the prior account in Exodus 40:34, 35 that describes the completion of the Tent of Meeting at Mount Sinai. Leviticus begins with God summoning Moses to hear his word spoken "from the tent of meeting."[2] What the Lord created at Sinai was a nation, formed by a covenant-relationship of trust, and he manufactured a home in their midst for his dwelling-place—that is, "the tent of meeting." In a word he established a relationship with the slaves who had been incarcerated in Egypt. This relationship was based on the redemption he achieved on their behalf by the blood of the Passover lamb. Salvation came before relationship. At the Red Sea the Lord liberated his people from Egypt's armies.

"The tent of meeting" was a portable tent. It was the transient epicenter of the world in the eyes of Israel. A movable ground zero, so to speak, so that the focus of Israel's attention was always directed toward the tabernacle that was at the center of their lives wherever they moved about. American life once made the fireplace or hearth the vital center of family life where meals were prepared and where the family enjoyed its light and warmth. Now living areas in our homes have the entertainment center as the focal point. The hub of ancient Israel's national life was the tabernacle, the visual reminder of God's presence. It was the vital center of Israel's experience and identity.

Before the people departed for their promised homeland in Palestine (ancient Canaan), the Lord spoke from the tent. The book of Leviticus is essentially the message that God spoke to his people at that time in preparation for their departure. The teaching of Leviticus was both revelatory and regulatory.[3] This message revealed more about their God and also regulated the relationship that he had established with them at the exodus. Repeatedly in Leviticus we are told that the Lord "spoke to [Moses]" (1:1).[4] Moses was the mediator of God's word to his people. Unlike any other person, the Lord met with Moses: "With [Moses] I speak mouth to mouth, clearly, and not in riddles, and he beholds the form of the LORD" (Numbers 12:8). At Sinai the mount was enveloped by a cloud that was identified as "the glory of the LORD" from which the Lord spoke to Moses. The language that begins the book is an exact echo of God's revelation to Moses at Sinai in Exodus 24:16: "The glory of the LORD dwelt on Mount Sinai, and the cloud covered it six days. And on the seventh day *he called to Moses* out of the midst of the cloud." Moses actually entered into the cloud on top of the mountain and remained there for forty days and nights (Exodus 24:18).

Although the people saw "the glory of the LORD," it was not a cloud of benevolent revelation for them: "Now the appearance of the glory of the LORD was like a devouring fire on the top of the mountain in the sight of the people of Israel" (Exodus 24:17). In fear they distanced themselves from the mountain (Exodus 24:17, 18). In the book of Leviticus we discover that the people, however, gladly saw "the glory of the LORD" after the priests prepared the way by instituting the first sacrifices in the tabernacle: "And Moses and Aaron went into the tent of meeting, and when they came out they blessed the people, and the glory of the LORD *appeared* to all the people. And fire came out from before the LORD and consumed the burnt offering and the pieces of fat on the altar, and when all the people *saw* it, they shouted and fell on their faces" (9:23, 24).

God has spoken that we might believe, and that believing we might see.

*From the mountain.* The Lord delivered the covenant (Exodus 20—24), instructions for building the tabernacle (Exodus 25—40), and the regulations found in the book of Leviticus at Sinai. The opening words of Leviticus assume the Sinai location, and the book concludes with a special mention of "Mount Sinai" (27:34). The people resided on the mountain for about a year and a half (cf. Exodus 19:1, 2; Numbers 10:11). During this period the Lord provided the regulations for worship and holy living in Leviticus across a month's time (Exodus 40:17; Numbers 1:1). The importance of "Sinai" for the setting of Leviticus shows the strategic magnitude of the revelation that God gave regarding worship and holy living. It was the site of revelation, promise, and command. It was the first place where Moses encountered the Lord (Exodus 3:1–4; Acts 7:30) and the place where the Lord gave Israel the two tablets of the Ten Commandments (Exodus 31:18). Jesus' Sermon on the Mount (Matthew 5—7) had parallel significance for Christians. It was the place of revelation. Jesus painted the profile of righteous citizenship for kingdom citizens. Moreover, the transfiguration of Jesus occurred on a mountain (Matthew 17:1–8). And a cloud too rested over Jesus and his disciples from which the Father spoke. Jesus' face and garments radiated the glowing majesty of God. Jesus as the Son of God embodied the glory of the Lord as truly God (2 Peter 1:16–18).

Israel associated "Sinai" with the majesty of God whose presence shook the earth and whose voice was like thunder (Exodus 19:16–19; 20:18–21; Deuteronomy 4:11, 12). The smoke and fire of God's appearance at the mountain forever marked the people's vision of God's blazing glory (Psalm 104:32; Habakkuk 3:6). Moses himself was utterly petrified with fear (Acts 7:32; Hebrews 12:21). But we who know the Lord Jesus have not come to Mount Sinai with trembling. The writer to the Hebrews declares that we who know Christ have come to the heavenly Mount Zion, the heavenly abode of all who have faith in the Lord (Hebrews 12:18–24). We have no fear but rather confidence in the eternal destiny to which our pilgrimage here on earth will lead. This heavenly citizenship was accomplished through the shed blood of our Lord Jesus Christ.

*From the tent.* Although the Lord was remembered for his revelation at the mountain, the people could not remain at the mount if they were to receive God's provision of the promised land. The mountain was immovable. There were no more "Sinai's" along the desert trek. The Lord therefore furnished a portable "Sinai," the tabernacle shrine where God might reside among his people wherever he might lead them. We are familiar with the advantages of portability in our high-tech society. For example, the popular computer-based iPod enables a person to carry on the small digital device up to 5,000 musical songs. Whenever the cloud that hovered above the tabernacle moved, the people knew to set off on another stage of their journey. The regulations of Leviticus fit between the two descriptions of the movements of the tabernacle in Exodus 40:36–38 and Numbers 9:15–23. Those two passages are like bookends that highlight the portability of the tabernacle but also reinforce the importance of God's presence among his people. They were not to take one step apart from the presence of God. Moses met with God at the tent and there received the assurance of God's word and presence.

That the Lord's revelation to Moses was as authentic at the tent as it had been at Mount Sinai was shown in two ways. First, there was a correspondence between the three divisions of the tent and the three circles of holiness that ascended to the summit of the mountain.[5] The tent consisted of two rooms, separated by a curtain. The inner room of the tent was known as "the Most Holy," and the outer room was simply "the Holy Place" (Exodus 26:33). The third division was the courtyard that encircled the tent (Exodus 27:9). Correspondingly, at the peak of the mountain, as in the Most Holy Place, the Lord spoke, and no one could approach God at the summit except Moses. In the same way, only the high priest could enter into the Most Holy Place (Exodus 19:20; 25:22; Numbers 7:89). Below the peak was the cloud to which Moses and the elders of Israel ascended. This corresponds to the Holy Place, the room that the priests could enter to assist the high priest in his duties (Exodus 20:21; 24:1, 2, 15, 16). Last was "the foot of the mountain" where the people stood (Exodus 19:17; Deuteronomy 4:11). Here was the equivalent to the courtyard where the laity could enter for sacrifice and worship (Leviticus 1:3; 8:3).

Second, the visage of Moses after speaking with God recalled his sojourn on the mountain. Whenever Moses entered into the presence of the Lord, his face glowed brightly as it had initially upon his descent from the mountain. His face reflected the effulgent glory of the Lord (Exodus 34:29–35). The significance of the opening words of Leviticus is that God continued to speak, although the forty days of revelation at the mount would come to an end.[6] The Lord continued to provide for his people regardless of their proximity to the mountain. By this perpetual presence among his people, the Lord provided for closeness between him and Israel. This continuous presence of the tabernacle assured Israel uninterrupted provision and protection.

God has made the same provision for us as Christians but in a much more personal way. The Apostle John drew on the imagery of the tent when he declared, "[T]he Word became flesh and dwelt among us, and we have seen his glory, glory as of the only Son from the Father, full of grace and truth" (John 1:14). The term "dwelt" translates the Greek term (*skenoō*), which is related to the word "tent" (*skene*) in our passage. Our Lord Jesus Christ became flesh—the incarnate God—who made his tent among us. By this habitation the Lord exhibited the glory of God. Whereas in the past God revealed himself by means of dreams, visions, and the prophets, he now has shown himself uniquely through the incarnation of his Son. Jesus is the very expression of God himself—fully God and fully human (Hebrews 1:1–4). There is no option for Christians to include other religious figures on the same stage as the Lord Jesus. It cannot be "Jesus and Caesar" or "Jesus and Mohammad."[7] By becoming a human being, our Lord Jesus assured us as human beings of God's salvation for all who will hear and believe the gospel.

## Through His Mediator

*His servant Moses.* If the book of Leviticus teaches us anything, it is that the Lord God demands that only qualified persons can commune with him. He is the awesome holy God who is unlike any other. It was long recognized that a go-between was necessary for men and women to relate to the Lord (Job 9:32, 33). It was at the risk of death that someone transgressed the sacred space that God inhabits, unless preparatory steps were taken to become fit to meet with God (Exodus 19:12–14). God permitted Moses to speak with him "face to face" (Exodus 33:11), yet elsewhere we learn that God prohibited Moses from seeing God's face: "you cannot see my face, for man shall not see me and live" (Exodus 33:20; cf. John 1:18). The descriptive language that God met with Moses "face to face" must mean that the Lord's presence was with him. Moses could not look upon the essence of God by viewing his face; he could only see his back and survive (Exodus 33:23). Yet, by his gracious mercies God made it possible for the people to know him despite their sinful condition as human beings.

The chief mediator or safeguard between the Lord and the people was Moses, who was the mouth of God. Moses enjoyed a special relationship with God. Initially, the Lord made himself available to Moses at any time from a special tent outside the camp. Progressively, Moses' access to God became limited once the tabernacle structure was built. Moses actually entered the cloud on Mount Sinai (Exodus 24:18), but when the Lord took up residence in the Tent of Meeting, the cloud so filled the tent that Moses could not enter (Exodus 40:35). He received the word of the Lord while standing *outside* the tent. It was from this position that the Lord gave to Moses the beginning revelation and regulations of the book of Leviticus (Leviticus 1:1). Later, at the induction of Aaron and his sons, Moses' role became a transitional link to the established order of the Aaronic priests who alone made intercessory sacrifices on behalf of the people (Leviticus 9:23). Especially, the ritual on the Day of Atonement restricted entrance to the Most Holy Place to the high priest alone who was an exclusive descendant of Aaron (Leviticus 16:11–14).

*His Son Jesus.* Jesus was "the second Moses," who delivered the word of the Lord to God's people. Despite Moses' great stature as the quintessential prophet (Deuteronomy 34:10), he was not able to mediate the glory of the Lord perfectly. He failed the Lord through angry disobedience and was prohibited from leading the people into the promised land (Numbers 20:12). Jesus exceeded even the great prophet Moses. Although Moses was a loyal *servant*, Christ was a faithful *son* (Hebrews 3:3–6). The divine son, Jesus, is the very image of God, fully divine and fully human (2 Corinthians 4:4; Colossians 1:15; Hebrews 1:1–3). He is the complete and perfect mediator (1 Timothy 2:5). Jesus fully revealed the Father (John 1:18; 6:46; 14:9). The radiant glory with which Moses' face shone was temporary, but those who gaze upon him will experience the permanent transforming power of Christ's glory (2 Corinthians 3:12–18). Those of us in the household of faith no longer stand outside the tent looking from afar; we are brought close to God through the sacrificial death of our Lord Jesus Christ. He performed flawlessly the vicarious death that removes our sin and reconciles us to God (Hebrews 7:27; 9:26).

## God Reveals His Glory

*From the tent.* The initial revelation that God gave Moses in Leviticus pertained to the steps necessary for Israel to receive the revelation of God's glory. The Lord had provided the tabernacle, but now there was the need for the proper features of worship. Leviticus spells out the five sacrifices that God ordained for worship, including atonement for their sin (Leviticus 1—7). Additionally, the Lord directed Moses to carry out the ordination of the priests who were to function at the altar where the sacrifices were carried out (Leviticus 8). After all had been revealed regarding the means of maintaining the relationship between the Lord and his people, the first sacrifices were performed by the newly consecrated priests, Aaron and his sons. Aaron carried out the animal sacrifices for his own sins and then offered up the sacrifices for the sins

of the people (Leviticus 9). It was only after the proper place, persons, and offerings occurred that the Lord showed his approval of the worship offered by
the people. By an amazing pyrotechnic display, God confirmed his presence
and pleasure:

> And Moses and Aaron went into the tent of meeting, and when they came
> out they blessed the people, and the glory of the Lord appeared to all the
> people. And fire came out from before the Lord and consumed the burnt
> offering and the pieces of fat on the altar, and when all the people saw it,
> they shouted and fell on their faces. (Leviticus 9:23, 24)

This blazing fire came from *within* the tent, presumably from the ark of
the covenant in the Most Holy Place (Exodus 40:21). It was a continuation
of God's presence demonstrated at Sinai where "the glory of the Lord" was
previously seen as "a devouring fire" (Exodus 24:17). The implication of the
passage is that the fire on the altar became a perpetual flame fed constantly
by the priests each morning and evening (Leviticus 6:12, 13). The prior seven
days of ordination sacrifices ensured that the altar maintained a constant smoldering fire from the daily sacrifices. But on the eighth day in a flash the whole
of the offerings were instantaneously burned up. By this the Lord approved of
the intercession of Aaron, and the people responded gladly that by means of
the tabernacle structure, the animal offerings, and the ministry of Aaron, the
Lord had indeed visited his people as he had promised.

*In the Lord Jesus.* At the incarnational appearance of our Lord Jesus
Christ, the glory of the Lord was found exclusively in him. There is no other
means by which we can behold the glory of the Lord. We have all sinned and
thus failed to live in accord with the majestic glory of God (Romans 3:23).
We must hear and receive the gospel, and once received we behold "the glory
of God in the face of Jesus Christ" (2 Corinthians 4:6; cf. 2 Corinthians 3:18;
2 Thessalonians 2:14). The enabling presence of the Lord in the life of Israel
led them to their reward in the promised land by the radiant glory of the cloud.
By the presence of the Lord in the life of the believer and the church, we too
will persevere in the knowledge and hope of our resurrected Savior, the Lord
Jesus Christ, who has called us for greater destiny—the eternal glory that is
ours at his coming (Colossians 3:4; 2 Peter 1:3).

Hear, receive, obey, and see with the eyes of faith the glory of our Lord
Jesus Christ. God has spoken that we might believe, and that believing we
might see.

# 2

# Commitment

LEVITICUS 1:2–17

THE WOMEN'S MAGAZINE *COMMITMENT* boasts that it is the number one magazine for women on the Internet. Although commitment is a valued goal in our society, it is rarely exhibited when we consider America's popular culture. Superheroes regularly fail to maintain their commitments to spouse and children. Sports figures typically renegotiate inked contracts. Politicians renege on campaign promises. Media outlets twist the facts. Perceived friends often betray confidences. People in our times are starving for the security of a loyal person, a person in whom they can put their trust (cf. Psalm 41:9; 109:5; Proverbs 17:9). What we don't find in others, we find in the Lord Jesus Christ. In turn he demands that his people commit themselves wholeheartedly to him and to one another in Christian love. We don't need to be afraid to surrender our life to the Lord. We can warmly embrace this obligation, for the Lord is worthy of such dedication. This act of supreme loyalty is depicted in the first offering called for, the whole burnt offering.

Worship always requires commitment. We cannot escape this fundamental feature of authentic worship. Commitment as the beginning place is reflected in the arrangement of the five sacrifices called for in Leviticus 1—7. The five sacrifices can be classified according to their motivation and necessity. The beginning three sacrifices are voluntary: the burnt offering, the grain offering, and the peace offering (chapters 1—3). The final two are required: the sin offering and the guilt offering (chapters 4, 5). The first offering is the burnt offering (chapter 1). As a voluntary offering, its presentation to the Lord by worshipers reflects their willing spirit to acknowledge the lordship of their God. Since the burnt offering was totally burned up on the altar (except the skin, which belonged to the priest, Leviticus 7:8), the layperson did not benefit from the sacrifice. It is an expression of complete surrender to the Lord, an act of total devotion. There was no holding back, no stingy parceling out of favors. It was a costly sacrifice. Worship begins with a devoted heart toward God. On your own accord you part with your possessions and disregard personal ambitions. The first divine word, then, from the tent was a call for complete submission to the Lord who accepted nothing less from those who loved him. The question that the passage asks us to answer is: Have you committed yourself and all that is yours to the Lord? Can we genuinely say, as the Apostle Peter said to Jesus, "See, we have left everything and followed you" (Mark 10:28)?

The Lord required the Israelite worshiper to bring the *proper gift* to the *proper place* and to worship him by the *proper presentation* of the offering. We will discover that the demands made of the ancient Hebrews were perfectly performed on our behalf through Jesus Christ who himself was the proper gift and the proper place and fulfilled the proper presentation of sacrifice for the forgiveness of sin. By his perfect obedience, we as Christians can worship with the perfect assurance that our worship is accepted by the Father.

### The Proper Gift (vv. 2, 10, 14)

"What do you want for Christmas?" is a typical question at the holiday season when we contemplate doing our shopping. Usually the children are the easiest to buy for since they have a ready (and perhaps endless!) list of possibilities. But "what is the proper gift?" is another question we put to ourselves when considering a gift for a friend, an employer, or an aging parent. Should it be personal? Costly? Traditional? For a friend, we may choose a gift in part based on how dear a friend. For an employer we ask, "How long have we worked together and what has been customary in that particular business setting?" For an aging parent, "What is something that she doesn't already have or probably has several times over?" The kind of gift usually reflects the kind of relationship the one giving the gift and the recipient have.

*A costly offering.* The gift that the worshiper offers the Lord requires the same and more important questions of us. What does the Lord require? What is the acceptable gift? The Israelite worshiper in this case had no doubt as to the demands of the Lord because a specific gift was called for. For the burnt offering the proper gift could come from one of two types of offerings—an animal from livestock (v. 2) or a bird (v. 14). Within the first option of domesticated animals, the worshiper could further select either a bull or a male sheep or male goat (vv. 5, 10). Also, there was a selection of birds permitted, either turtledoves or pigeons (v. 14). This variety in animals conveyed that God always required a sacrifice of value from the worshiper, but that the economic value varied based on the ability of the worshiper to give. A poor Israelite had the option of offering an inexpensive bird. The wealthy person gave a costly gift. A person could not worship "on the cheap," as we would say today.

The famed pastor W. A. Criswell told the story of a father and his son who went one Saturday to the local county fair where they splurged on the midway rides, the games, and plenty of cotton candy. The next morning the father and his son attended the Sunday church service, and the father placed a pittance in the offering place as it passed. "What did this teach the lad?" Dr. Criswell rhetorically asked. The sad lesson learned that morning was that the county fair's amusements were more important than the worship of God. King David said it best: "I will not offer burnt offerings to the LORD my God that cost me nothing" (2 Samuel 24:24). Every person should give and should give sacrificially to the Lord's work if there is to be true worship.

If the worshiper offered livestock, the animal had to be "a male without blemish" (vv. 3, 10). The significance of the male beast was more symbolic than the actual value. Practically, the female animal was more valuable since it produced milk and was essential to reproduction. The male, however, was viewed as the symbolically significant animal since it was representative of the whole herd as the chief animal and the most virile. By calling for the male animal, God demanded the best of the worshiper's herd as a token of the worshiper's all. Although the animals and birds varied in value, each creature—whether from cattle, sheep, or fowl—was accepted by the Lord; it was deemed "a pleasing aroma to the LORD" (vv. 9, 13, 17). The poor Israelite's inexpensive bird received the same approval as the costlier bull. God provided a system of offerings that enabled all economic classes to present a gift that the Lord welcomed. What was required was the worshiper's heartfelt devotion.

Giving that is commensurate with a person's economic status is a principle that was commanded for Christians, too (1 Corinthians 16:2; 2 Corinthians 8:12). We give what we have. God does not demand that we give what we do not have. Jesus commended a widow who gave only two coins because she gave all she had (Luke 21:2–4).[1] Can the Lord's church succeed without my gift? Yes, because all has its source in him, and I am dependent on him. The better question to ask ourselves is, can I succeed in Christian living without giving? Erwin W. Lutzer, senior pastor at The Moody Church in Chicago, once commented that the remedy for stinginess and greed is giving all our possessions to the Lord. We no longer own them, and their loss is not a challenge because the Lord is the one who owns and manages our welfare. The money that we present is not counted loss because it's not ours.

*A perfect offering.* "I am easily satisfied with the very best" was one of Winston Churchill's humorous quips. Usually for us as human beings the "best" is whatever gives us personal satisfaction. Divine demand for the best, however, is not exploitation for self-aggrandizement but the only proper demand if worship is to have any meaning at all. As the psalmist declared, it "befits the upright" to praise the Lord (Psalm 33:1; cf. 147:1), and we would add in that vein, it is fitting that we give the Lord our best. Anything short of a sacrificial offering signals that the Lord is not worthy of our all. This is not sincere worship. That the animal had to be unblemished spoke again to the worth of the gift. It had to be pristine in condition and not defective in appearance. A deformed animal had less value and thus was taken as an offense to the Lord (Leviticus 22:25; Malachi 1:8, 9). It would be like giving your child a broken toy at Christmas, although you could afford a new one. A broken toy is a castoff. A flawless animal was the appropriate service rendered to God as an act of total commitment. The same Hebrew term translated "without blemish"[2] describes the Lord's salvation: "His work is *perfect*" (Deuteronomy 32:4). It is also used of the upright whose lives are "blameless" before the Lord: "O LORD, who shall sojourn in your tent? Who shall dwell on your holy hill? He who walks *blamelessly* and does what is right and speaks truth in his heart" (Psalm 15:1, 2).[3] Those who claim to be loyal subjects to the Lord show themselves worthy of that claim when they offer up the best to God.

## The Proper Place (vv. 3, 5)

*At the Tent of Meeting.* The proper offering, if it were to be accepted, had to be presented at the proper place—at the "the entrance of the tent of meeting" (Leviticus 1:3). "The tent of meeting" refers to the worship center, also called "the tabernacle."[4] The tent of meeting was geographically, structurally, and theologically the centerpiece of Israel's tribal life. Geographically, the tent of meeting was in the focal point of the twelve tribal camps, with three tribes encamped at each side of the tent of meeting. Structurally, it consisted of two major parts: a courtyard and a sacred tent that sat inside. The courtyard was enclosed by a linen screen that measured 150 feet long and 75 feet wide. For comparison, the length of the courtyard was half the length of an American football field, measuring from the goal line to the fifty-yard line, and a little less than half the width of a football field. The altar was located near the entry to the courtyard. The courtyard faced east as did the sacred tent, which was situated at the back of the courtyard. So upon entry into the courtyard, the worshiper saw the altar and could see in the background the sacred tent. The symbolic message was plain: to approach God, the Israelite first made a sacrifice at the altar.

Theologically, the tent of meeting was central to Israel's life because it served as the primary symbol of God's presence among his gathered people. Inside the sacred tent there were two rooms. The front room was "the Holy Place" where authorized priests functioned. The back room was "the Most Holy Place" where the ark of the covenant, which represented the Lord God, resided. The sacrifice could not be made at just any place, since the offering must be presented where the Lord inhabited his people. The layperson was permitted to enter the courtyard for the purpose of presenting his gift to the Lord. However, he could not venture any farther. Only the approved priests could enter the sacred tent. In bringing the offering to the tent of meeting, there could be no confusion as to whom the presentation was made. The Lord God of Israel alone was the recipient of the gift—and no other nation's god. The tent of meeting was sacred because of God's presence, for he was (and is) the only true God.

*At the altar.* When the Israelite came into the courtyard, he first viewed the altar that was in the foreground. Next to the tent itself, it was the most dominating structure. The architectural arrangement of the structure conveyed a theological message. Since the altar first came into view upon entrance into the courtyard (Exodus 40:33), it reminded the worshiper that God first required a sacrifice. Altars were common features of worship in ancient times, set either inside enclosed sanctuaries or constructed at open sites. The construction material of Israel's altar was wood from the acacia tree, overlaid with bronze (thus sometimes called "the bronze altar," Exodus 38:30). The altar's dimensions were seven and a half feet square and four and a half feet high.[5] At each corner was constructed a horn that protruded beyond the corner. The horn signified strength (cf. Amos 3:14). The altar was hollow and was transported by means of two poles that fit into four bronze rings on the four corners. The bottom half of the altar consisted of a network of bronze grating (Exodus 27:1–8; 38:1–7).

Since the burnt offering was the most common offering, the altar was often identified as "the altar of burnt offering" (Exodus 30:28). The famous Assyriologist A. Leo Oppenheim commented that Mesopotamian religion was essentially "the care and feeding of the god."[6] The Biblical picture of sacrifice, however, is not the feeding of a god, such as was found among the nations, but a symbolic act of worship by the Israelite. All food and drink offerings were presented on the altar in the courtyard, a distance away from the tent where the Lord symbolically resided (Exodus 40:6). Thus the sacrifices were not presented to God in his residence to feed him.[7]

The sight of the altar produced conflicted emotions in the Israelite worshiper.

The altar signaled *sorrow* by virtue of its identity as the place of death. The burnt offering was the regular daily offering, offered each morning and at twilight (e.g., Exodus 29:39, 42).[8] The animal smoldered on the altar all night (Leviticus 6:9). Yet, the altar was also a place of great *joy*, for sacrifice characterized festivals of celebration (Numbers 10:10). The psalmist understood the altar as the place of meeting with God who was his perpetual joy (Psalm 43:4), and the prophet Isaiah depicted the future day when all nations would come in joy and receive acceptance at the altar of the Lord (Isaiah 56:7). Like the cross of Jesus Christ, the altar had the dual effects of repelling and attracting the worshiper (2 Corinthians 2:16, 17). The altar was a perpetual reminder of human sin but also a provision of divine grace that resulted in the joy of receiving forgiveness (Psalm 32:1, 2).

The cross of our Lord Jesus was a testimony to the *sorrow* produced by our sin and the undeserved suffering Jesus endured for our crimes. Yet, it was also a sign of the *joyful* victory that Jesus achieved on our behalf by paying for our sins, liberating us from guilt and death. But what corresponded with the Jewish altar was not Mount Calvary where Jesus hung on the cross. Rather, the proper place of sacrifice for the Christian is through the sacrificed *body* of Christ who is our spiritual altar (Hebrews 10:5–10; cf. Romans 12:1; Hebrews 13:15). Christians do not have a material, physical altar, but the writer to the Hebrews noted that: "We have an altar from which those who serve the tent have no right to eat" (Hebrews 13:10). This altar, the body of our Lord Jesus Christ, surpassed the tabernacle's altar because Jesus secured eternal spiritual benefits.[9]

## The Proper Presentation (vv. 4–17)

If the gift were to be accepted, it must also be offered in the proper way. Any departure from the prescribed course of action resulted in the rejection of the offering. The Lord required strict observance to show the importance of approaching him for the purpose of worship and for the forgiveness of sin. Proper protocol when receiving a dignitary evidences respect for the person and for the office that person holds. All governments have offices of protocol, including the United States, which advises officials such as the President of the United States, the Vice President, and the Secretary of State on official matters of national and international protocol. Protocol is part of recognizing a person's significance in the life of a community. By fulfilling the proper presentation of the animal offering, the Israelite acknowledged the ruling presence of God. Moreover, the proper procedure symbolized weighty theological teaching that the Israelites learned through the observance of worship. The pictorial nature of the ritual was an ancient PowerPoint presentation, so to speak, that was pedagogical. Symbols can be powerful tools of communication. The US flag, fondly referred to as "Old Glory," is such a symbol, a national symbol that speaks to those who honor it as today's patriots. The US Flag Code of 1924 provides for the proper treatment of the flag. The church too has its symbols of spiritual realities—Christian baptism and the Lord's Supper. The tabernacle and its worship services were an earthly copy of heavenly realities (Hebrews 8:5).

*The worshiper.* In the presentation of the burnt offering, the layperson and the officiating priest each played vital roles. Both were essential to the success of the ritual. Their respective parts in the ritual alternated between layperson and officiating priest. There was a symbiotic harmony between the worshiper and the officiating priest.[10] The choreography of the ritual began at the initiation of the worshiper. The layperson, not the priest, selected the appropriate animal from the permitted species and brought it to the Tent of Meeting. Although we are not certain to what extent women entered the tabernacle courtyard to bring animal sacrifices, we know that the purity rite for the new mother after childbirth requires it (Leviticus 12:6–8). The worshiper placed his hand on the head of the victim, indicating his identification with the animal. By this signal, the animal became a formal substitution for the man (vv. 3, 4).[11] There is no explicit command in our passage for the worshiper to confess his transgressions, although in the rite of the Day of Atonement the high priest confessed the sins of Israel (Leviticus 16:21; also cf. 5:5; 26:40; Numbers 5:5–7). The worshiper slew the animal and carved it up into pieces for their placement on the altar's fires (vv. 5–7).

The term "kill" (*shachat*) is a technical term that describes a ritual slaying of an animal. Precisely how this occurred can only be inferred from the Bible.[12] Later Jewish tradition specified the nature of the act. The animal remained in the same position where the layman laid his hand, and he slit its throat. The tradition was that the animal and the worshiper faced the sacred tent, perhaps symbolizing by this that the animal belonged to the Lord.[13] After slitting the throat and opening up the carcass, the man washed off the feces and filth of the animal's entrails and legs (v. 9). This cleansing of the animal offering was necessary to meet the standard of an untainted animal. The animal then was burned up on the altar. If the offering were an animal from the sheepfold, the same procedure was followed (vv. 11–13). One practical difference between the offering of cattle or sheep was the location of the slaughtering of the animal in relation to the altar in the courtyard. The preparation of the sheep occurred on the "north side of the altar" (v. 11), but when the offering was of cattle the layperson probably slaughtered it in any part of the forecourt. This permitted the more convenient handling of larger animals.[14]

By carrying out this procedure, the Israelite identified closely with the innocent victim. The blood of the animal would have gushed from the neck, splattering the worshiper. The sounds, smells, and blood would have indelibly marked the memory of the Israelite's worship of God. The person's transgressions had cost the life of another creature. How much more disturbing is it for the Christian when we contemplate the ordeal of our Savior whose blood streamed down "the old rugged cross," pooling at the feet of his mother and mourners. George Bennard's third verse in his beloved hymn "The Old Rugged Cross" says, "In that old rugged cross, stained with blood so divine, A wondrous beauty I see, For 'twas on that old cross Jesus suffered and died, To pardon and sanctify me."

*The priest.* At the slaying of the cattle or sheep by the worshiper, the priest caught the blood, presumably in a receptacle, and poured it out at the base of the altar (v. 5). This action symbolized that the animal's life had been forfeited by the worshiper as a costly gift presented to the Lord. The blood did not fall to the ground as if it were of no consequence, but the priest showed by the symbolic act that the blood was devoted to God.[15] After the layperson cut up the beast, the priests placed and arranged its parts on the altar, including the head and fat (v. 8). The text specifically remarks that the whole of the animal was burned up as a gift to the Lord (v. 9). The ritual offering of the sheep or goat (vv. 10–13) involved the same procedure by the priest. However, there was a significant departure from the procedure when a bird was the offering of choice. Since the bird was small, either a dove or young pigeon, the priest carried out the full procedure once the individual had presented the gift to him (vv. 14–17). The officiating priest, having accepted the bird, tore off its head, removed its gullet with its impurities,[16] and burned it upon the altar. The gullet was tossed aside on the east side of the altar in the nearby ash heap. The ash heap consisted of the burned residue from the many animals offered on the altar (esp. the burnt offering, Leviticus 6:10, 11).[17] Specifically, the priest tore open the carcass, but not so as to sever the bird into two parts (cf. Leviticus 5:8). The blood was treated with the same deference as the previous sacrificial gifts. It was drained out (but not thrown, cf. vv. 5, 11) on the side of the altar (v. 15), so that the blood ran down the wall of the raised structure, pooling on the ground. This careful treatment of the blood showed that the life of the victim, whether it was the larger or smaller animal, was precious since life and death were divine prerogatives. The bird represented the guilty person whose life was of incomparable value in God's eyes.

*The purpose of sacrifice.* Only by making the proper presentation did the act of worship achieve its purpose for the Israelite. Ceremony requires an explanation. Otherwise the people who observe it do not understand its meaning. Jesus, for example, explained the spiritual significance of the elements at the Last Supper for his disciples as they ate bread symbolizing his body and drank wine symbolizing his blood (Matthew 26:26–29). Sometimes a symbol or ritual is continued although its meaning has been lost or reinterpreted. In some church traditions the monogram "IHS" (or "IHC") may be prominently displayed by liturgical symbols such as lectern or pulpit hangings, clergy crosses and robes, and commission linens. In antiquity it was wrongly thought to mean "Jesus, the Savior of men," and today many think that it means "In His Service," while others have no idea. The letters IHS are the first three letters of Jesus' name in Greek.

Our passage makes clear the purpose of the ritual: The animal offering was "to make atonement" (v. 4). The word "make atonement" (*kipper*) indicated an act of reconciliation with an aggrieved individual.[18] In this case, the offended party was the Lord, not the worshiper. The worshiper angered God by his sin against the Lord, and the atoning sacrifice pacified the Lord's anger. The English word *atonement* reflects this idea of reconciliation. *Atonement* indicates "at-one-ment." However, we must be clear that the blood of the animal by itself did not merit God's forgiveness.[19] God by his unmerited grace bestowed forgiveness in response to the repentance and obedience of the offender. The ritual shedding of blood was a symbolic gesture of obedience, not an actual transference of value that warranted God's forgiveness.

The writer to the Hebrews made this clear: "For it is impossible for the blood of bulls and goats to take away sins" (Hebrews 10:4). The basis for the taking away of sins is the blood of our Lord Jesus Christ, whose perfect sacrifice alone is adequate to win the forgiveness of sins. James Earl Massey reminds us that "Christ did not come into the world to confirm us in our sin but to save us from our sins" (cf. Matthew 1:21).[20] When we come to the Lord, we must first encounter the blood-smeared altar. For "without the shedding of blood there is no forgiveness of sins" (Hebrews 9:22). The blood of our Lord Jesus Christ has made it possible for us to receive acceptance. There is no bloodless gospel in the Bible. It is not surprising that many people today resist a gospel that has a gruesome cross at its heart. But a gospel without the cross is not good news at all, for without the death of the slain "Lamb of God" (John 1:29; Revelation 5:9–12) there is no forgiveness of sin.

When the person and the officiating priest properly carried out the ritual, the result was "a pleasing aroma to the Lord" (vv. 9, 13, 17).[21] The same expression described the response of God to the grain, peace, and drink offerings (Leviticus 2:2; 3:5; Numbers 15:7).[22] That the priest accepted the sacrifice presented by the individual was the first sign that the person could be accepted by the Lord. However, the expression "pleasing aroma" conveyed the certainty of God's pleasure at the completion of the offering. By this set phrase, the passage indicates that the Lord had fully accepted the offering with approval. When Noah left the ark, he presented burnt offerings that assuaged the anger of God, resulting in the Lord "[smelling] the pleasing aroma" (Genesis 8:21; cf. Ezekiel 20:41). The worshiper could leave the precincts of the tabernacle with the same assurance that the Lord had shown favor toward him and his gift. The expression "pleasing aroma" is a figure of speech and is not to be understood as a literal description of smelling. The picture of a satisfying fragrance may be derived from the practice of adding incense to offerings (e.g., Leviticus 2:1), although that was not specifically stipulated for burnt offerings. Additionally, the tent contained an altar of incense that stood outside the veil of the Most Holy Place, and its smoke symbolized intercessory prayers on behalf of the people (Exodus 30:1–10).

The Greek Old Testament's translation of our phrase is important to us as Christian readers.[23] It translated the Hebrew phrase as "sweet aroma," which is the same language used by the Apostle Paul when describing the atoning sacrifice of Christ: "Christ loved us and gave himself up for us, *a fragrant offering* and sacrifice to God" (Ephesians 5:2). Unlike the animal slain on behalf of the worshiper in Leviticus, the sacrifice offered up by our Lord was wholly voluntary. He "gave *himself* up." That the Father fully accepted the atonement of Jesus was proven by the resurrection of the Lord. We who have entrusted ourselves to Christ by faith can have the same assurance of acceptance with the Father.

Moreover, when the Philippian church sent its monetary support to Paul in prison, he characterized their sacrifice with the same language used of our Lord's death: "*a fragrant offering*, a sacrifice acceptable and pleasing to God" (Philippians 4:18; cf. 2 Corinthians 2:14–16). As Christians we too offer up ourselves when we present our monetary gifts to the Lord as an act of worship. The Bible views such gifts as an indication of our commitment to the Savior. Giving is not incidental to Christian living but a core value in the life of a devoted disciple of Christ. There is no legitimate claim to commitment if there is no costly consecration to God.

# 3

# Thank You, Lord!

LEVITICUS 2:1—3:17

A SECRETARY ONCE TOLD ME that "please" and "thank you" went a long way in her book. Does it go a long way in your book? Have you ever thought that "thank you" goes a long way in God's book? George Whitefield, the famed evangelist and companion of John Wesley, preached a farewell sermon to the passengers of the ship *Whitaker*, anchored near Savannah, Georgia in 1738, entitled "Thankfulness for Mercies Received, a Necessary Duty." After four months of open seas, sailing from England, he characterized their adventure this way: "At God Almighty's word, we have seen 'the stormy wind arise, which hath lifted up the waves thereof. We have been carried up to the Heaven, and down again to the deep, and some of our souls melted away because of the trouble; but I trust we cried earnestly unto the Lord, and he delivered us out of our distress.'" But it was what Whitefield acknowledged about the telling character of human ingratitude that caught my attention: "Numberless marks does man bear in his soul, that he is fallen and estranged from God; but nothing gives a greater proof thereof, than that backwardness, which every one finds within himself, to the duty of praise and thanksgiving."[1] Luke's Gospel recalls the healing of ten lepers by Jesus, but only one returned to give him thanks. The Lord remarked on the ingratitude of the nine; the one who expressed thanksgiving alone received Jesus' confirming grace: "Rise and go your way; your faith has made you well" (Luke 17:19).

The grain and peace offerings were an individual's voluntary offerings of thanksgiving for the Lord's bounty. On either side of the instructions for the grain offering were directives for the meat offerings (the burnt offering) in chapter 1 and the fellowship offering (ESV, "peace offering") in chapter 3.

The grain offering usually accompanied a burnt offering, and baked bread was required for the peace offering with its roasted meat. The grain offerings supplied the bread products that completed the symbolic meal given to God and the shared community meal of the peace offerings. The association of thanksgiving with the bread of a meal was a tradition that Jesus and the church continued. When he fed the multitudes, he offered thanks before parceling out the bread (Matthew 14:19; 15:36), and he did the same for the bread of the Lord's Supper (Matthew 26:26), which we practice to this day. It was the practice of the Apostle Paul (Acts 27:35). The principle of thanksgiving is extended to all things and all circumstances: "And whatever you do, in word or deed, do everything in the name of the Lord Jesus, giving thanks to God the Father through him" (Colossians 3:17; cf. 1 Thessalonians 5:18). The fellowship meal in the church (Acts 2:42; cf. "love feasts," Jude 12) also involved thanksgiving, and this was typical of the practices of the early Church Fathers.

We will learn anew from our passage that worship involves an attitude of thanksgiving to God, praising him for the provisions he has made for us, materially and spiritually. We cannot worship our Creator and Savior if we neglect thanksgiving.

### "Give Us Our Daily Bread" (2:1–16)

The Lord's Prayer recognizes that the ultimate source of our daily sustenance is the Lord God: "Give us . . . our daily bread" (Matthew 6:11). By presenting grain offerings, the individual Israelite expressed recognition and thankfulness for God's grace in providing his everyday blessings. Jesus remarked that disciples should not obsess over acquiring the basic needs in life because the Lord will care for them (Matthew 6:25, 26). In our affluent times we forget that some societies struggle for daily food. The grain offering offered by the Israelites was the simplest and most common offering because everyone, even the poorest of the poor, could present a measure of flour. Flour, for example, was acceptable for sin and guilt offerings by the very poor who could not afford animals or even birds (5:11; 14:21). Bread products, not meat, were the common food on the table for most people. Meat was a delicacy enjoyed by royalty and the wealthy. If enjoyed at all by common families, it was reserved for special occasions.

*Icing on the cake (vv. 1–3).* The worshiper could bring *uncooked* (raw) grain consisting of "fine flour" derived from wheat; oil and frankincense were added. Oil and frankincense symbolized joy and topped off, so to speak, the gift as a happy occasion. Oil had the additional feature of making the flour combustible. Frankincense was a white resin of pleasant fragrance that was highly valued (Matthew 2:11). After the preparation, the individual presented it to the priest at the main altar, and he took a handful as a representative portion to burn up. This memorial portion signified God's portion and served as a reminder to the worshiper of God's gracious provisions. The remainder, identified as "a most holy part" (vv. 3, 10), was the priests' portion. The description "most holy part" meant that only the consecrated priests could eat it and only in the sanctuary, probably near the altar. Grain offerings were the daily staple for the priests as their stipend for their service at the Lord's house.

*Cooking up the batch (vv. 4–10).* If the flour was cooked, the layperson chose the culinary means of cooking, either by oven, griddle, or pan. That no frankincense was required for the baked goods enabled the poor to make their gift without the undue hardship of adding the costly spice. The passage reiterates that the priest received the gift and burned a portion on the altar. That the text says specifically that the layperson brings the bread "to the LORD" (v. 8) was another reminder that the gift was not merely bringing groceries to the preacher but was an act of worship directed first and only to the Lord God. The acceptance of the gift by the priest with its memorial portion burned on the sacred altar symbolized the acceptance of the offering by God. Sometimes we forget that the appeal made in our churches for tithes and offerings is an appeal *for the Lord's work*, not primarily for meeting budgetary items to sustain the programs of our church. If we discover that we do not support our church by giving because we are not confident in the leadership's conscientious use of the funds, we should find a new church where we can give liberally to the ministry of the church. Holding back our offerings until the church staff meets our expectations is a form of holding the church hostage.

*Covenant commitment (vv. 11–13).* Chief among the ingredients for the grain offerings was the required addition of salt. Its presence was not only for flavoring but was a reminder of God's covenant with his people. Salt's quality of permanency indicated the perpetuity of God's commitment to Israel (Numbers 18:19). The same idea describes God's love for King David (2 Chronicles 13:5). This implied that the people too must remain loyal to their Covenant Redeemer. By bringing seasoned offerings in accordance with the Lord's instructions, the people exhibited their obedience to and love for the Lord. The salt reminded the worshiper of the reason for bringing the gift. In the history of Israel's worship the people would carry out the ritual but lose sight of the relationship. Religious rites are proper only if they reflect the authenticity of a relationship with God through our Lord Jesus Christ. The prophets and Jesus scolded those who kept the ceremonial laws but were morally and spiritually corrupt.

This notion of corruption is also addressed by the ingredients of the grain offering. Whatever is presented to the Lord must be pure and whole. The dough could not have yeast or honey.[2] Yeast, known also as leaven, is a fungus that when introduced into a batch of dough provides fermentation and changes the physical properties of the dough. Yeast enables the dense blob of dough to rise into a light loaf, strengthens the bread dough, and provides flavor. Thus it is a foreign agent added to the basic mixture of flour and water that "corrupts" the mixture. Leaven became a symbol for the evil that corrupts the people of God (Mark 8:15; 1 Corinthians 5:8). The prohibition against honey is not explained. Since the context refers to "firstfruits," it was probably the sweet syrup coming from fruit. Bees' honey, no doubt, would have been understood as included. It too could corrupt the dough because of its sweetness that leads to fermentation.[3] Still others believe that since honey was a common feature in pagan offerings to the gods, it could lead to confusion with idolatrous offerings. The grain offerings of the Israelites were different in appearance and taste.

*The first and the best (vv. 12, 14, 15, 16).* Instructions for the grain offerings provided the opportunity to address directives for the firstfruits of the harvest. The "fresh ears" (v. 14) were the first ripened ears (probably from barley), which were roasted and then crushed. The firstfruits were the first and best produce of an Israelite's crops (Exodus 23:19). They belonged to the Lord (Exodus 34:26). It was part of the Feast of Firstfruits (Leviticus 23:9–14) and Feast of Weeks (Leviticus 23:15–21). We have a similar tradition in weddings when the newly-wed couple will be the first of the wedding party and guests to eat the wedding cake. The bride cuts the first piece of cake with the "help" of the groom, and they each feed the other with representative portions. As their first task as husband and wife, this symbolic gesture represents their joining together in covenant unity. By presenting the firstfruits, the Israelites recognized that the Lord had granted them the land and its produce for their enjoyment. The worshiper recounted the great deliverance from Egypt that the Lord gave Israel and the bestowing of the land (Deuteronomy 26:1–11). By offering the firstfruits, the worshiper was returning but a portion of the bounty to the rightful owner of the land, the Lord God. The general principle of firstfruits coincides with the New Testament's teaching to give ourselves and our best to the Lord  (2 Corinthians 8:5; 9:7). Jesus was the firstfruits of the resurrection, and we will join him as the firstfruits of his new creation (1 Corinthians 15:20, 23; James 1:18). All creatures belong to God, but the first and best are those who are born anew through the salvation offered by the word of the Lord.

I remember my father telling of his early married days during the Depression era when finances were especially tight. His refrigerator went on the blink, and he had just enough money to get it fixed—if he postponed writing his weekly tithe check to the church. He decided to give to the church first and hoped that the money for the appliance repair would come from somewhere. The next morning after writing the check to the church, his refrigerator "came back from the dead." It spontaneously went into working order. My point is *not* that paying your tithe first will always result in your car or some household item experiencing miraculous "healing." The point is that my dad made a decision to give God his due, an early gesture in his married life that became the pattern for the sixty-seven years of his marriage. And he bequeathed to me, a youngster at the time, through recounting the story the lesson that God must come first in our lives by showing proper gratitude.

### "Blest Be the Tie That Binds" (3:1–17)

Reverend John Fawcett pastored a small Baptist church in Wainsgate, Yorkshire.[4] When he accepted the call in 1772 to take a prestigious church in London, he preached his farewell sermon. When he was packed and ready to depart his beloved parishioners, the sad good-bye was overwhelming. He reversed his decision on the spot and chose to remain at his Wainsgate church, where he resided until his death and was buried in 1817. The humble minister wrote the words to the now-famous hymn "Blest Be the Tie That Binds." It was published in 1782 and has been tearfully sung by generations of church fellowships. The opening stanza reads:

> Blest be the tie that binds
> Our hearts in Christian love;
> The fellowship of kindred minds
> Is like to that above.

Fawcett penned these words out of his experience but also out of his recognition that Christians enjoy a rich fellowship with the triune God and with fellow saints in a communion of love and devotion. First John 1:3 reads, "[T]hat which we have seen and heard we proclaim also to you, so that you too may have *fellowship* with us; and indeed our fellowship is with the Father and with his Son Jesus Christ." In ancient Israel the fellowship offering, traditionally known as the peace offering, was a voluntary expression of the worshiper's praise for God's deliverance in his life. Whereas the grain offering was thanksgiving for God's bounty generally, the peace offering was usually related to a specific incident of blessing. It was the only offering that both the priests and the worshiper ate, signifying the fellowship of the Israelite and

God (Leviticus 7:31–35). It was a communal meal shared with the worshiper's family and invited guests (Deuteronomy 26:12, 13). The peace offering could be one of three kinds: a thanksgiving offering for answered prayer, a vow offering after a vow has been completed, and a freewill offering that is freely presented without reason other than celebrating the largesse of the Lord (Leviticus 7:11–16). The writer to the Hebrews refers to this practice: "Do not neglect to do good and to *share* what you have, for such sacrifices are pleasing to God" (Hebrews 13:16).[5] Service to the members of the body of Christ is the normal experience of a believer.

*Peace with God (vv. 1–5).* The worshiper could choose the animal that he brought to the Lord, either from the herd or from the flock or a goat (vv. 1, 6, 12). The procedure closely resembled the burnt offering. The worshiper placed his hand on the victim, signifying the transference of his sin to the animal. Afterward the Israelite slew the animal, and the priests retrieved the blood, which they cast against the sides of the altar. The purpose of casting the blood against the altar was to show that the life of the animal belonged to the Lord. Moreover, the worshiper removed the kidneys and liver from the animal's carcass and especially the fat, and the priest burned them up on the altar. By burning up the organs and fat on the altar, the priest indicated that these portions belonged to the Lord exclusively. The fat was important due to its association with the best portion of an animal and its symbolic value indicating the robust power of the animal (Genesis 4:4; 2 Samuel 1:22). The kidneys and the liver also were prized portions since they were vital to sustaining life (Job 16:13; Proverbs 7:23). The kidneys were seen as the seat of the emotions, much like we refer to the heart as the center of feelings (Psalm 73:21). The liver is the largest and heaviest internal organ in the human body; the ancients practiced divination with animal livers, known as hepatomancy. This form of pagan sorcery was prohibited in Israel (Deuteronomy 18:10–12). By giving the liver to the Lord by fire, the Israelite worshiper showed his exclusive commitment to the Lord. He trusted in the word of the Lord as revealed to Moses for his life's direction, not in the world of the magical arts.

The entrails and pieces of the animal were placed by the priest on top of the daily burnt offering, which had already burned and was left smoldering on the altar. That the burnt offering preceded the peace offering conveyed to the worshiper that the basis for his fellowship with God was the atonement and forgiveness of sin that the burnt offering had represented (3:5; cf. 1:9; 6:12). This was anticipatory of the Christian fellowship we enjoy with God and the church; our fellowship is founded on the atoning work of Jesus Christ (Romans 5:1). The heart of Christian fellowship is not a social event at the church where the folks enjoy their coffee and pastries. Christian fellowship is a spiritual dynamic that can only be experienced by those who have been spiritually regenerated. We are enabled to love all people, but the call to Christian love among the brothers and sisters of faith is of a higher order that calls for greater sacrifice (2 Thessalonians 2:13; Philemon 5, 7; Hebrews 13:1; 1 Peter 1:22; 1 John 3:11, 14, 16).

*Fellowship with the Lord (vv. 6–15).* The peace offering also was symbolic of a shared meal with the Lord. Because the priest and the worshiper with his family and guests all partook of the animal's meat, it indicated that God had provided a means to have fellowship with his people. This was the desire of the Lord in forming a relationship with and in redeeming his people. The idea of a shared meal is shown by two aspects of the passage. First, the text repeatedly says that the offering was a "food offering" given to the Lord (vv. 3, 5, 9, 11, 14, 16).[6] This did not mean that the Hebrews believed that the Lord actually consumed the food from the altar. The nations believed that the animal sacrifices and drink libations fed the gods and won their favorable response. The Scriptures show otherwise, for the Israelites recognized that their God transcended earthly and human institutions (1 Kings 8:27; Psalm 50:12, 13). The prophets condemned the false notion that God could be manipulated through food offerings. "Food offering" is a figure of speech, alluding to the fellowship of the worshiper with the Lord in the setting of a shared meal. The importance of a shared meal has always pointed to a covenant loyalty and agreement between two parties. An example is the covenant meal shared by Jacob and his uncle Laban who formed a non-aggression pact (Genesis 31:51–54).

The inauguration of the new covenant was founded upon the shed blood of our Lord Jesus Christ. The symbolic force of the Lord's Supper reflected the new fellowship with the Lord and with one another that a covenant meal represented to his disciples. The language "Take, eat; this is my body" and "Drink of [the cup] . . . for this is my blood of the covenant" (Matthew 26:26–28) meant a spiritual communion with God provided by the very offering of the Lord's body. Jesus postponed the partaking of the Supper with his followers until he had completed the salvation that his sacrifice would bring: "I tell you I will not drink again of this fruit of the vine until that day when I drink it new with you in my Father's kingdom" (Matthew 26:29). The taking of the Lord's Supper in our churches is full of spiritual meaning and proclamation. The Apostle Paul said, "For as often as you eat this bread and drink the cup, you proclaim the Lord's death until he comes" (1 Corinthians 11:26).

*Forever with the Lord (vv. 16, 17).* The prohibitions against consuming the fat and blood were "a statute forever throughout [Israel's] generations" (v. 17). By this declaration the Lord ensured Israel that his desire was to enjoy Israel as his people for all time. He is not fickle like human monarchs or today's politicians; his promises are reliable. The mention of God's intent to maintain this caring relationship is reflected in the expression "in all your dwelling places." This meant that God provided for the migration of the people and eventual arrival in the promised land where they would succeed in establishing a homeland. The fat and blood of their offerings, that is, their worship, would always be devoted solely to the Lord.[7] He was their caretaker, and their worship belonged only to him. The phrase "statute forever" occurs here for the first time in Leviticus. A "statute" describes royal and legal enactments that must be kept. These enactments included laws and customs pertaining to Israel's life in the land, such as the tradition of keeping Passover (Exodus 12:14). Observance of the decrees of the Lord meant a secure and prosperous life in the land (Deuteronomy 30:16).

The fellowship that the Lord provided Israel was eternal in purpose but not eternal in actuality, however. The relationship was broken by the failure of Israel to keep the covenant statutes (Isaiah 43:24). Yet there remained the promise of a new covenant (Jeremiah 31:31), which the Lord established by his own blood so that all who believe might enter into the salvation and fellowship of the Lord forever (1 Corinthians 11:25; Hebrews 9:15). This eternal relationship with God is secured through our Lord Jesus Christ. It cannot ever be jeopardized by our disobedience because we receive the credit of Christ's perfect obedience to the statutes of the Lord.

# 4

# Purging the Soul

## LEVITICUS 4:1—5:13

DO YOU KNOW HOW to avoid the common cold? On average preschool children have nine colds a year and adults seven colds a year. The only way to insure that you don't pick up one of the many cold and flu viruses is to die! Cold viruses, of which there are many kinds, are contracted through hand-to-hand contact with an infected person or touching the surface of an object that has been touched by an infected person, such as the handle of a grocery cart or the coffee cup extended to you by a fast-food server. In other words, catching a cold is inevitable regardless of the care you take to avoid coming into contact with the annoying cold virus. There are preventative steps you can take, including regularly washing your hands—but watch out for the bathroom's door handle!—or staying fit through good nutrition and exercise—but beware of the germs lurking on the treadmill's grip at the gym! We can't see cold viruses, but they are unavoidably enveloping us. And as we might be a victim of a cold virus, we are as likely to be the purveyors of a nasty cold virus.

What can be said about the common cold virus and the human condition is true of the spiritual condition of each one of us. By virtue of our human condition as sinners we are all—each and every one of us—inevitably committing sinful thoughts and making sinful choices. Even if our sin is not premeditated and if we are most fastidious to avoid iniquity, we cannot escape the inevitability of committing sin. The Bible clearly tells us that the human soul stands in need of purging from sin and guilt. The first letter of John observes, "If we say we have not sinned, we make [God] a liar, and his word is not in us" (1 John 1:10). The sacrificial system that is detailed in the book of Leviticus made an accommodation for the unavoidable human condition of sin. The sin offering was God's gracious provision for the guilty person by which his or her sin was purged and by which he or she received divine forgiveness. The corruption of human sin polluted the tent and required a cleansing. The offering should be thought of as an offering of purification. But the sacrifice of an animal only purged the corruption of the outer person, the body, the book of Hebrews tells us (Hebrews 9:13, 14). What was needed to purge the malignancy of the inner person, the soul? We will discover that the Lord has made a sure and eternal means of forgiveness for each one of us through the death of Jesus Christ, whose sinless life made it possible for our iniquities to be purged from our souls.

### "But I Didn't Know!" (4:1, 2)

Ignorance of the law does not absolve a person of guilt for committing an infraction. Perhaps a softhearted parent, teacher, or employer will accept the special plea, "But I didn't know!" But try that with a traffic officer and see how far that gets you. Citizens are expected to conform to the civil law, rather than the law conforming to our behavior. It is our responsibility to know the law and obey it. The sin offering was given to remedy the sins that were committed "unintentionally." The word "unintentionally" can be translated along the lines of "mistake, error, or inadvertence," meaning a misjudgment or misstep. But whether a person broke the covenant law through neglect or ignorance, he was still guilty of transgression (4:22, 27). In order for there to be a lasting relationship between God, who was without sin, and his people, who inherently were sinners, there was the perpetual necessity of a means whereby that great divide could be bridged. It is just as impossible for God to deny his inherent holiness as it is for a human being to escape his inherent sinfulness. The sin offering made it possible for God to remain among his people because there was a gift made that reconciled the offender to God.

How could unintended sins have occurred?[1] Four such situations are listed in 5:1–4 to illustrate ways the common people sometimes failed in their duty. (1) A person failed to appear in court to serve as a witness. (2) A person touched a dead animal. (3) A person touched human uncleanness. Or (4) a person spoke a rash oath. The first and last cases deal with violations against court proceedings, and the middle two examples pertain to transgressions of religious law.[2] In today's world for comparison, an unintended error might be when a person fails to file proper court papers required by law or misjudges when making out a tax return. When it comes to offenses against religious law, the text is speaking of persons who became ritually unfit to worship the Lord.

In the Bible we have one case of violating the cultic law, which can be used as an example for us.

Persons who made a special vow of commitment to the Lord, known as the Nazirite vow, dedicated themselves to the Lord's service. During the time of their dedication, such persons were not to cut their hair, eat or drink anything made from grapes, or become ritually unclean. Samson and Samuel, for example, were lifelong Nazirites.[3] But what would happen to a Nazirite who failed to keep the oath through a mistake or an unavoidable situation? Just such a case is hypothesized in the Bible: Suppose a person died unexpectedly in the presence of the Nazirite person; the vow would be violated because the Nazirite became unclean through proximity. The reasoning behind this custom is theological. Since the Lord God is the God of the living, it would be unfitting for a person especially dedicated to the Lord to touch or be in the presence of the dead. Not all was lost if a Nazirite became unclean because the Law provided a way to remedy the violation, which among other things included the gift of a sin offering (Numbers 6:1–12).

As you can tell, it would be inevitable that the Israelite people would commit sins through no premeditated fault of their own. Nevertheless, according to the standards of holiness set by God, the offender was guilty. What we learn from this passage is the frightful reality that every one of us stands in this guilty state. It is the universal human condition. Apart from God's gracious forgiveness, we are in constant peril of offending God through our sins. We aren't exonerated on the basis of our ignorance or well-meaning efforts. This is because there is an objective standard whereby we are measured, and we always come up short. The insidious power of sin can be summed up in the admonition of the Puritan theologian John Owen: "Be killing sin or it will be killing you."[4] But God did not then and does not now leave us without a means of reconciliation to him. By an animal offering as a symbolic act of substitution, the animal bore the consequence of sin by which the Israelite received forgiveness from the Lord. This innocent animal foreshadowed the death of the Lord Jesus Christ who voluntarily, though without sin, became a sin offering for the guilty (2 Corinthians 5:21).

## Purging for the High Priest (vv. 3–12)

An important aspect of the purification offering was the recognition that some inadvertent sins were more damaging than others. This is because mistakes committed by some persons can have far-reaching repercussions for others, such as we find today when a restaurant or a grocery store sells contaminated food. From time to time we hear news reports about an outbreak of E. coli bacteria. Often this is contracted through eating contaminated food, such as undercooked ground beef, that causes mild to severe symptoms. This bug in the food chain can impact dozens of innocent people, if not more. In a similar way, a sin committed by the high priest symbolically had serious repercussions for others because the priest held the key role of intermediary between God and the people. If the priest failed in his role as mediator through some oversight, the ordinary people also bore the consequences of his sin (v. 3).

*The blameless bull (v. 3).* The ceremonial law therefore required a more stringent purification process for the priest than for the sin of the common person. It called for the priest to present a most costly animal, a bull "without blemish." That the animal must be perfect in its appearance and whole in its health makes sense when we remember that symbolically the animal portrayed a sinless substitute. If the animal were defective, it would hardly do for it to be offered in the place of the flawed offender. This reminds us of the unblemished Lord Jesus whose spiritual credentials were flawless. Jesus "who knew no sin" (2 Corinthians 5:21), that is, did not commit sin, bore the guilt of our sin. Repeatedly the Scriptures point out the innocence of Jesus (e.g., Hebrews 4:15; 1 Peter 2:22; 1 John 3:5). Our blessed Savior was "the righteous [who suffered] for the unrighteous" (1 Peter 3:18).

*The blood inside the tent (vv. 4–7).* In addition to the costly animal, the extent of the priest's sin required special handling of the animal's blood. The priest retrieved some of the blood of the slain animal, probably captured in a vessel, and transported the blood *inside* the sacred tent itself. The high altar was located in the outer court, but the Tent of Meeting housed the two most sacred areas—the Holy Place and the Most Holy Place. This was a dramatic departure from the ritual of the sin offering for the ordinary Israelite person. The blood in that case was smeared on the high altar in the outer courtyard. But by requiring the blood *inside* the tent's Holy Place, the Law indicated that the priest's offense was so penetrating that it was necessary to cleanse the tent itself of sin. In other words, the sin of the priest contaminated the sacred tent as well as the outer altar. Why did the effect of the priest's sin reach beyond the altar to *inside* the tent? Because the priests alone could enter into the tent to carry out the duties of mediation. The average person was not allowed into the tent. The tent represented the very presence of God, and there had to be cleansing for the place where the priests carried out their exclusive duties.

Once the priest had entered the tent, he dipped his finger in the blood and sprinkled it seven times "in front of the veil of the sanctuary" (v. 6). He also smeared some blood on "the horns of the altar of fragrant incense" (v. 7). The altar of incense was located inside the tent and was not to be confused with the larger high altar in the courtyard. Both the number "seven" and the locations of placing the blood in front of the veil and on the altar of incense held special significance. The number "seven" is the number often used in the Bible to indicate perfection and wholeness. By sprinkling seven times, the priest symbolically showed that the removal of the sin was complete and that the tent was restored to its status of holiness. The veil and the altar of incense were closely related because the altar stood in front of the veil. This screen separated the two inner rooms in the tent—the Holy Place from the Most Holy Place. In the first room were the three pieces of sacred furniture—the table of bread, the lampstand, and the altar of incense. This altar was perpetually aflame, burning the soothing odors of incense, the ascending of which symbolized the prayers of God's people before the Lord. The private room, the Most Holy Place, was behind the curtain where the most sacred furniture was stationed. The ark of the covenant was the only furniture in this room. It represented the very presence of God, and its most sacred status restricted anyone from entering with one exception. Only the high priest, and no other priest, and only on one day of the year, the Day of Atonement, could go behind the veil (Leviticus 16). In our passage, by bringing the blood to the precipice of the Most Holy Place, the priest brought the blood as close to God's presence as possible, short of actually going behind the curtain into the Most Holy Place.

*The blood and body outside the tent (vv. 8–12).* Upon completing the ritual inside the tent, the priest exited the tent and returned to the high altar where the animal had been initially slain. There he poured out the remainder of the blood at "the base of the altar of burnt offering" (v. 7), indicating that the life of the animal was sacred and belonged wholly to God. The priest next butchered the beast and carefully separated its fat from the internal organs. The fat plus the kidneys and the lobe of the liver were fully burned up on the altar. Since the animal was offered for human sin, it would be inappropriate for the Israelite to benefit from his sin, such as eating its meat or using its hide for leather goods. The priest should not derive benefit from his own sin. Therefore, the remaining parts of the carcass were removed from the camp altogether to a ceremonially "clean place" (v. 12). This place, known as "the ash heap," was where the parts were cremated. The animal had to be burned up at an officially "clean" location since it was a holy offering presented to the Lord and could not be desecrated in any way.

The order in the steps of the ritual conveys an important message spiritually. Why did the priest start at the high altar where he slew the animal, enter the tent with blood, and then exit the tent to return to the altar to complete the butchering? Why did the ritual end with the remaining parts of the carcass delivered outside the community where they were burned up? These movements symbolized the staggering effects of sin in God's eyes and the drastic steps necessary for the sin to be removed from God's presence. That the priest brought the blood inside the tent *before* applying the blood to the high altar showed that the sin of the priest that had polluted his intercessory work inside the tent had to be removed before his mediation at the altar could continue. For the Christian, however, we have no worries that the priesthood of the Lord Jesus Christ is sullied by his sin, for he had no sin of his own for which to atone. Our access to God when provided by Jesus can never be threatened. If we are yoked to the Lord Jesus Christ through faith in him, we have a permanent home in the heavenly Tent of Meeting because Christ our Savior and High Priest resides even now at the right hand of the Father, making perpetual intercession for us and cleansing us from our sin.

## Purging for the Whole Congregation (vv. 13–21)

A second set of instructions follows, describing the offering made for the sins committed by the whole congregation. Again the sin is an unintended transgression, and the ceremonial remedy for it is similar to what we have just described for the high priest. We learn from these instructions some additional insights about the purification offering that teach us more about the nature of sin's insidious hold on us.

*Community guilt (vv. 13, 14).* Sin not only attacks an individual person but also can condemn a whole assembly. In the ancient world there was a greater emphasis on the idea of community responsibility than is found today in our American culture. We celebrate the idea of individuality that stresses individual rights and independent responsibility. Although we in our culture champion individual freedoms, we still recognize that individual behavior can injure a whole community. For example, leaders of a country may plunge a nation into war, and after suffering defeat, the whole nation may be enslaved or placed under economic penalties. The Treaty of Versailles in 1919 officially brought World War I to a close. In the agreement between the Allied Powers and Germany, the treaty assigned the blame of the war to the German Empire and required the German state to make war reparations to the Allies for damages. The poor decisions of the German high command led to the humiliation of the people, many of whom were not directly responsible for the war. Perhaps something similar occurred in ancient Israel when a leader, perhaps even the high priest, failed to instruct the congregation in some aspect of God's Law or made a decision that led to the assembly's transgression of the Law. The whole congregation as a consequence had to make atonement for its sin. This was accomplished through the offering presented by the elders of the assembly who represented the whole congregation (v. 15).

Although the congregation did not intentionally offend the Lord, they came to "realize their guilt" by some means unstated here (v. 13). The translation "*realize* their guilt" reflects the subjective aspect of guilt, but most translations render the language in the objective sense of guilt, such as, "to incur guilt," "are guilty," or "become guilty."[5] The significance of the objective sense of guilt is that even if they do not *feel* particularly guilty or even know of their guilt, they are still guilty before God. Although the book of Leviticus does not explain explicitly how their sin was discovered, an example of this can be seen many centuries later during the days of the monarchy. When King Josiah of Judah read "the Book of the Law," which had been discovered in the ruins of Jerusalem's temple, he realized that the previous kings and leaders of the nation had failed to lead the people in the ways of the Lord. The whole nation had suffered as a result and faced even greater risk if the nation continued in its ways. Josiah tore his clothes in repentance and called upon the nation to join him in renewing their commitment to God (2 Kings 22, 23). By reading God's Word they came to understand that they had committed sin against the Lord, and by it they recognized their guilt. God's Word is like a light that exposes our sin and incites us to confess and reorder our lives in obedience (1 John 1:5–9).

*Atonement and forgiveness (vv. 15–21).* The sin offering for the assembly was the same as that described for the sin of the high priest. That the ritual was the same probably indicates that the guilt of the assembly was related in some way to the ill-advised leadership of the priest. By carrying out the ritual, the result is explicitly stated in our passage: "The priest shall make atonement for [the congregation], and they shall be forgiven" (v. 20). "Atonement" (*kipper*) is a "church word" that does not always speak to our contemporary audience, but if we look at the word carefully we can see why the English word *atonement* is a correct translation. When we pronounce the word "atonement" in its compound parts, saying, "at-one-ment," we recognize the meaning of the passage. *Atonement* means the reconciliation of two conflicting parties through an act of appeasement. When a dispute separated two people, it was resolved through a settlement, as when a person pacifies the wrath of a king with a gift (Proverbs 16:14). For example, the patriarch Jacob "appease[d]" (*kipper*) the wrath of his aggrieved brother Esau by presenting a gift (Genesis 32:20). Sometimes we say today to a person with whom we have quarreled, "please accept my peace offering" or we extend an "olive branch." The gift that alone could appease an offense against God's holiness was the shedding of blood. A substitution death had to occur because the judgment against the offender was death. A pastor friend names the shedding of blood as one of the "Indispensables" to saving faith. As the writer to the Hebrews pointed out, "without the shedding of blood there is no forgiveness of sins" (Hebrews 9:22b).[6]

The result of the purification offering was that the people were "forgiven" by God (v. 20).[7] The blood purged the tent of the sin of the people, making it possible once again for the Lord to dwell at peace among his people. This did not mean that the ritual itself achieved the forgiveness received by the people. Forgiveness was solely a gift from God, an act of grace. The priest did not provide forgiveness; he only mediated forgiveness. In the Old Testament the word translated here "forgive" (*tsalach*) is only used of God as the one who forgives. This term is never used of a human forgiving another. The idea of forgiveness is the "release" of a person from the guilt brought about by the transgression.[8] The Lord ensured a means of forgiveness through the ritual of blood, but the ritual was just a symbolic act. It was necessary that the people turn from their sins and confess their sins (Leviticus 5:5; 16:21; 26:40). This is implied in the ceremony when the guilty person placed his hand on the head of the animal before the animal was slain.[9] By this action the person symbolically transferred his guilt to the animal, which was then slain on his behalf.

We must address another aspect of the passage as readers of the New Testament because we are told in the New Testament that sins could *not* be forgiven by "the blood of bulls and goats" (Hebrews 10:4). But in Leviticus we are told that forgiveness was granted. The necessity of repeatedly presenting the sin offering showed, however, that the ritual was not totally effective for purging the stain of sin. Moreover, the sin offering was only for the unintentional sins that polluted the house of God and condemned the wrongdoer; there was no specific ritual designated for *intentional* sins of rebellion (Numbers 15:27–31).[10] The sin offering of an animal was only *provisional* until an eternal and fully effective atonement could be made. This fully perfect atonement was supplied by the blood of our Lord Jesus Christ. The animal ritual was only effective for cleansing the outer person (Hebrews 9:13, 14), but the cleansing provided by the blood of Christ purged the inner person. His death was once, and the atonement achieved was eternal, never to be repeated out of necessity (Hebrews 7:27; 9:28; 10:2, 10). It was the blood of the eternal Son of God whose perfect life and obedience made him alone a worthy substitute for the sins of all who repent and call upon his name for salvation. The Apostle Paul explained that the blood of Christ made complete atonement (Romans 3:25; Hebrews 9:5),[11] for Jesus was our perfect sin offering (Romans 8:3; Hebrews

13:12). As the priest took the blood of the animal into the earthly tent to purge the tent of its impurities and restore its holiness, the Lord Jesus took his own precious blood into the heavenly tent before the presence of God to cleanse our sin, making us holy in God's sight forevermore (Hebrews 9:12; 10:10, 14).[12] By this unsurpassed act of sacrificial love, the Lord became our sin offering whereby we who believe have received the righteousness of Christ (2 Corinthians 5:21), never to be condemned again (Romans 8:1).

## Purging for the Leader (vv. 22–26)

The third set of instructions concerns a community leader who sins. Like the high priest, a civic leader, too, was especially influential in the community and therefore received special attention in the law of the sin offering. The ritual pertaining to him was the same in most aspects but differed in two significant ways. First, the animal required of him was a male goat, not the more costly bull. Second, the blood of the goat was *not* brought by the priest into the holy tent. Rather, the blood was smeared on the four protruding horns of the main altar in the courtyard. We learn from these differences that the sin of the community leader did not have the same intensity of contamination as in the cases of the priest and the whole community. The priest and community were held to a higher standard, and therefore their sin was more potent in its corruption. Symbolically, it was necessary in those cases to bring the blood closer to the Lord's presence because the effect of the sin was graver.

Certain sins are more severe in their outcome because of how destructive they are to other people. The book of Proverbs names, for example, the so-called "seven deadly sins" that are "an abomination" to the Lord (Proverbs 6:16–19). This explains in part why today's church leaders must meet demanding moral and spiritual requirements. A teaching elder, for example, is responsible for teaching right doctrine and for exhibiting right behavior. Those who fill this difficult role are worthy of "double honor" (1 Timothy 5:17). Most of us are leaders, either in our homes or in the fellowship of the church, and our influence for good or ill impacts many others, including across generations. The Bible reflects this principle when it expects that future generations will commit the good or sin of their fathers and receive their just punishment too: "[The Lord] keep[s] steadfast love for thousands, forgiving iniquity and transgression and sin, but . . . will by no means clear the guilty, visiting the iniquity of the fathers on the children and the children's children, to the third and fourth generation" (Exodus 34:7). Because of the consequences of leadership's behavior, a distinct category in the ritual of the sin offering addressed offenses by Israel's leaders.

### Purging for the Common Person (vv. 27–35)

We have thus far spoken of leadership and the collective guilt of the community, but what about the common man and woman? What provision was made for them? We learn from this fourth set of instructions that the Lord bestows his forgiving grace on individual common people, regardless of their status. That they are not in leadership positions means that the value of the animal slain can be less because the impact of their sin is less damaging. They are to bring either a female goat or female lamb. Now, the text does not say that the sin of the average person is of little interest to God, because the same procedure of killing the animal and smearing its blood on the altar of burnt offering is required. On the contrary, this is a recognition that all men and women have sinned and are in need of atoning grace. The Apostle Paul expressed it this way: "None is righteous, no, not one" (Romans 3:10), and "all have sinned and fall short of the glory of God" (Romans 3:23).

### Purging for the Poor (5:1–13)

We have already mentioned the specific sins listed at the beginning of chapter 5 that are representative of the kinds of sins people make without malice. They all share in common the sacrifice of an animal, either a lamb or goat. But what about the people who cannot afford a lamb? Is there no hope for them? As in the case of the common person, the Lord provides for the poor and for the poorest of the poor. The poor were permitted to offer inexpensive birds, either two doves or two pigeons (v. 7). One bird served as the sin offering, purging sin, and the second as a burnt offering, expressing devotion to God. This gives us some insight into the family of Jesus when we recall that Mary and Joseph brought baby Jesus to the temple in Jerusalem for Mary's purification rites. They presented birds as a sacrifice (Luke 2:24). Even though the family of Jesus was not wealthy, they were not among the most impoverished.

For those who could not even afford birds, the sin offering was only a measure of "fine flour" (v. 11). This would be the minimal level of subsistence for a person in that day. According to the Law, landowners were instructed to leave stalks of grain at harvesttime for the poor to gather for food (Leviticus 23:22). For the very poor, the officiating priest took a representative portion of the flour and burned it up on the altar as a gift to God; the leftover flour was reserved for the priest's rations (v. 13). By accepting the flour, the priest demonstrated symbolically that the gift had been received by the Lord. Although the offerings of the poor and very poor were not animals, whether birds or merely flour, they were still called in the text "a sin offering" (vv. 9, 12). Therefore they were burned up on the altar as an act of atonement.

What this provision for the poor in the Law tells us is that the forgiveness that God provides was not dependent upon a person's wealth or status. Jesus witnessed a poor woman who gave all that she possessed, her very livelihood, although it was just a penny, and our Lord gave her his highest commendation because of her heart, not the measure of her gift (Mark 12:41–44). Such is the mathematics of the kingdom of God. One's economic or social position does not advantage or disadvantage a person in receiving God's forgiveness (Acts 10:34). Men and women could receive forgiveness by bringing an offering in hand. The Lord accepted them because of their repentant hearts and confessions of sin. The same is true of the salvation that the Lord Jesus Christ extends to each person today. There is no excuse for those who do not experience the forgiving grace of God for salvation, since it is a free gift to us, purchased through the shed blood of Christ and offered to all persons who entrust themselves to the Lord. Jesus gave this assurance when he said, "whoever comes to me I will never cast out" (John 6:37b). There is no one who is outside God's loving desire that we come to him in repentance, receiving his gracious mercy.

# 5

# Debt-Free

LEVITICUS 5:14—6:7

HAVE YOU EVER FAILED to make amends for a debt? Robert Nuranen made amends, but it was forty-seven years late! He returned a borrowed book from his local library, paying the late fee of $171.32. In the ninth grade Robert checked out the book *Prince of Egypt*, but while cleaning the house his mother misplaced it. From time to time across the years the family discovered the book anew but did not return it. He commented, "I figured I'd better get it in before we waited another ten years. . . . Fifty-seven years would be embarrassing!" The librarian who received the long-overdue book remarked, "It's never too late to return your books."[1] We commonly make mistakes as humans, and when we do, we must pay back whatever indebtedness we bear. Robert didn't mean to avoid his responsibility, but he was negligent in his obligation. Once he was convinced that he needed to make things right, he returned the book and paid the fine.

The sacrificial system in ancient Israel provided a way to make things right for the person who committed transgressions against others. Traditionally, it is called the "guilt offering" or "trespass offering," but since there is a monetary penalty involved, it is sometimes referred to as a "reparation offering."[2] There were two important differences between the sin offering and the guilt offering. First, the guilt offering remedied the particular offense of fraud, whereas the sin offering was broad in scope. Second, the guilt offering always required the payment of money to compensate for indebtedness, whereas the sin offering did not.

To defraud someone meant to take from a person his good name or property. By blaspheming the "holy things" of God (5:14–19) or by blaspheming the holy name of God through a false oath (6:1–7), a person stood guilty for depriving God of his sacredness. These crimes are called acts of sacrilege, which means disrespecting God and the holy things pertaining to the worship of God. An example of this today would be arsonists who burn a church building or thieves who rob and deface burial places. It was also possible to defame the Lord in another way—by defrauding another human being. When an Israelite cheated a fellow Israelite, the crime involved defrauding God by taking the Lord's name in vain through a false oath. The way a person claimed his innocence was through swearing an oath in the name of the Lord. If we were to find a modern parallel, we might consider how people sometimes heatedly say, "I swear this is true!" Or in a formal court setting an oath to tell the truth is accompanied by swearing on the Bible. In effect a witness is saying that God will judge him if he fails to tell the truth. In ancient Israel when a cheater swore falsely, he made the name and reputation of the Lord worthless.

Our passage will show that the Lord takes seriously the way we treat him and the way we treat our neighbor. Since blasphemy meant the ultimate penalty of death, the Israelite offender put himself at risk (Leviticus 19:8; Numbers 18:32). But thanks be to God, he provided a means whereby the offender could be reconciled. We will see that God has made this possible for us through Jesus Christ who became our guilt offering by his sacrificial death. He has canceled our debt to God.

We will first look at the charge of defrauding God and then will see how the people defrauded their fellow covenant members.

## Defrauding God (5:14–19)

*Disloyalty in "holy things" (5:14–16).* The text shows us that the crime committed against "holy things" could be by "anyone" (v. 15), not just the priests or leaders. The guilt offering was required for everyone because everyone at some time or another would express disloyalty to God or to a fellow neighbor. The nature of the crime is not specifically noted in the passage, but we can piece together probably what was in mind from a number of clues.

First, the translation "breach of faith" (v. 15) accurately captures the meaning of the original language. It is a term that is common in the Bible and often appears in texts that describe a transgression of religious law. This explains why the language "breach of faith" says explicitly that it is "against the LORD," as in 6:2 (also, e.g., Numbers 5:6). The offense is also described as "sin" in verse 15. The translation "he has done amiss in the holy thing" describes the crime committed by the transgressor in a vague way, allowing for any number of specific cases under this category. The word "amiss" translates the most common word in Hebrew for the word "sin."[3] That the offense is taken personally by the Lord is shown in Leviticus 26:40 where the Lord speaks of treachery against him in the first person, "treachery . . . committed against me." Probably the best way to understand the essence of the phrase "breach of faith" is the use of the expression in human relationships. Numbers 5 describes a suspicious husband who charges his wife with "breaking faith" (Numbers 5:6, 27) by committing adultery. A test is implemented to learn if the charge against the woman is true, which may result in her guilt or in alleviating the man's jealousy. "Breaking faith" then meant acting disloyally, betraying a trust. The offense is against an innocent husband.

A second feature of the offense against the Lord is that the sin is committed "unintentionally" (v. 15). The guilt offering does not make amends for what the Bible calls high-handed sins. Numbers 15 differentiates between sins committed by mistake and sins that are deliberate acts of rebellion against the Lord. Such a person "reviles the LORD" and "despise[s] the word of the LORD" (Numbers 15:30, 31). The difference between unintentional and willful sins is not so much the sin per se but the attitude of the offender toward his sin. The person who commits unintentional sin and confesses his sin offers up an animal sacrifice in connection with a remuneration (Leviticus 5:5; Numbers 15:22–26). The person who has no remorse cannot receive forgiveness.

A third feature of the offense is the nature of the thing transgressed—the "holy things" of God (v. 15). Typically this phrase refers to the sacrifices presented at the Tent of Meeting.[4] These are deemed "holy things" because they are offered exclusively for the Lord's service. Defrauding God of his rightful due could occur by sins of omission or commission. In the days of the prophet Malachi, for example, the people withheld their tithes from the service of God. They were guilty of robbing God because the tithe exclusively belonged to the Lord (Malachi 3:8–10).[5] Sins of commission would be unlawful eating of the sacrifices. Persons who came into contact with "holy things" who were *not* qualified to eat them were guilty of offending God (cf. esp. Leviticus 22:1–16). These items belonged to him, and when taken unlawfully the offender robbed God of his holy prerogatives. For example, unlawful eating of holy offerings robbed the Lord. Sacrifices were given to the Lord by burning them on the altar, but he assigned a portion of them to the priests for their livelihood, and in some cases the worshiper, too, could participate (the peace offering). If unqualified priests or laypeople ate unlawfully, they impugned the holiness of God. In effect the holy reputation of God had been defrauded by the illicit actions of the offender.

A fourth feature of the offense was the gracious provision of a pardon for the crime. Even the profaning of the Lord's holiness could be forgiven if it were committed as an unintended mistake. A ram could be offered up as an atoning sacrifice. This atonement secured the reconciliation of the offender to God, releasing the guilty person from his debt to God. Since the offense was defrauding God of his rightful due, the guilty party compensated the Lord for depriving him of his holiness by making a payment. This meant adding a 20 percent surcharge to the value of the item that was defrauded. A payment of money was delivered to the priest for the service of the Lord's house. "And he shall be forgiven" (5:16, 18) describes the outcome. If the offender repents of his sin and expresses his repentance by obeying the demands of the sacrifice, he is free from his liability.

How do we today as Christians run the risk of defrauding God of his rightful due? It is not appropriate to equate the Old Testament teaching on holy places and holy things with the worship practices of the Christian today. Although we may refer to things pertaining to worship as "holy," such as "holy vestments" worn by the clergy, this is born out of tradition, not the direct teaching of the New Testament. A holy place and its things of worship are no longer deemed "holy." Rather, the Lord Jesus himself is the holy temple of God, and he alone is the pure and perfect sacrifice that pleases God (John 2:20–22; Hebrews 10:1–14). The New Testament describes the church collectively as God's holy temple (1 Corinthians 3:16, 17; Ephesians 2:21), and individually Christians are the temple of the Lord and present themselves as holy sacrifices (Romans 12:1; 1 Corinthians 6:19).[6] We can draw some implications from our passage for us today since the New Testament confirms what can be gleaned from the passage.

First, we defraud the Lord of his rightful due when we withhold or pervert the worship of God. First Corinthians 11:27 describes the failure of Christians to honor the Lord when they observed the Lord's Table unworthily. The Apostle Paul warned those who worshiped idols (2 Corinthians 6:16) or angels (Colossians 2:18). Today the worship of God must be done in the name of the Lord Jesus Christ and in a respectful manner. We do not have a "generic god" that we worship; we worship specifically the triune God, "the God and Father of our Lord Jesus Christ" (1 Peter 1:2, 3).

Second, we defraud God of his rightful due when we compromise a life of holiness by choosing a lifestyle that betrays the gospel and the claims of Christ on our lives (James 4:1–10).[7] When we act as unbelievers do, living for the pleasures of this world, we rob God, for we have been purchased by the blood of Christ and belong exclusively to Jesus (1 Corinthians 6:20; 7:23; 1 Peter 1:18–20). As one person told me, he drives his father's car with a special awareness that his father has a bumper sticker that proclaims "Jesus is Lord!" He accepts the responsibility of behaving well on the road lest he stain the name of Christ. Misbehavior or defiance by Christians brings disrepute on the Lord Jesus in the eyes of those who would slander him  (1 Timothy 6:1; 1 Peter 3:16).

Third, we defraud God when we fail to give him our *all*. Our all means first to give our service to him, for we are to commit ourselves to righteous living and to the expansion of the gospel. And we are to give of our financial resources to enable the ongoing work of the kingdom. Giving ourselves and our monies is a testimony to the lordship of Jesus Christ over our lives: "For the ministry of this service is not only supplying the needs of the saints but is also overflowing in many thanksgivings to God" (2 Corinthians 9:12). The result of giving ourselves and our resources to the kingdom's work is that it brings glory to our Savior, honoring him as our Lord and recognizing him as our great Provider. If we deny the Lord our lives and monies, we are doing more than shirking the church—we are defrauding the Lord of his rightful due.

Fourth, we can trivialize the name of the Lord, robbing him of his magisterial honor, when we wrongly credit him with some action that is destructive or hurtful, although we are not in a position to make such a judgment. Job's friends, for example, insisted that God had punished Job for his sins, which alone in their eyes could explain Job's misery. However, the Lord himself corrected the friends, angrily scolding them: "You have not spoken of me what is right, as my servant Job has" (Job 42:7). It is a precarious position to take on if we assign to God specific responsibility for natural disasters or suffering (e.g., AIDS). It does not advance the cause of God to assign blame, usurping his role as Judge.[8]

*Disobedience of God's commandments (vv. 17–19).* A person also suffered guilt if he disobeyed any of God's commandments. The opportunity for this was vast, as we see from the enormous number of commandments found in Leviticus. The passage describes these infractions as actions that "ought not to be done" (v. 17). This indicates that the transgression pertained to a sin of some improper deed. Again specific infractions are not named; rather, the passage only describes the nature of the infractions. The sin committed cannot have been a consciously deliberate violation with premeditation. The passage says that the person "realizes his guilt" only after the fact (v. 17).[9] How he came to know his guilt is unstated. It appears to be through his conscience, or possibly some previously unknown information comes to him. Although initially the offender did not intend to disobey, he still "shall bear his iniquity" (v. 17). This sad news occurs again in verse 19, where the text says the transgressor "incurred guilt before the LORD." By saying "before the LORD," the passage shows the severity of the infraction. This phrase "before the LORD" is typical of describing worship at the Tent of Meeting. So the crime must be related to a violation in carrying out the worship of God. The Lord regarded the transgressor guilty despite his ignorance of the crime.

This degree of culpability is striking for the contemporary reader because we tend today to excuse mistakes when made in ignorance. The Scriptures show, however, that sins are endemic to humans; we are rightly called "sinners" because capacity to sin and the practice of sins are a part of who we are. Leviticus shows us that God does not wink at our sins. He is characterized by perfect holiness and requires it of all who are in his family of faith. That men and women are sinners and that God demands that we *not* be sinners shows the grave impasse that our sins have created between God and us. Because of our sins, men and women are consigned to judgment, resulting in death.

There is good news in the passage, however; it is not completely a dark canvass. There is a means of escape. God, through commissioning an animal sacrifice, as we see in verses 18, 19, provided hope for a guilty person. The priest slaughtered a ram *in the place of* the guilty person. By means of substitution the penalty of wrongdoing was shouldered by the ram, and the guilty person therefore was relieved of debt. The priest's action provided "atonement," and the Israelite received forgiveness (v. 18). However, the Israelites' continuing to present offerings to the Lord on a daily basis because of their sins demonstrated that this provision was temporary at most. The guilt offering was not a permanent fix for disobedience. It nevertheless gave a short-term answer and looked ahead to the final full resolution.

Complete forgiveness for human sin and guilt was fully and finally paid for by the blood of Christ. We sing the old hymn entitled "Jesus Paid It All" to recall the completed salvation that Jesus' death has achieved for us who believe. We are no longer in debt for our sins. Isaiah's Servant is described as a "guilt offering"[10] that yields his life, making atonement for others (Isaiah 53:10). This is what Jesus has done for us at the cross. The Apostle Paul referred to the imagery of paying off debt when he said of Jesus' death, "And you, who were dead in your trespasses and the uncircumcision of your flesh, God made alive together with him, having forgiven us all our trespasses, by canceling the record of debt that stood against us with its legal demands. This he set aside, nailing it to the cross" (Colossians 2:13, 14). For those who have had the "monkey" of debt on our backs, there was no greater sense of relief than when we made that last payment or received forgiveness from a creditor. This debt of sin paid by Jesus is not just a reduced debt or a reconsolidation of our debt but the complete termination of *all* debt. The invoice reads "paid in full"! The very "record of debt" itself has been shredded; there is no charge standing against those who have received this forgiveness.[11]

## Defrauding Your Neighbor (6:1–7)

Another way in which the Israelites sinned against the Lord was their misbehavior toward their neighbors. We are not surprised that the text turns to the question of treating a neighbor since the Bible is replete with exhortations to love our neighbor. Leviticus 19:18 commands, "love your neighbor as yourself." We can't love our neighbor if we are cheating our neighbor of his rightful due. Jesus taught that loving God and loving one's neighbor go hand in hand (Matthew 22:37–40). The same description of "a breach of faith" concerning the holy things of God (Leviticus 5:15) is used for describing "a breach of faith" toward one's neighbor (6:2). Verse 2 says explicitly that an offense against your neighbor is also an offense "against the LORD." A people in covenant with God have been formed into a covenant community with shared obligations toward one another as well as toward God. To offend one is to offend the other. The same is true of the Christian community who are bonded together as servants of the same one and living Lord Jesus Christ (Ephesians 4:4–6). We have obligations toward one another as brothers and sisters in Christ. The Apostle Paul chastened the Christians at Corinth for bringing lawsuits against members of their fellowship: "But you yourselves wrong and defraud—even your own brothers!" (1 Corinthians 6:8). When the tax collector Zacchaeus became a follower of Jesus, he declared that he would make up for his mistreatment of the poor and would make good "fourfold" any injustice he had committed (Luke 19:8). A true signal of a regenerated heart is the way in which commitment to Jesus changes our behavior toward others. Occasionally we hear of church leaders who steal from church funds or appear in court for swindling an employer or fellow citizen. This brings disrepute on the name of Christ, and we as Christians fall under suspicion by those who want to slander the gospel.

*The crimes (vv. 1–3).* Our text gives representative examples of how the Israelites defrauded fellow covenant members. These examples had a legal implication since they are described as the result of "swearing falsely" in verse 3. This means that the offense was connected with making a false statement in a matter of a neighbor's loss of property.

The first crime listed was "deceiving" a neighbor (v. 2). The word is used frequently to mean "to lie." It indicates in our passage the "distorting" or "dissembling" the truth of a matter.[12] Two specifics follow in the text: First, a neighbor had left an item with a person for a deposit or pledge, but the person refused to acknowledge it; second, a person robbed another by seizing his property. Exodus 22:7–13 instructs the Israelites in the matter of receiving a deposit of money or an animal for safekeeping. For example, if an animal was in a person's custody, but it was stolen by a thief or injured by a wild animal, the person holding the property had to demonstrate his innocence, showing that he did not steal the animal for himself. In some cases there was a monetary restitution required if the holder of the property had acted neglectfully in the loss of the property.

Another crime was "oppressing" a person (v. 2), which has usually been understood as extortion. Extortion means to obtain something from someone through force or intimidation. This means of stealing was prevalent in suppressing the poor (e.g., Micah 2:2). Someone in a position of power can take advantage of another through threats, thereby gaining something dishonestly. Christian employers and supervisors must especially beware of using their power base for obtaining their ends through pressuring employees directly or subtly. Extortion of money, gifts, or inappropriate actions makes us guilty before God.

Another way to gain advantage over a person is through misleading him. This crime was the result of finding an item that had belonged to a neighbor. Instead of returning it, however, the offender kept the item and when asked about it lied about the discovery. Deuteronomy 22:1–4 legislates the correct procedure for the discovery and return of a lost animal. If the lost animal's owner is known, it should be returned to him right away, but if he lives too far away, the animal should be kept until the owner comes inquiring for the animal.

*The restitution (6:4–7).* When the violator "has realized his guilt" (v. 4), he must follow a procedure for restitution of the defrauded property. It is not clear how the person "realized" his crime. We surmise that he came to acknowledge his guilt because of his injured conscience. His remorse for his behavior led to his confession. Or he was suspicious, having guilty feelings, that he had committed an offense. To ensure that he did not continue in his guilt, he went through the procedure for restitution. Job exemplified this pious impulse when he offered sacrifices on behalf of his children, thinking, "It may be that my children have sinned, and cursed God in their hearts" (Job 1:5).

Another question of interpretation is imagining how someone could defraud a person unknowingly. An example is the dispute of the patriarch Jacob and his father-in-law Laban. Laban charged Jacob with stealing his household idols, but Jacob swore that he had not. Unknown to Jacob, however, his wife

Rachel had taken the idols and hid them without her husband's consent. Jacob misled Laban but not in malicious intent (Genesis 31:32–37). Also, since the guilt offering atoned for unintended sins, it is puzzling that crimes are listed that were surely deliberate sins, such as stealing or lying. How could this be? The answer probably lies in the attitude of the criminal. Because of his remorse and confession, the offender could receive forgiveness. The crime therefore could fall under the provision of the guilt offering, and restitution could be made.

The first step involved the admission of his sin; he must return the stolen property to the owner along with a 20 percent additional charge (vv. 4, 5). The reason for the additional charge was to compensate the owner for the loss of the use of the property during the time it was withheld. This restoration of property and additional money must be returned promptly—"on the day" the transgressor acknowledges his sin. Any further delay will further wrong the victim. Moreover, a prompt response showed the genuineness of the person's remorse. Jesus taught in the Sermon on the Mount that there is a relationship between acceptable worship and any indebtedness that we have toward another person (Matthew 5:23, 24). Before an act of worship can be received by God, the worshiper must reconcile any wrong he has committed against another. First, reconcile with your neighbor and then make your offering at the altar. When we convene to worship, the question of our relationship with God is impacted by the honesty that we show others. At the same time, what should be our reaction to the person who has wronged us and comes seeking our forgiveness? Our response must be to forgive if we are to expect the same in turn from God. In the same sermon Jesus said, "For if you forgive others their trespasses, your heavenly Father will also forgive you, but if you do not forgive others their trespasses, neither will your Father forgive your trespasses" (Matthew 6:14, 15). We must be as anxious to reconcile with an offending person as God is anxious to reconcile us to himself.

The second step was the violator's presentation of a ram as a guilt offering. The offering was presented "to the Lord" (v. 6) as the trespasser's just "compensation." The animal was offered on the altar by the priest at the Tent of Meeting. The guilt offering was made to the Lord, meaning that the offense against a person's neighbor was also an offense against the Lord. To restore the property and make the monetary payment is not enough to appease God. Reconciliation required setting things right with God as well as with the person wronged. Defrauding God and a neighbor was such a serious violation that God demanded the loss of life for the offender. By God's grace, however, the violator could make restitution and substitute an animal offering to make atonement. Sacrificing a costly ram evidenced the gravity of the person's guilt in the eyes of God.

God requires nothing less for our sins and guilt before God. Our sin cannot be satisfied by any act of penance, sincere or not. Our best efforts fall short of the demands God expects of his people. Our guilt cannot be erased by the blood of animals or merely by the remorse we have for our sins. Yes, remorse is our appropriate reaction to our human sins, but remorse alone does not absolve us of guilt. The only means by which we are debt-free is by the cancellation of our debt through the blood shed by our Lord Jesus Christ.

# 6

# Handling Holy Things

## LEVITICUS 6:8—7:38

WHEN I WAS A YOUNGSTER, my family's folk customs had designated certain religious practices and items as sacrosanct, requiring special care. When it came to our Bibles, it was generally accepted that it would be disrespectful to write in or mark up one's Bible. And even when church services were not in progress, it was irreverent for the kids to run up and down the aisles or crawl under the pews of "God's house." Today there are still a few taboos in some church traditions, but the trend toward casual dress and laidback behavior in our culture has also left its mark on the perception of how to handle the "holy." The impression, however, of a demarcation between the common and the "holy" has been retained in some important ways. It is still generally considered a most dastardly crime to commit an atrocity in or against a sanctuary, be it a church, synagogue, or mosque. There is a heightened sense of outrage against the person who defames religious icons, and in some quarters it is still considered coarse to speak the name "Jesus" in a profane way. But with the coming of Jesus who inaugurated the kingdom of God, the meaning of what is "holy" has changed from the external to the internal life of the believer.

We will discover that the instruction on handling holy things in ancient Israel has a relevant message for us whose lives are devoted to the Lord as his holy people today. There is a temptation to reduce the meaning of holiness to a set of moral values, but Christian holiness is an encompassing commitment of one's life to the service of the Lord. Our passage will teach us about what is genuinely holy and will encourage us to live a life of purity in our moral life and deep devotion to God.

### Handling Holy Fires (6:8–13)

The priests had the daily responsibility of maintaining the altar's holy fires and ensuring that a lamb as a whole burnt offering was offered each morning and each evening. The daily offering was called in Jewish tradition the *Tamid* (pronounced *tah-meed*) offering because the Hebrew word means "regularly," indicating a continual burnt offering (Exodus 29:38–46). The offering was coupled with grain and drink offerings, which provided a pleasing aroma to the Lord. The aroma's being pleasant indicated that the Lord accepted the offerings. The perpetual burning of the altar's fires symbolized the perpetual need of sacrifice if the people were to enjoy the continued presence of the holy God in their midst. You may know of the eternal flame that marks the grave site of former President John F. Kennedy in Arlington Cemetery where he is interred. It symbolizes the constant memory of the slain President in the minds of the American people. The perpetual fires on Israel's altar and the daily offerings were a continual demonstration of the people's worship of the living God who symbolically had taken up residence in the Tent of Meeting among his people.

As a burnt offering the animal was completely burned up, showing that the people dedicated themselves wholly to the service of the Lord. Since the offering was given to God, even the residual ashes from the roasting were considered holy. So the priest dressed specifically for the task by putting on white under- and outer garments. His full appearance in white conveyed the purity of God and of the offering presented to him. The priest scooped up the ashes and placed them beside the altar, indicating that the ashes too were sacred and must be handled properly. Once he had changed again into his normal priestly attire, the priest transported the ashes to outside the community, where he deposited them in a place designated "a clean place" (v. 11) because of the sacred state of the ashes. Our passage specifies how the priests were to maintain the fires, too. The priests placed fresh wood on the altar each morning, which would have stoked up the simmering fires of the offering presented the night before. Next the burnt offering was placed on the arranged wood followed by the fat pieces derived from peace offerings presented by worshipers. This fat functioned as combustible fuel to assist the burning process. Little or nothing was left to chance or human invention. That detailed instructions were given to the priests tells us that the worship of God is not a casual matter that can be treated carelessly. The psalmist says as much when he invokes the congregation to "Sing to [the Lord] a new song; play *skillfully* on the strings, with loud shouts" (Psalm 33:3).

Although we witness in this offering God's grace by providing this perpetual flame, the reality was that the daily sacrifices were not sufficient since they had to be renewed each morning and evening. This was a constant reminder to the priest and the congregation that a permanent solution to human sin and ritual impurity was needed. The recurring sacrifices indicated to the people that the present arrangement was only temporary and that a final deliverance was yet to come. This is fulfilled in the perfect sacrifice, our Lord Jesus Christ, whose death on the cross resulted in a complete removal of our sins and a final solution to our guilt. The writer to the Hebrews makes this point:

> And every priest stands daily at his service, offering repeatedly the same sacrifices, which can never take away sins. But when Christ had offered for all time a single sacrifice for sins, he sat down at the right hand of God. . . . For by a single offering he has perfected for all time those who are being sanctified. (Hebrews 10:11–14)

The fact that we have received an eternal mediation through Christ, our perfect High Priest, encourages us to live with full assurance that our sins are forgiven.

## Handling Holy Food (vv. 14–23)

Next to the burnt offerings, the grain offerings were the most common gift presented by the Israelites. Grain products usually accompanied burnt offerings, together providing meat and bread at the sanctuary. The gift of a baked or cooked product expressed the worshiper's thanksgiving to God for supplying the person's physical needs. It reminds us of our Lord's Prayer: "Give us this day our daily bread" (Matthew 6:11). Our passage refers to the grain offerings as "[God's] food offerings . . . most holy . . ." (v. 17). In our culture we have divinity candy and angel food cake or the TV show *Divine Design* on the House and Garden TV network. We might hear Oprah say on her TV show, "Oh, I do think it is simply divine, darling" when referring to some "pink bubbly." This is a common way today to speak of something that is so special, it is called "divine."

But the nations in antiquity believed that their offerings actually fed the deities. Was this true of Israel's theology? No; the Bible makes it clear that the Lord God is not like the false deities who are beholding to their human servants. The Lord in Psalm 50:12 said, "If I were hungry, I would not tell you, for the world and its fullness are mine." The Lord owns the world and is not dependent on the animal and grain offerings to survive. On the contrary, all humanity is dependent on God to survive. Another evidence that the Hebrews did not conceive of their God as just another one of the gods is the restriction

on the priests to eat sacrificed food offerings only in the courtyard. They were
not to take the food into the inner sanctum where the Lord was understood to
dwell. Blood was brought into the tent but never food. The reference to God's
"food offerings" is best interpreted as a figure of speech drawing on the imagery of sharing a meal with a friend—dining together with God. The reason
that it is deemed "most holy" by our text is because it is a food gift that was
eaten by the priests. By eating the grain offering, the priests were saying that
the gift and the worshiper had been accepted by God.

Since the priest ate a portion of the offering, the instructions of when,
what, and where the portions were to be eaten were crucial. After the priest
burned up a small memorial portion of flour (v. 15), the remaining flour belonged to all the priests as their stipend for service (v. 18). They cooked the
flour without leaven into a variety of bread products and ate them in the courtyard of the Tent of Meeting. Only in this especially holy area could they consume the bread. That the bread was holy can be seen by the last statement in
verse 18: "Whatever touches [the food offerings] shall become holy" (also
v. 27). This means that the holy bread symbolically communicated holiness
to whoever ate the bread (for touching the altar, see Exodus 29:37; 30:29).[1]
For laypeople to eat the bread would put them in peril since the bread was
designated for only priests to eat.[2] The priests alone as especially holy servants
could legitimately consume the food offerings of the Lord. They were the only
authorized persons to represent the Lord, and they therefore alone could eat
the Lord's food. The food offering belonged to the Lord, but he gave of his
food to the priests. The warning does not spell out the consequences, but we
can surmise from other occasions when the holy things of God were trivialized
that the penalty included death (see Leviticus 10:1, 2).

That the priests benefited from the grain offerings reflects an important
principle in the Scriptures. The priests received their primary source of sustenance through the grain offerings. Since the priests were consecrated to the
service of the Lord, they did not own land from which they could produce a
livelihood. They were dependent upon the gifts presented to God. The Leviticus instruction ensured that the priests would receive the major portion of the
gifts so they could give their full attention to the work of the Lord. The Apostle
Paul in his defense of the rights of apostleship remarked to the Corinthians,
"Do you not know that those who are employed in the temple service get their
food from the temple, and those who serve at the altar share in the sacrificial
offerings? In the same way, the Lord commanded that those who proclaim the
gospel should get their living by the gospel" (1 Corinthians 9:13, 14; also see
1 Timothy 5:17, 18). By providing for the minister's material requirements,

the congregation frees the minister to give full attention to the spiritual needs of the people he serves. A wise congregation provides sufficient income so that the pastor attends to the caring of their souls and is not diverted by the sorry financial state of his family.

This does not mean that the minister has no obligation to give of his resources. The priests, too, had an obligation to give to the Lord. This is illustrated in the following instructions regarding the installation service of a new high priest into office (vv. 19–23). He and the priests give a cooked grain offering, one in the morning and another at evening, from the first day of his installation. It is prepared with oil, grilled, and broken into pieces that are fully consumed on the altar. The passage emphasizes that the grain offering must be burned up, and no portion is retained for the priests for food. This reminds us that the food offerings are first given to the Lord, and the worshiper—in this case the priest—could not benefit from his own offering. It is not a gift if the priest ultimately receives it back. The sole exception to this practice is the fellowship offering, which is a special rite in which a fellowship meal occurs.

## Handling Holy Blood (6:24—7:10)

Since the offerings typically included the slaughter of animals, an excess of blood had to be dealt with. Blood represented the life force of an animal, and since life is the sole propriety of the Lord, the priests had to be careful in honoring the victim's life. The proper handing of the blood evidenced the priests' recognition that God is the giver of life and that he has demanded the death of the sacrifice to make atonement for the sin of the guilty person or to purify the ritually impure person. The sin and guilt offerings had more in common with each other than with any of the other offerings: "The guilt offering is just like the sin offering; there is one law for them" (7:7a). So we can comment on the two together. These instructions for the sin and guilt offerings describe in detail the regulations for disposing of each part of the victim's anatomy. For example, the fat and entrails of the animal must be burned up on the altar. As "most holy" offerings (6:25, 29; 7:1, 6), the priests must eat the prepared meat in a clean place in the courtyard. At the slaughtering of the animal, the victim's blood must be drained and caught in a receptacle for proper removal. The blood was either poured out at the base of the altar (sin offering) or cast against the sides of the altar (guilt offering). This ritual act indicated that the life belonged to God as his gift. If in the process some blood splattered on a garment, it had to be washed in a holy place, which meant that it was cleansed in the courtyard of the tabernacle. And when the residue of blood from the cooked meat seeped into the porous earthenware pot, the vessel had to be broken. But if it was prepared in a bronze pot, the container could be scrubbed and washed for future reuse. The difference in the two regulations was that the clay material absorbed the holy blood and therefore could not be separated from the pot. The bronze pot, however, did not soak up the blood and could be cleansed (6:27, 28).

So that the priests would not get it wrong in caring for the blood, the regulations reminded the priests that special precautions must be undertaken when the ritual of the sin offering required that the blood be transported inside the tent. According to the procedure of the sin offering, when the priest offered the animal for his sin or for that of the whole community (4:3–21), the blood of the sin offering was applied to the horns of the altar of incense, located inside the tent (4:5–7, 16–18). The priests therefore were not permitted to eat any part of the animal (6:30). This goes back to what we said earlier. The priest should not benefit from his own sin, and as a member of the community he cannot benefit from the sins of the community. After describing what to do with the blood and fat, further instructions followed that clarified when the priests could obtain benefit from a person's burnt offering or grain offering (7:8–10). Although the burnt offering required the burning up of the entire animal, the hide was reserved for the officiating priest as his remuneration for serving at the altar. He presumably could sell the leather or use it for himself. The grain offerings too could be enjoyed by the officiating priest, and in one case the grain offering was provided for all the priests.

The sacredness of sacrificial blood is paramount in the teaching of the Old Testament. The Apostle Peter reflected this special attention to innocent blood when he spoke of Jesus' sacrifice: "knowing that you [Christians] were ransomed from the futile ways inherited from your forefathers, not with perishable things such as silver or gold, but with the precious blood of Christ, like that of a lamb without blemish or spot" (1 Peter 1:18, 19). The payment for our sins cannot be the offering of money, such as we sometimes see in the Mosaic law for ransoming a transgressor (Exodus 21:22, 30). Our salvation was achieved by the uniquely offered blood of our Lord Jesus Christ. One of the most sober warnings in Scripture is the reproach against those who have heard the gospel but neglected it:

> For if we go on sinning deliberately after receiving the knowledge of the truth, there no longer remains a sacrifice for sins, but a fearful expectation of judgment, and a fury of fire that will consume the adversaries. Anyone who has set aside the law of Moses dies without mercy on the evidence of two or three witnesses. How much worse punishment, do you think, will be deserved by the one who has trampled underfoot the Son of God, and

has profaned the blood of the covenant by which he was sanctified, and has outraged the Spirit of grace? For we know him who said, "Vengeance is mine; I will repay." And again, "The Lord will judge his people." It is a fearful thing to fall into the hands of the living God. (Hebrews 10:26–31)

Can there be any more heinous crime in the eyes of God than despising or blaspheming the blood of his only begotten Son?

## Handling Holy Communion (7:11–38)

After the instructions regarding the handling of the holy blood of the sin and guilt offerings, the text turns to the peace offerings. The order of the three offerings communicated an important message: The sin and guilt offerings came first, providing atonement and ritual cleansing, after which the worshiper could enjoy fellowship with the Lord and also peace with his neighbors. The peace offerings expressed communion between the worshiper and God. They were the only offerings from which the offerer could eat a portion of the sacrificed animal. The extent of the details in our passage was necessary since the fellowship meal could be eaten by the laity. This meant that the priests were especially needed to oversee that all was carried out according to the right ritual procedures. The priests too enjoyed designated portions, and together the meal was a fellowship feast to which the offerer invited friends and family members. It was a celebratory feast acknowledging the peace that the worshiper and all those who ate of the meal had in joyful fellowship. Unlike all the other sacrifices, the peace offerings entailed three subtypes, each distinguished by the motivation for the gift: the thank offering, the vow offering, and the freewill offering.

*Thanksgiving offering (vv. 11–15).* When we in North America hear the word *thanksgiving*, we immediately think of the holiday season by that name celebrated in late November. As in the original sentiment of the pilgrims' Thanksgiving, the thanksgiving offering in Israel recognized that the Lord had provided for the needs of the worshiper. It was presented to the Lord out of gratitude for the Lord's goodness, probably rejoicing at his answer to the worshiper's prayer. The thanksgiving of the Israelites was not a word of grace prayed over a meal or the casual "Thank you, Jesus" we sometimes hear. The offering of praise included the ritual practice of costly sacrifice and verbal testimony to God's goodness to the worshiper (Psalm 66:13–16).[3] The Hebrew word for "thanksgiving" (*todah*) is derived from the word "to confess, declare" (*yadah*). It was an integral part of the public act of thanksgiving. The ceremony concluded with a joyful communal meal, involving the worshiper, family, priests, Levites, and the poor (Psalm 22:25, 26). Psalm 107 calls on the congregation to offer thanksgiving when in distressful times they had cried out to God and he delivered them, such as from the trials of a desert journey, from cruel imprisonment, from near-death illness, and from drowning on the open seas.[4] Psalm 100 was written to be performed by the pilgrim's act of worship upon entering the temple grounds: "Enter [the Lord's] gates with thanksgiving, and his courts with praise" (Psalm 100:4).

The spiritual teaching of thanksgiving offerings was reflected in the psalmist's description of the person who makes this offering: "The one who offers thanksgiving as his sacrifice glorifies me [the Lord]; to one who orders his way rightly I will show the salvation of God" (Psalm 50:23). The parallel expression to giving thanksgiving in this verse is "order[ing one's] way rightly." Ritual sacrifice had to be matched by the worshiper's consecrated life. Thank offerings were symbolic acts of a person's authentic devotion to God (Psalm 50:12–15). Participation in the thanksgiving meal pointed ahead to the Lord's Communion table. As participants in the body of Christ we partake of the "cup of blessing" and the broken "bread" (1 Corinthians 10:16).

Although the Lord brought an end to the practice of animal sacrifice by his perfect sacrifice, once and forever given, the Christian life continues to present sacrifices of thanksgiving and praise. The sin offering of Christ has been offered, and now we as forgiven Christians enter into a fellowship with him and with the family of God.[5] We present spiritual gifts, ". . . that is, the fruit of lips that acknowledge his name" (Hebrews 13:15). As in the peace offering in which the community joins in the eating of the animal sacrifice, the worshiper today also extends to others both spiritual and material blessings. As the writer to the Hebrews said, "Do not neglect to do good and to share what you have, for such sacrifices are pleasing to God" (Hebrews 13:16). Our offering of saying grace over a meal is not therefore a perfunctory custom (1 Timothy 4:4), but a praise offering given out of a total life shared with the Lord and sacrificed for others.

*Vow and freewill offerings (vv. 16–18).* The other two fellowship offerings are the votive offering and the freewill offering. The votive offering was a sacrifice made in celebration of the completion of a vow by a worshiper. A vow was made by an Israelite to God regarding a promise entailing a special act of devotion. When the vow was made, it usually entailed a sacrifice, but not always. A vow often was made in the context of a prayer request. Once the vow was completed, the worshiper expressed his gratitude by giving the votive sacrifice. The freewill offering also was not a religious obligation and was offered to the Lord simply out of a joyous heart of generosity. The psalmist

David, for example, pledged a freewill offering for the deliverance he received from his enemies:

> With a freewill offering I will sacrifice to you;
>   I will give thanks to your name, O LORD, for it is good.
> For he has delivered me from every trouble,
>   and my eye has looked in triumph on my enemies. (Psalm 54:6, 7)

As peace offerings the votive and freewill offerings were communal meals. Therefore, our passage provides directives on the handling of the sacrificial meat. Regulations concern the time permitted for the eating of the meat, so as to avoid the eating of spoiled meat. Any meat that still remains by the third day must be burned up. The penalty for transgressing this regulation meant that the worshiper not only is denied God's favorable acceptance, but the person actually bears guilt. Symbolically it would be a great offense to the purity of God if the worshiper or the guests of the celebratory party ate tainted meat, for the communal meal was a meal shared with God himself.

There is a correspondence between the Lord's Table in the Christian church and the ancient practice of communal meals in Israel. The inauguration of the Christian ordinance was at the Passover meal celebrated by the Jews from earliest times, remembering the deliverance of their ancestors from Egyptian bondage. The symbolic eating of Christ's blood and body by consuming the fruit of the vine and the broken bread conveyed a message of fellowship with God that was based on the sacrificial death of Jesus. The Lord's Table, too, signified a holy communion with others in the body of Christ. As in the case of the peace offerings, specific instructions in the New Testament address the proper handling of the Lord's Supper. There were stern warnings by the Apostle Paul against defiling the sacredness of the ritual.

> Whoever, therefore, eats the bread or drinks the cup of the Lord in an unworthy manner will be guilty concerning the body and blood of the Lord. Let a person examine himself, then, and so eat of the bread and drink of the cup. For anyone who eats and drinks without discerning the body eats and drinks judgment on himself. That is why many of you are weak and ill, and some have died. (1 Corinthians 11:27–30)

The warning pertains to any person who mistreats the bread and wine in a manner that nullifies the message of the Lord's Table. Turning the sacred moment into merely a meal of feasting results in the guilty person's opposing the death of the Lord.[6] The implication for us is clear: with all diligence, let us not trivialize the sacred message of Jesus' death and resurrection.

*Dangers of communion (vv. 19–27).* The text turns to the potential risks that the fellowship meal presents for the participants. Two dangers must be avoided or the worshiper "shall be cut off from his people" (vv. 20, 21, 25, 27). The first danger was contaminating the holy food by the food coming into contact with an impure thing or by the worshiper in an impure state eating the meat of the offering (vv. 19–23). According to ritual law, uncleanness was a contagion that made whatever the unclean touched also unclean. The severity of an unfit person consuming meat was greater than the meat polluted by touching an unclean thing. The pollution of the meat by touching some unclean thing could be eliminated by burning up the corrupted meat. But in the case of an unclean person, the holy food had been eaten, and the only remedy was to penalize the person who ate unworthily. This was achieved by cutting off the person from the camp of the Israelites. This act of "cutting off" has been variously interpreted, either referring to the execution of the person or the exile of the person from the community. Exclusion from the camp was in effect a symbolic sign of death since the person who was exiled was considered outside the protection of the community. This was the complaint of the murderer Cain who killed his brother and was exiled by God to live as a vagabond, ostracized from the shelter of society (Genesis 4:12–14).

Perhaps we can point to a similar incident in the life of the Corinthian church that involved the penalty of excommunication. A man had committed the grievous sin of having sexual relations with his stepmother (1 Corinthians 5:1), and Paul in concert with the congregation resolved "to deliver this man to Satan for the destruction of the flesh, so that his spirit may be saved in the day of the Lord" (1 Corinthians 5:5). The object of Paul's instruction was to purify the gathered community by their not associating with such immoral people (1 Corinthians 5:6–11). This exclusionary move was meant also to alarm the immoral culprit so that he might repent and thus be restored to the congregation that provided spiritual defenses against wicked powers (2 Corinthians 2:5–11).[7] The warnings in Leviticus had the same message: beware of offending the Lord God by profaning his holiness.

The second danger regarded the unlawful eating of fat and blood (vv. 22–27). This prohibition is a recurring subject in Leviticus because of the importance attached to the fat and blood of a sacrifice presented to God (3:17; 17:10–14; 19:26; cf. Genesis 9:4; Deuteronomy 12:23). The fat was reserved for the Lord and was to be consumed by fire on the altar as his rightful portion. This was likely because the fat was deemed the best part of the meat and served as a fuel that fed the altar fires. An exception to eating the fat was if the animal in question was *not* a species permitted for a food offering (vv. 22–25).

If the beast was a type that could be offered but it had been made unfit by its natural death or torn by wild beasts, the animal's fat could be used for purposes other than worship, such as oil for lamps. But under no circumstances could the fat be ingested. The blood, too, was owned by the Lord; it was most precious since it represented the life of the animal. All creatures belong to God; he determines life and death. For a person to eat blood would be a false claim on the life of the victim that would usurp the Lord's sole right as Creator.

Why did the Lord require such detailed procedures for handling the fat and blood? Because spiritual truth can be understood more readily by people if tied to a specific concrete act with which the people are familiar. Parables have the same effect since they are stories of common human experiences—like a lost sheep, a wedding, or a vineyard—that reveal unseen things about the kingdom of God (Luke 8:10). The power of symbolic rituals left visual images that stamped the people's memory. But Israel's ritual was not magical. Magic invokes self-power, but Israel's animal sacrifices represented underlying spiritual realities. This is why it would do no good to go through the rites of worship without authentic commitment to God. It would be as useless as a person who says his wedding vow of cherished love, "'til death do us part," when all the while he has no intention of such enduring love. Or a judge who officially recites the oath of integrity at his installation but has every intention of using his new position for personal aggrandizement. The Hebrew prophets insisted that external religious acts must reflect a life of genuine obedience, not a substitute for devotion (e.g., Hosea 6:6).

*Supporting the worship of the Lord (vv. 28–38).* The final directives in this chapter address the ongoing support of the ministry at the tabernacle. If there is to be a worship service with offerings for atonement overseen by God-called ministers, there must be responsibility on the part of the worshiper to contribute to the material aspects of the worship service. The meat of the peace offerings was a vital means for supporting the work of the Lord. An Israelite, when making his offering, gave the breast and thigh of the animal to the priests as their portion of the celebration. The word that appears in verse 35, translated "portion," occurs only in this passage in the whole Old Testament. The word was carefully chosen by the author because of its connection to the related word translated "anointed" that appears in verse 36. That verse refers to the ordination service of the priests who received anointing oil as a sign of their unique role as mediators of the offerings made to the Lord. By this wordplay the text ties the exclusive "portion" of the gift to the exclusively ordained ministers.[8]

The order of the distribution of the gifts communicates the divine means of providing for the practical aspects of the worship service. The worshiper by "his own hands," the text says, brought the gifts to the Lord (v. 30). That the presentation was made to the Lord is shown by the worshiper's taking the fat with the breast and lifting up the breast heavenward. By this symbolic gesture, the gifts were transferred from earth to the divine realm.[9] The officiating priest then burned up the fat, which was the portion reserved exclusively for the Lord. The worshiper handed over the breast to the priestly family for their portion, and he took the right thigh and gave it to the officiating priest for his compensation. The distribution pattern of the animal's parts communicates the way in which God enabled the sanctuary to operate. The layperson offered the contributions to the Lord, not directly to the priest. It was *the Lord* who reassigned select portions for his ministers whereby they obtained their daily livelihood. "For the breast that is waved and the thigh that is contributed I [the Lord] have taken from the people of Israel, out of the sacrifices of their peace offerings, and have given them to Aaron the priest and to his sons, as a perpetual due from the people of Israel" (v. 34). This provision for the servants at the tabernacle was perpetually supplied by the Lord (vv. 34, 36). The priests had no other means of income since they did not own land. They were totally dependent upon the Lord to provide their needs. How did the Lord do this? He provided through blessing his people who in turn out of gratitude to God presented contributions to him that the Lord shared with his ministers.

The New Testament Scriptures confirm this pattern for supporting the practical work of carrying forth the gospel. Paul acknowledges that as Christians today we are to first give ourselves *to the Lord*—all that we are and all that we have. Then we give out of our means as the Lord has provided us (2 Corinthians 8:3–5; 9:9–11). The gifts will be used by the Lord to sustain his ministers and to enable the church's mission. Paul taught his churches to give liberally from their resources (1 Corinthians 9:13, 14; also Galatians 6:6; 1 Timothy 5:17, 18). We who benefit from the bodily sacrifice of Christ and from the worship of the Lord by his church have the obligation to contribute to the life and service of the church. Some church members are disobedient by neglecting to offer monies to the work of the Lord. But if we have truly given ourselves, our families, and our destinies into the hands of the Lord, surely we can entrust our pocketbooks to his care. When we give, we give *to the Lord*; and through wise oversight the church distributes the monies to sustain the various ministries of the church.

Our gifts are to be as peace offerings, tangible acts of praise lifted up to the Lord. Our motivation, like that of the ancient Israelites, is to express heartfelt thanksgiving and adoration, "for God loves a cheerful giver" (2 Corinthians 9:7).

# 7

# The Mediator

## LEVITICUS 8:1–36

WE ARE ACCUSTOMED TO the notion of arbitration and mediation in our world because conflict is commonplace between nations, businesses, and individuals. The National Mediation Board (NMB), established by the 1934 amendment to the Railway Labor Act of 1926, provided the first government agency for resolving labor and management disputes in public transportation. Since then the profession of mediation has blossomed into elaborate specializations: divorce mediation, employment disputes, neighborhood mediation, and government disputes over trade. One principle of mediation is the assumption that the mediator is an independent individual whose goal is to achieve a mutually satisfying outcome between two aggrieved parties. If we think of Israel's priest as a literal mediator in the modern sense, we will get the wrong impression.[1] The chief role of priestly mediation was not between two aggrieved persons but with only one offended party. God alone had the right to be offended by the disobedience of his people Israel. God was faithful to his people, but they were not loyal to him. The people had no legitimate grievance to bring against their God.

Also, the priestly mediator was not a dispassionate observer of the dispute. He himself was part of the problem. He too was a sinner and required a resolution to his own offense against God before he could represent the Israelite individual or the nation before the Lord. Moreover, the priestly mediator did not seek compromise or enter into negotiations so as to nudge God one way or the other. It was not a two-way street. There were no negotiations to be sorted out. The Lord demanded the only means of resolving the dispute. As we say today, it was his way or the highway. At first blush some may think that the Lord is cruelly stringent in his demands for strict compliance. "Doesn't

God bend, even a little?" we might ask. We must remember, however, that the whole order of worship was a *provision*, not a ploy of entrapment. In that way we can consider that the tabernacle, its sacrifices, and its priests were God's gracious "bending" toward sinful men and women. For apart from this provision, they would have faced the consequences of unforgiven sins.

So that Israel might come to the Lord in worship, there was the necessity of a qualified mediator to represent them before the Lord. Thus, the Lord after providing the authorized sacrifices in Leviticus 1—7 established an authorized priesthood to carry out the sacrifices properly. Leviticus 8 describes the inauguration of Aaron, Moses' brother, as the father of the priestly family. The Lord prescribed an ordination service that was conducted in the presence of all Israel (in fulfillment of Exodus 29). The ritual ordination entailed a whole week. Repeatedly the text says, "as the LORD commanded Moses," underscoring the divine origin of Moses' instructions (vv. 9, 13, 17, 21, 29; cf. v. 5). Ministers don't call themselves into Christian service. The gifts of a minister are gifts endowed by the Spirit. Beware of the person who calls himself to a ministry. From our passage we see the necessary demands on priest and people for their acceptance by God. The message of the ordination service of the Hebrew priests serves as a picture of the nation as a whole that ministered to the world of nations. It also speaks to the priestly role of the church as the people of God today and, most important, to the ministry of our Lord Jesus Christ who intercedes on our behalf as Christians.

Although most Christians are not ordained members of the clergy, the depiction of Aaron and his sons is especially important to every Christian. The Bible characterizes Christians as priests, drawing on the imagery of the priesthood in Israel. The church bulletin of Grace Lutheran Church in Destin, Florida, lists the church's various ministers by personal name, which is typical of most churches, but distinguishes the church by beginning with this general identification: "Ministers: *All God's People*."[2] Each person among the people of God is gifted and empowered by the Holy Spirit to minister to the church and to the nations. Israel as a nation collectively was appointed by God to function as "a kingdom of priests" to the nations (Exodus 19:5, 6). The church, too, is called upon to be a witness of the gospel of Jesus Christ to the nations (1 Peter 2:5, 9; cf. Romans 15:16). Also, we will learn the superior character of the Lord Jesus' priestly role in our behalf versus that of the temporary Jewish priesthood (Hebrews 7:11–28).

## The Preparations for Ordination (vv. 1–9)

The aphorism "Clothes make the man" could be a title for the opening verses, which describe the vestments received by the priestly family. Moses, however, was not a fashion designer. The articles of clothing worn by Aaron and his sons not only distinguished them as priests but also symbolically communicated important spiritual lessons. A constant feature of instructions for proper worship involved appropriate preparations that indicated the spiritual preparations of those who supervised and participated in the worship of God. For today's Christian we can rest at ease that God himself through his Son has made the way open for us to worship the Lord. At the same time, the call to purity is still a legitimate expectation for Christians today. The Apostle Paul says in 2 Corinthians, "Since we have these promises, beloved, let us cleanse ourselves from every defilement of body and spirit, bringing holiness to completion in the fear of God" (2 Corinthians 7:1). We too must undergo spiritual preparation for worship before we enter into his presence through prayer and praise. Our passage is a reminder that as Christians we must give more attention to our spiritual readiness when we worship the Lord. The Apostle Paul spoke of those who received the Lord's Table in "an unworthy manner" (1 Corinthians 11:27–31), which resulted in sickness and death for some of the offenders. Worship is a serious matter that must be viewed as a grave risk for the careless.

*Community ceremony (vv. 3, 4).* Therefore the ceremony of robing Aaron and carrying out the ordination sacrifices were public rituals (vv. 3, 4) from which Israel was to learn about God and the role of the priestly mediator. The goal of the ceremony was not to flatter Aaron but to teach the community about God's holiness. So it is with those in the service of Christ today. The spiritual gifts that the Lord provides his people are not for the indulgence of the recipient but are designed to strengthen the people of God (Ephesians 4:12).

*Cleansing (v. 6).* Aaron first underwent a ceremonial washing, indicating the moral purity required of a priest. In Levitical law ceremonial purity was emblematic of personal moral purity (cf. 1 Peter 3:21). Aaron could not approach the holy God unless he himself was spiritually prepared. This corresponds to the symbolism of an unblemished animal that the priest alone could offer up (e.g., Leviticus 1:9; 8:21).

*Clothes for Aaron the high priest (vv. 7–9).* The distinctive priestly vestments bestowed on Aaron and his sons gave them "glory" and "beauty" in the eyes of the people (Exodus 28:2, 40). We are accustomed today to the formal dress of the military services whose uniforms, medals, and ribbons symbolically convey valor in the service of our country. The Navy Cross, for example, is given for heroism, second only in distinction to the Congressional Medal of Honor. The ribbon of the Navy Cross is navy blue in color with a center stripe of white, the latter representing the purity of selflessness. The dress of the priestly family conveyed important meaning and attracted the respect of the people for what the vestments signified. All priests wore a "coat" (v. 7) made of fine linen, but Aaron's coat possessed distinctive embroidery (Exodus 28:4, 39; 39:27).[3] Some vestments were worn exclusively by the high priest, Aaron.[4] These included five special items.

First, a "robe" (v. 7) made of blue cloth possessed an opening at the top so that the priest slipped the garment over his head. Around the bottom hem of the robe were alternating decorative pomegranates made of blue, purple, and scarlet yarns and small golden bells (Exodus 28:31–34). Not only did the priest attract attention visually, but his physical activities also created accompanying sounds of tinkling bells. The bells had the practical purpose of preserving the high priest's life when he ministered in the restricted area known as the Most Holy Place on the sacred Day of Atonement. At his entrance and exit the bells assured the people that he had fulfilled his duty and had not been struck dead before the Lord (Exodus 28:35). The high priest had an embroidered "sash" (v. 7) of blue, purple, and scarlet yarns that tied the coat at the waist (Exodus 28:39; 39:29).[5] The colors of the garments matched the colored threads of the tabernacle's curtains and veil (Exodus 26:1, 31). The tabernacle as the place where the high priest ministered explains the correspondence between the two in appearance. Have you seen mother-daughter pictures in which the mother and daughter dress identically? One impression this gives is that the parent and child belong together; the child belongs to the mother and not another. Likewise, the high priest's distinctive apparel showed he belonged to God in the Tent of Meeting.

Second, the "ephod" (v. 7) was a sleeveless garment, made also of fine twisted linen and woven of gold, blue, purple, and scarlet yarns (Exodus 28:6–35). The gold thread gave a brilliant luster to Aaron's appearance. A waistband made as part of the ephod was of the same material (Exodus 28:8; 39:5). It probably was worn at the shoulders, extending down to the waist or possibly below to the thigh. Two gold shoulder pieces for attaching the garment possessed two onyx stones set in gold filigree; each stone was engraved with six names of the tribes of Israel (Exodus 28:9). Additionally, there were two golden rope-like chains connected to the settings.

Third, attached to the ephod at the shoulders by a blue cord looped through golden rings was a breastpiece (v. 8) made of the same colored yarns as the ephod. On the front of the breastpiece were twelve gemstones in four rows of three, each stone engraved with the name of a tribe (Exodus 28:29). It was made in a perfect square of about nine inches and folded over to double its thickness. Consequently, the breastpiece formed a pouch in which was placed the fourth distinctive feature of Aaron's apparel. The pouch of the breastpiece contained two sacred dice, the Urim and Thummim. These two stones were instrumental in discerning the will of God (Exodus 28:30; Numbers 27:21), and thus the breastpiece was called "the breastpiece of judgment" (Exodus 28:29, 30). The sacred Urim and Thummim are particularly mysterious to us, because the Bible does not specify how the stones were used. Among the most prominent theories is that the stones were cast like lots. They were marked with the words equivalent to our English terms *yes* and *no* (cf. 1 Samuel 14:41). Therefore the stones were useful in answering only "yes/no" kinds of questions.[6] Since the breastpiece showed forth the inscribed names of the twelve tribes, the high priest bore the names of the tribes over his heart, and whenever the high priest came into God's presence they were present too (Exodus 28:15, 29, 30). In the same way, the Lord Jesus, the perfect High Priest, bears our names in the presence of the Father (Hebrews 6:19, 20; cf. Matthew 19:28).

A fourth garment unique to Aaron was his headwear.[7] It was a linen turban (v. 9) on which at the forehead was tied a "plate" of pure gold by a blue cord (Exodus 28:36; 39:30).[8] The plate possessed the engraving "Holy to the LORD," which meant that Aaron continually mediated in behalf of Israel whenever he came before the Lord, bearing "any guilt" and securing acceptance for God's people (Exodus 28:36–38).

The brightly colored, dazzling garb of the high priest communicated the holiness and majesty of God. It was a constant reminder of the distinctive role that the priest was called upon to fulfill on behalf of the nation. By the mediator's vestments, Aaron symbolically brought the people into the presence of God each time he performed the rites of sacrifice. The qualifications of the priestly intercession of our Lord Jesus Christ, however, did not include a dress code. His was not merely a symbolic gesture of reconciliation (Hebrews 4:14; 6:20). Rather, in his very person Jesus as the very image of God (Hebrews 1:3) was the perfect conciliator between God and humanity—"the man Christ Jesus"—who perfectly performed the eternal sacrifice on behalf of all those who place their faith in him (1 Timothy 2:5, 6). Our Lord Jesus reigns in the presence of God his Father (Acts 2:33, 36; Hebrews 9:24; 1 Peter 3:22; cf. Acts 7:55). Because Christians are "in Christ," the Apostle Paul could speak of our dwelling-place as "in the heavenly places" (Ephesians 2:6; cf. Philippians 3:20). We have been clothed in Christ (Galatians 3:27).

## The Ordination Ceremony (vv. 10–36)

After distinguishing Aaron and his son as the solely authorized mediators, Moses prepared the tabernacle and the priests for administering the first sacrifices. The ordination ceremony involved symbolic cleansing of the place and the persons involved in carrying out the sacrifices. The place was the tabernacle with its furnishings and the altar where sacrifices would occur. The persons who underwent the ceremonial consecration were Aaron and his sons. In other words, all the persons, items, and places important to administering the sacrifices of worship were sanctified. Nothing was left to chance. All must be made holy for the sacrifice to be acceptable to the Holy One of Israel. Otherwise, the offering would be desecrated by the impurities of the procedure. The ceremony events of anointing with oil, animal sacrifice, and the smearing of blood converged on the final consecration of Aaron and his sons (v. 30). In our day we are familiar with decontamination technologies, such as fumigation and antimicrobial products, that make a polluted site once again inhabitable for human life. But in Israel's case the blood does not literally cleanse; rather it symbolizes the spiritual cleansing that can only be accomplished by the spilling of blood, that is, at the cost of a life. As a public ritual it made understandable to the people that the Lord was holy and that the priests were the sole designates who were adequately cleansed to serve before the Lord. This ritual picture showed the necessity of spiritual cleansing as preparatory for authentic worship in the presence of the Lord.

*Consecrating the tabernacle and the priests (vv. 10–13).* The Lord had already assigned Moses the task of anointing the place of worship and the priests (Exodus 30:22–33; 40:9–16). Now Moses carefully carried out the assignment in the ordination service (cf. Exodus 37:29). The anointing oil was made up of an exclusive formula. It could not be utilized for any other purpose, nor was any other formula to be used for the anointing rite. This reminds me of my high school days when I worked for a fruit juice stand named Orange Julius. By its name you can guess that it specialized in an orange beverage that had a special concoction of ingredients that distinguished it from any other orange drink. There was a "special powder" that made the key difference in the sweet, foamy drink. The mother company sold the powder to authorized franchise owners. Supposedly only a few people in the company knew the formula, but that did not stop us kids from speculating, and some even attempted to duplicate it. The anointing oil followed a divine recipe made up of measured portions of fragrant spices (myrrh, cinnamon, cane, and cassia) that were mixed in about four quarts of olive oil (Exodus 30:22–25). This mixture was designated "a holy anointing oil" (Exodus 30:25), not because of inherently sacred ingredients but because the oil was uniquely related to the holy worship of God.

The term "anoint" in our passage indicates a smearing of the oil on the surface of the tabernacle and its furniture. The text highlights "the altar" and its sevenfold anointing (v. 11). The altar was the location where the priests daily made sacrifice to atone for the sins of the people. The procedure varied with persons. Moses "poured" oil over the head of Aaron, resulting in the oil bathing his face and shoulders (Exodus 29:7; Leviticus 21:10). The act of pouring was reminiscent of the ministry of the priests who poured oil for the rites of the grain offering and the cleansing of lepers (Leviticus 2:1, 6; 14:15, 26). The blood of sacrificial animals was also poured out (Leviticus 8:15; 9:9). All was done for the effect of consecrating the place and the person of mediation. To consecrate one and not the other would be of no benefit. Both must be cleansed. This was true of our Lord Jesus who was the sanctified offering and at the same time the official who entered into the holy throne room of Heaven, bringing his precious blood before God his Father (Hebrews 7:26; 9:11, 12).

The significance of the anointing oil was its symbolic association with the Spirit of God (1 Samuel 16:13; Isaiah 61:1). Priests, kings, and prophets received the Spirit, and in many cases they were simply known as "the anointed." The oil represented the power of the Spirit that enabled the priests to carry out their duties. The Spirit's presence distinguished the priests from regular members of the congregation. The same significance is attached to the indwelling presence of the Holy Spirit in the life of the individual Christian and the Christian church as a whole today. John's first letter tells us that Christians "have been anointed by the Holy One" as their distinguishing mark (1 John 2:20; cf. 2:27). This anointing is a spiritual anointing that comes with the presence of the Spirit in the life of each believer and is secured by the Lord Jesus Christ (2 Corinthians 1:21, 22). This anointing is provided for all believers, not just those who are clergy. All Christians are enabled by the Spirit and the gifts of the Spirit to be witnesses for Christ and to serve as the conduit of intercession for the nations.

Especially important was the anticipation of the messianic king who as God's Anointed One would bring to pass the establishment of God's kingdom. For this reason the early church referred to Jesus as "anointed" (Acts 10:38). Jesus himself in the synagogue at Nazareth quoted Isaiah's prophecy, referring it to himself: "The Spirit of the Lord is upon me, because he has anointed me to proclaim good news" (Luke 4:18). The Lord bore the responsibility of interceding for the world through the revelation and salvation that he uniquely presented to the nations. We, as his emissaries, are called upon to do the same. We are his designated witnesses for the spiritual kingdom that is offered today through the preaching of the gospel.

*Consecration offerings (vv. 14–30).* With the altar prepared with anointing oil, Moses could now offer up animal sacrifices. The *first* was a bull for the sin offering in behalf of Aaron and his sons (vv. 14–17; cf. Exodus 29:10–14;

Leviticus 4:3). By placing their hands upon the head of the animal, the priests depicted the transfer of their sin to the substitute victim. Although the priests were dressed in holy garments and the high priest had received the oil of consecration, Aaron and his sons had not yet received atonement for their sins. There remained the need to deal with their own sin before they could step into the role of mediators for the sin of the people. Because they were in a leadership position, the proper offering was the costly male bull. The blood from the animal made atonement first for the altar as the instrument of atonement made in the Tent of Meeting. Blood was necessary for the cleansing of the altar and for cleansing the priests who conducted worship. The colorful finery of their dress and the fragrant perfume of the anointing oil could not redress sin (Hebrews 9:22). Only the death of a substitute victim could do that, for as Paul said, "the wages of sin is death" (Romans 6:23). This requirement of death was fully satisfied on our behalf by the blood of our Lord Jesus Christ (Colossians 1:20) who gave himself as a sin offering (2 Corinthians 5:21).

The *second* animal sacrifice was a ram for the burnt offering (vv. 18–21; Exodus 29:15–19). As in the former case, the priests placed their hands upon the head of the animal, and the blood of the animal was applied to the altar. Two differences in the procedure from that of the bull offering were the removal of the bull's hide and entrails to outside the camp where they were burned up and the washing of the ram's legs and entrails, which were then wholly consumed on the altar. This followed the pattern of the purpose of the burnt offering that was wholly burned up as a sign of complete dedication to the Lord.[9]

The *third* animal was another ram, here designated "the ram of ordination" (vv. 22–30; Exodus 29:27–31). With blood from the slaughtered beast, Moses applied some to the lobe of Aaron's right ear, the thumb of his right hand, and the big toe of his right foot.[10] Aaron's sons received the same rite (vv. 23, 24). Moses "threw" blood against the sides of the altar (v. 24). The symbolic significance of these acts pertained to the roles of the priests and the altar as the functionaries and the place for atonement. The physical extremities of the ear, hand, and foot were smeared with blood so as to represent their complete cleansing. There was also a connection between the body part and the priests' distinctive role as mediators. The ear indicated the confessions of the people that the priests heard, the hand was involved in the handling and the preparations of the holy offerings, and the foot signified the holy environs in which they served. The central place for their activities was the brazen altar that received the blood for cleansing.

Next, Aaron and his sons presented a *wave offering* that consisted of a combination of portions of the ram offering and a grain offering (vv. 25–29). Moses' role was the preparation of the wave offering. He took the fat of the entrails and the right thigh of the ram. The fat of animal offerings was devoted to the Lord exclusively, forbidden for human consumption (7:23–25; 17:6). The objective of the prohibition was so no person could benefit from the sacrifice. On top of the animal portions he placed three grain products—a loaf of bread, a second loaf made with oil, and a thin wafer. All three were prepared without yeast in accordance with the typical practice of regular grain offerings (2:11). Yeast was a prohibited item since it represented a corrupting influence and thus was unacceptable as an offering burned on the altar before the Lord (6:17; cf. 1 Corinthians 5:6–8).[11] Moses placed the animal and grain portions in the hands of Aaron and his sons, who waved them as a gesture of presentation to God. After that Moses took back the offerings from Aaron and placed them on top of the burnt offering (the first ram) that remained burning on the fires of the altar. Moses, as the officiating priest, received the breast of the ram of ordination as his portion, which he presented to the Lord as his own wave offering. Last, Moses took anointing oil and blood from the altar and sprinkled them on the priests and their clothes. Thus, the priests were speckled with the mixture of oil and blood, a sight that signified the cleansing of the mediators. At the completion of the ritual, Moses had "consecrated" the priests, thus designating them holy in the eyes of God and the people. The people could now have confidence in the holy and pure condition of the priests, who were essential to their acceptance before the Lord. We who have the Lord Jesus as our perfect Mediator can have perfect confidence that we have total acceptance with God (Ephesians 3:12).

*Ordination meal (vv. 31, 32).* The last phase of the ordination service was the ordination meal eaten by Aaron and his sons. The meal consisted of cooked meat and baked goods from the ordination offerings. Cooking the meat at the entrance to the Tent of Meeting meant the people could witness the consumption of the meal. The priests' participation in the eating of the sacred offerings symbolized their fellowship with the Lord by virtue of partaking in the holy sacrifices offered up to him. What they did not consume was burned up that same day so that the food would not spoil and to show that no one else was qualified to eat the ordination meal.

*Seven days (vv. 33–36).* The ordination service lasted seven days. The procedure outlined above was practiced each of the seven days. The numerical symbolism of "seven" indicated that the ordination ritual was complete. It was imperative that the priests remain in the holy precincts during the whole week or they would suffer the deadly judgment of God. Since the process of ordination involved only holy elements, the priests could not leave the sacred grounds, which would subject them to ritual impurity. Although the priests received reward and recognition for their status in the community, they undertook a heavy responsibility that involved the risk of life and death. Those who lead the community of God today enjoy the blessing of ministry but also the burden of ministry (1 Timothy 3:1–7; 4:14–16; 5:22; 2 Timothy 1:6). Church leaders, whether they are ordained members or laypeople who undertake leadership roles, face accountability before God and before the church.

# 8

# The Glory of the Lord

LEVITICUS 9:1–24

IF YOU ARE A DEVOTEE of the old crooner Frank Sinatra, you know the 1960s hit song "Get Me to the Church on Time" by Lerner and Loewe:

> I'm gettin' married in the morning . . .
> Get me to the church on time.

For all the pomp and ceremony planned for a wedding, the necessary essentials are really only these three: the presence of the bride, the groom, and the minister. Without the appearance of them, there is no point in all the preparations. The guests may enjoy the music and the beautiful flowers and eat the bridal cake. But there is no marriage, only a wedding party. Up to this place in Leviticus, all that has gone before was preparatory for this central event—the appearance of God among his people. The sacrifices delineated, the priests ordained, and the cleansing of the sanctuary and of the people made it possible for the Lord to accept the worship of his people. The presence of God was often described as the appearance of the glory of the Lord. The purpose of this inaugural worship was ". . . that the glory of the LORD may appear to you [the people]" (v. 6), and the outcome was just that: "the glory of the LORD appeared to all the people" (v. 23). These two passages are the only two places in the book of Leviticus that include the word "glory." By this sign of the fiery glory of the Lord, the people could know that the Lord was present and that he had received their worship.

Worship meant communion between God and his people. This is why we as the people of God gather for worship—to behold the glory of the Lord

87

and to know his acceptance of our worship. The purpose of the tabernacle and the sacrifices was to safeguard the relationship initiated by the Lord with the Israelites. We will discover through the exposition of this first occurrence of worship in the Tent of Meeting that we too as Christians enjoy the glory of the Lord and have full assurance of his approval of us and our offering of worship. Ministers lead the congregation in worship, approach God through the atoning blood, and bring God's word of blessing to the people. Worship leads to the congregation's assurance that the Lord is among them and receives them.

### The Call to Worship (vv. 1–6)

Moses, as the chief mediator between God and Israel, followed the Lord's directions by calling for Aaron, his sons, and the representative elders of the people to prepare for the first formal act of worship in the Tent of Meeting. Although Moses and Aaron played crucial roles in the worship service, it must never be forgotten that the Lord himself gave these directions to Moses (v. 6).[1] Worship begins with God's instructions, not with the ideas of men and women. When we come before the Lord in the proper way, we will have acceptance. When we come according to human devices, we put at risk the assurance of acceptance.

*The inaugural service (v. 1).* The service began on the "eighth day," that is, the day following the seven days of priestly ordination (Exodus 29:35; Leviticus 8:33). All the events of the first communal service occurred on this one day.[2] The significance of "the eighth day" in Israelite law was its ceremonial role as a day of giving to the Lord. For example, the firstborn of oxen and sheep remained with their mother for seven days and then were fit for offering to the Lord on the eighth day (Exodus 22:30; Leviticus 22:27). The sign of the covenant was circumcision of the male children born to the Hebrew people. On the eighth day this rite was performed (Leviticus 12:3). The eighth day was also a day of purging an unclean Israelite from his pollution after a seven-day period of isolation (Leviticus 14:8–10, 23).[3] It is striking that the traditional Christian day set aside for worship has been the first day of the week, that is, the eighth day following a seven-day segment of time (Acts 20:7; 1 Corinthians 16:2). It was the day of our Lord's resurrection (Luke 24:1–3), the initiation of the new creation that displaced the old seven-day creation.

*Offerings for Aaron the priest (v. 2).* The offerings for Aaron as the officiating priest consisted of "a bull calf for a sin offering and a ram for a burnt offering" (cf. Leviticus 4:3; 8:2, 18; 16:3). The sin offering was for cleansing from impurities and the burnt offering for atonement. According to the sacrificial regulations of chapters 1—7, the sin offering was required of all worshipers, but the burnt offering was a voluntary offering. The necessity of offering these animals for Aaron before he could perform his duties underscored the limitations of Aaron and his sons (cf. Hebrews 5:3). Although consecrated to the service of the Lord, they were persons who still had impurities and committed sins. The ordination service, which lasted for seven days, included their ritual cleansing, but it was not a once-for-all purging (contrast Hebrews 7:27). Purging from sin was a daily requirement. The priests must be purged of their sins and forgiven before they could adequately intervene on behalf of the people. God did not tolerate anyone less than a consecrated and forgiven clergy. If the high priest sinned against the Lord, the people suffered the guilt of the priest too, unless the priest was purged of his sin. For this reason the elders must have been especially concerned about the spiritual status of the high priest. We too must have blameless clergy whose lives match their leadership role (Titus 1:6, 7). It is a fruitless endeavor for an unregenerate minister to lead a church.

*Offerings for the people (vv. 3–5).* Although Moses spoke directly to Aaron, he did not speak directly to the people concerning their offerings. He commanded Aaron to provide instructions for the offerings to the people. From the start of the ceremony Aaron functioned as a mediator, here as the go-between of Moses and the people. The reason for turning to Aaron was to elevate the high priest in the eyes of the people. Aaron and his household were the priestly order. There would not be a Mosaic order of priests. The service was the public act of worship.[4] The offerings for the people included animal sacrifices and a grain offering. All of the regular five offerings were given except the guilt offering, which involved restitution and was a private ceremony. An explanation for the offerings follows: "for today the LORD will appear to you" (v. 4b). This remark assumed that the people well understood that communion with God required the implementation of sacrifices. The Hebrew word translated "appear" (from *ra'ah*) in verse 4 occurs four times in our passage, three times describing the appearance of "the glory of the LORD" (vv. 6, 23, 24). An "appearance" of the glory of the Lord was a visible manifestation of God's presence. Theophany, which means the outward show of God, involved a visible light or fire. The best known to Bible students is the burning bush in which God appeared to Moses in the desert (Exodus 3:2). What our passage echoes, however, is the blazing appearance of God at Sinai when he revealed his law to Moses. The tent was in effect a portable Sinai.[5] The Apostle John described the incarnation of Jesus in similar imagery (John 1:14). Our Lord embodied the presence of the glory of the Lord and thus was a tabernacle.

Sometimes the Christian community overlooks the importance of sacrifice when coming to the Lord in worship. We do not witness the slaughter of animals today in our worship services, but our worship is predicated on the blood sacrifice of the Lord Jesus Christ. There is no acceptance, and there is no worship without spiritual cleansing and the forgiveness of sin afforded by the death of the Lord Jesus. It is only by God's acceptance of us through Christ's atonement that we can share in the glory of the Lord (John 17:22–24).

*Purpose of worship (v. 6).* The purpose of the sacrifices was to prepare for the coming of "the glory of the LORD," which occurred in dramatic fashion at the end of the ritual offerings (vv. 6, 23, 24). The fire of the Lord broke forth from the Tent of Meeting and consumed the smoldering animal portions that had remained upon the altar. Levitical law required the priests to maintain the fires on the altar perpetually (6:12, 13). Our passage shows that the altar's fires came initially from God himself (9:24). The expression "the glory of the LORD" was a technical expression for the "manifest presence" of God among his covenant people, Israel.[6] In essence the glory of the Lord was equivalent to the person and name of the Lord. Where his glory appears, he is present. The glory was something that could be seen by the human eye and inhabited a visible cloud (Exodus 16:10). God's "glory" was associated with a fiery display of blazing majesty. At Sinai the Lord appeared before the people and spoke from the flaming mountain (Exodus 24:17; Deuteronomy 5:24). Also, the Lord's "glory" was manifested in a cloud that filled the Tent of Meeting at the completion of its construction (Exodus 40:34, 35). When the Lord spoke through his prophet Moses at the Tent of Meeting, the Lord made visible his glory to the congregation (Numbers 14:10). By the visible coming of the glory, the people knew that the Lord had taken up residence in the Tent of Meeting.

The Lord's disclosure of himself to his people, however, had its fullest expression in the person of Jesus Christ. By his human incarnation, the glory of God became known to those who believed (John 1:14; Hebrews 1:3), and especially through Jesus' death and resurrection the glory of the Lord became manifest (Romans 6:4; Hebrews 2:9). But whereas the majesty of God's glory in Old Testament times often instilled fear in those who witnessed his awesome power and heard his thunderous voice, the Lord Jesus came in humble trappings and preached the grace and truth of the kingdom. Our sure hope in the glory to come sustains us in our present sufferings (2 Corinthians 4:17; 1 Peter 5:10). The presence of the Spirit among us as we worship assures us of both present and future acceptance with God (cf. Leviticus 26:12 with 2 Corinthians 6:16).

## The Cleansing of the Priests (vv. 7–14)

After the planning and gathering of the elements for worship, the priests first underwent ritual cleansing—a sin offering followed by a burnt offering. The order of the offerings is significant. The sin offering made the worshiper's gifts acceptable for the service of the Lord. Our sin must be dealt with before we can offer ourselves and our gifts to the Lord.

*Sin offering for cleansing (vv. 7–11).* The offerings were to remove sin from the priests and cleanse the altar where they were to function (v. 7). The death of the animal was a strong reminder of the costly suffering of an innocent life on account of the priest's sinfulness. Aaron in accordance with the normal regulations for the sin offering (4:3–12) presented a bull calf for himself (v. 8). He applied its blood to the altar's four protruding horns at the corners of the altar. He next poured the blood at the base of the altar, signifying that the blood of the victim belonged to God (v. 9). The power of life was in the blood, and thus the blood belonged exclusively to God since he is Creator of life (17:11, 14). The belief that divine prerogative determines life and death has shaped Western civilization's view of *all* life as sacred. Aaron burned up on the altar the fat, the kidneys, and the lobe of the liver; the flesh and hide he carried outside the camp, where he burned them up in a designated clean place (vv. 10, 11).[7] This would have been the first recorded time in the passage that Aaron left the confines of the tabernacle after his seven-day ritual of ordination. Completely reducing the animal to ashes showed that the priest was not to benefit from the meat or the hide. Aaron was guilty of uncleanness, and the animal victim was wholly sacrificed as a complete substitute for him.

*Burnt offering for atonement (vv. 12–14).* The second animal was the ram for the burnt offering that was cut into pieces. The message of the burnt offering was the person's total dedication to the Lord and the forgiveness of sin. The high priest himself slaughtered the animal because it was an offering made on his behalf. His sons as before presented to him the blood. But with this burnt offering he cast the blood against the sides of the altar rather than pouring it out at the base (v. 12). This casting of the blood was in accordance with the normal procedure for the burnt offering (1:5, 11). It was also the case in Aaron's ordination service, except that the ritual included Moses tossing blood on Aaron's clothing (8:19, 24). The priests gave him the animal's butchered pieces including the ram's head for incineration on the altar (v. 13). What remained were the entrails and the legs. These Aaron washed with water to remove any debris, making them suitable for an offering (v. 14). These in turn were burned up with the burnt offering. As in the sin offering offered first, the animal was fully incinerated, but in this case at the altar.

## The Cleansing of the People (vv. 15–21)

*Sin and burnt offerings (vv. 15, 16).* Only after the cleansing of Aaron could the offerings be presented on behalf of the people. For the people a goat for the sin offering was called for in accordance with the typical sin offering for an individual person (4:27, 28). A major difference, however, was that the sin offering for the layperson was a female goat, but for a leader of the community a male animal was required (4:22, 23). That the people offered a male goat showed that the male victim was to be a representative of all the people, including the community's elders. The burnt offering for the people included a calf and a lamb, both male yearlings (v. 3), which Aaron presented according to the regular procedure for burnt offerings.

*Grain and peace offerings (vv. 17–21).* Additional offerings of grain and peace sacrifices followed, both of which were part of the regular sacrifice system (chapters 2, 3). Both of these offerings were voluntary gifts as signs of commitment and thanksgiving to God. The grain offering consisted of fine flour over which was poured oil and was sprinkled with incense (2:1). Aaron took a handful of flour as a memorial portion (2:2), which he placed on top of the morning's burnt offering (the daily offering, Exodus 29:38–40) and burned it up on the altar (v. 17). Last, he took the animals for the peace offering, slaughtering the ox and ram. As in the former cases, the blood of the victims was thrown against the sides of the altar (v. 18). These two offerings provided the daily livelihood of the priests. The baked goods belonged to the officiating priest and the other priests. Also, select portions of the peace offerings could be consumed by the priests, but there were specific prescriptions for when and where the eating could occur. Failure to fulfill the proper etiquette meant excommunication from the community (Leviticus 7:9–21). The fat and blood of the peace offerings could not be eaten by anyone, priest or not; they belonged to God exclusively. The sons of Aaron placed the fat portions on the animal's breasts on the altar, and Aaron burned them up, but the breasts and the right thigh Aaron took and presented as a wave offering (vv. 19–21). By the priests eating the grain and peace offerings, the ritual showed that the Lord accepted the offerings. Again, because of the public nature of this inaugural worship service, the priests performed the duties that otherwise were the customary role of the individual layperson (7:30).

## The Worship of God (vv. 22–24)

*Priestly blessing of the people (vv. 22, 23a).* Worship resulted in a blessing for the congregation. Aaron invoked a blessing with uplifted hands, perhaps worded similarly to the traditional priestly blessing:

> The LORD bless you and keep you;
> the LORD make his face to shine upon you and be gracious to you;
> the LORD lift up his countenance upon you and give you peace.
>       (Numbers 6:24–26)

The posture of uplifted hands in prayer indicated that the Lord was the recipient of the supplications offered by the person praying. The psalmist declared, "Let my prayer be counted as incense before you, and the lifting up of my hands as the evening sacrifice!" (Psalm 141:2; also 1 Kings 8:22; Psalm 28:2). This important feature of public blessing is a standard element in the church service to this day. The meaning of "blessing" in the Bible may include material prosperity but always implies spiritual and general welfare.[8] The Lord promised the congregation material favor for obedience to the law of the Lord (e.g., Deuteronomy 28:1–14). As the priests ministered before the Lord, they had the duty of invoking blessings on the people (Deuteronomy 10:8; 21:5). Moses joined Aaron in the tent and upon exiting shared in proclaiming another blessing. Why the two men were in the tent is unstated, but it is consistent with the tenor of the service that they were praying on behalf of the congregation.[9] That the two joined in the blessing showed the solidarity of the great prophet Moses and the high priest Aaron (v. 23a). This demonstrated to the people the approval of Moses on the proceedings. Today, through the ministry of reconciliation based on the blood of Christ, Christians receive and declare the peace that Christ affords those who entrust themselves to the Lord (2 Corinthians 5:18–20; Colossians 1:20). This peace is not material fortune but *spiritual* prosperity in the church's present service to Christ. When we worship the Lord, we receive the blessing of God's presence, and we depart the worship service with the joy and comfort of knowing that God's favor rests upon us.

*The glory of God (vv. 23b, 24a).* After the blessing was proclaimed by Aaron and Moses, the Lord responded to the people's worship, dramatically showing his power and majesty. The glory of God "appeared" (v. 23b) to the people as a blazing fire that originated from the tent, presumably from the Most Holy Place where God resided.[10] The fire consumed the smoldering offering and fat on the altar in a fiery blast (cf. Leviticus 6:9). The purpose of the inaugural worship (v. 6) was fulfilled by the appearance of God, proving to the people that the Lord indeed resided among them. This remarkable sight recalled the theophany of God at Mount Sinai where the glory of the Lord "was like a devouring fire" (Exodus 24:17; cf. 2 Chronicles 7:3; Ezekiel 1:27, 28). The God of the mountain had become the God of the tent in their very midst. A similar occurrence at the inaugural service in Solomon's temple reflects the same purpose (2 Chronicles 7:1).[11] God's residence was in the newly built temple. But there the fire that consumed the offerings came down from Heaven itself!

The worship of the congregation at Sinai was rooted in the blood offerings provided. The efficacy of the blood's atonement that purged and reconciled the people ensured that the Lord was present according to his promise: "There [at the Tent of Meeting] I will meet with the people of Israel, and it shall be sanctified by my glory" (Exodus 29:43). Now the people had full confidence in the adequacy of Aaron's priesthood. God had accepted the mediation of Aaron and the offerings of the congregation. For us as Christians we have a more secure acceptance with God since his presence in our lives and in the universal Church are guaranteed by the sacrifice of our Lord Jesus Christ. The writer to the Hebrews affirmed that the sacrifice and mediatory role of Jesus was perfectly offered and perfectly accepted by the Father (Hebrews 7:22—8:2; 9:11, 12). "But when Christ had offered for all time a single sacrifice for sins, he sat down at the right hand of God, waiting from that time until his enemies should be made a footstool for his feet. For by a single offering he has perfected for all time those who are being sanctified" (Hebrews 10:12–14). The mystery of God's regal majesty and awesome authority are sometimes lost today in our worship. Although the fire of God's glory is not seen by the naked eye today until the Lord bodily returns, the eye of faith affirms the presence of God in Christ who is ever present with his people. When we meet to worship, we meet in the name of the Lord, based on the atoning sacrifice of Christ alone. There is no basis for acceptance apart from the reality of God offering himself in Christ as the purging and reconciling offering for our sins. For this reason all peoples from all different ethnicities, languages, and cultures have a common place at the foot of the cross. There is simply no rhyme or reason to a segregated worship in the local body of a church. To exclude someone from a worship service based on such extrinsic criteria as economic standing, racial features, or cultural background flies in the face of the meaning of God's gracious provision for sinners whereby he unifies his people in his very person. The embodiment of God's presence among his people is in the body and person of our Lord Jesus Christ, not in any physical building, social stratum, or creedal statement.

*The response of the congregation (v. 24b).* Such gracious actions resulted in the spontaneous praises of the people at the spectacular confirmation of God's presence in their midst. Their response was both vocal and visible. At the sight of God's glory, they shouted, and they humbly bent down (to their knees?) upon their faces. A similar response occurred at the temple inauguration service, at which the people declared, "For he is good, for his steadfast love endures forever" (2 Chronicles 7:3).[12] There may be a series of sound plays in the Hebrew language that accentuates the theology of the passage. When the Lord "appeared" (*wayye'ra'*) and the people "saw" (*wayyar'*) the blazing fire, the congregation "shouted" (*wayyaronnu*). The worship of God resulted in both praise and humility. There was joyful acclamation but also hushed silence. This is the appropriate reaction of those who have witnessed the glory of the Lord. Whether we are in public worship or private devotions, our response to God must be characterized by prudent praise. We must worship enthusiastically and wholeheartedly but informed by our knowledge of the awe-inspiring God we serve (Psalm 33:1; Habakkuk 2:20). *Casual* dress in public worship is the trend in our times, but we must not mistakenly think that we are free to treat *casually* God's demands for authentic worship.

John Stott in his book *The Incomparable Christ* concludes with a story that the late Donald Coogan, the former Archbishop of Canterbury, told.

> There was a sculptor once, so they say, who sculpted a statue of our Lord. And people came from great distances to see it—Christ in all his strength and tenderness. They would walk all around the statue, trying to grasp its splendor, looking at it now from this angle, now from that. Yet still its grandeur eluded them, until they consulted the sculptor himself. He would invariably reply "There is only one angle from which this statue can be truly seen. *You must kneel.*"[13]

# 9

# The Priestly Mission

## LEVITICUS 10:1–20

DR. STEPHEN R. COVEY'S BEST-SELLING book *The 7 Habits of Highly Effective People* brought him center stage as an acclaimed leader in organizational management. He is recognized as one of the fathers of the mission statement movement known throughout the world. Mission statements are characteristic now of most organizations, large and small, including businesses, educational institutions, churches, and civic groups. The ideal mission statement addresses customer needs and inspires action to meet stated goals. The Bible is replete with mission statements such as Jesus' declaration, "For even the Son of Man came not to be served but to serve, and to give his life as a ransom for many" (Mark 10:45) and commissioning admonitions such as "Go therefore and make disciples of all nations" (Matthew 28:19). God gave Aaron and his sons a mission statement, so to speak, when he commissioned them to serve as spiritual authorities over and teachers of the people of God: "You are to distinguish between the holy and the common, and between the unclean and the clean, and you are to teach the people of Israel all the statutes that the LORD has spoken to them by Moses" (Leviticus 10:10, 11). In effect the priests protected the sanctity of the people through regulating and teaching godly behavior. Their role was critical to the survival of the community because they stood between the expectations of God for Israel and the sin of the people. There could not be a continuous fellowship between the Lord and the people if the priests did not exist or failed to carry out their ordained assignments properly (4:3). Symbolically, they bore the sins of the people and provided atonement through ritual sacrifice: they "bear the iniquity of the congregation, to make atonement for them before the LORD" (10:17).

Isaiah, too, recognized this when he described the Suffering Servant as the One who "bore the sin of many" (Isaiah 53:12). Because Jesus is our perfect High Priest and sacrifice who "bore our sins in his body on the tree" (1 Peter 2:24), he guaranteed the heavenly acceptance of all who put their trust in him (Colossians 2:14). Hebrews 9:11, 12 says, "But when Christ appeared as a high priest of the good things that have come, then through the greater and more perfect tent (not made with hands, that is, not of this creation) he entered once for all . . . thus securing an eternal redemption." But because of the weaknesses of the priests who served in the sanctuary, this rock-solid assurance was not one that the people of Israel could enjoy. Our passage illustrates how Aaron's sons failed in their duty, experienced divine judgment, and then completed the task. We will see that Jesus accomplished what they could not. We will also recognize that many of the same spiritual principles that guided the priests are in the New Testament for Christian leaders today.

### Leadership's Failure in Mission (vv. 1–7)

*Judgment against disobedience (vv. 1, 2).* The sons of Aaron, Nadab and Abihu, had an irreplaceable duty: They were the intermediaries between the Lord and the people of Israel. They were specially selected by the Lord, and yet they miserably failed in fulfilling their calling to service. Priests were commanded to take hot coals from the main altar and use them to burn perfumed incense in a hand-held censer. The smoking incense symbolized the rising prayers that the people offered to God (Psalm 141:2). Although Nadab and Abihu were divinely ordained laborers in the Lord's work, they met with immediate death because of their mistreatment of holy things. Since the incense was part of tabernacle worship, it was holy to the Lord. The fire for the same reason had to come from the anointed altar in the central courtyard, where the Lord first ignited the fires of worship: "And fire came out from before the LORD and consumed the burnt offering and the pieces of fat on the altar, and when all the people saw it, they shouted and fell on their faces" (Leviticus 9:24). Our passage characterizes the fire presented by Nadab and Abihu as "unauthorized," meaning that it did not come from the source sanctioned by God. The word "unauthorized" means "strange, foreign." The same word is used for a person who is a "stranger" to a family, that is, someone who is "outside the family" unit (Deuteronomy 25:5); it also names a "forbidden woman" who was outside a person's marriage (Proverbs 2:16).

The priests offered illicit fire from an undisclosed source. No motivation is cited, and it is puzzling why they did so. For the purpose of the passage, however, it is not crucial that we know. Sometimes even the best intentions will take us in a hazardous direction. They believed that the specific command to present the offerings in the precise way prescribed by the Lord was not to be followed here, or they may have been unaware of their error. Ignorance was not excused because they held a leadership position that required more of them. By priestly example the people would learn about the holy demands of the Lord. The same is true of Christian leaders, whether in the home or the church, who are required to be blameless examples of godly living (Titus 1:6, 7).

A similar account occurred in King Uzziah's reign in Judah when he unlawfully attempted to offer incense to the Lord (2 Chronicles 26:19). He was not an authorized priest (Exodus 30:9). God struck the king with the skin disease leprosy, which he bore the remainder of his life. A significant difference is that King Uzziah deliberately sinned, but the text does not specify that Nadab and Abihu were even conscious of their mistake. Ananias and Sapphira also intentionally deceived the church and lied to the Holy Spirit (Acts 5:1–11). The outcome of producing fear and respect for the Lord in the church was the same outcome of the deaths of Aaron's sons. Nadab and Abihu were authorized, in fact being the first and second born in Aaron's house (Numbers 3:2), but they did not follow the Lord's command completely. Since they held the most important place in the worship of the Lord, their judgment was the ultimate penalty of death. The severity of the penalty showed the seriousness that sin has for the person who approaches God. It must be in obedience to the directives of the Lord. Sin exacts its costs: "For the wages of sin is death" (Romans 6:23). The writer to the Hebrews warned his readers not to trivialize the blood of Christ by rejecting his bodily sacrifice, for "it is a fearful thing to fall into the hands of the living God" (Hebrews 10:31).

It was fitting that fire coming from the Lord consumed them since they had neglected the holy fire of God. The fire that had elicited such joy and blessing from the people initially (Leviticus 9:22–24) now was a source of death and fear. We have probably had this experience with a parent who was both benevolent and at times the needed disciplinarian in the family. The proverbial "Wait until your father gets home!" signals what probably lies in store for an unruly child. Paul reflected this idea when he spoke of "the kindness and the severity of God" (Romans 11:22). This should not fuel any misconceptions of the Lord today who is thought by many to be a policeman just waiting for us to fail. Remember that the Lord Jesus came to save people and not to condemn those who already lived under sin's condemnation (Mark 10:45; John 3:17, 18). "There is therefore now no condemnation for those who are in Christ Jesus" (Romans 8:1). For the redeemed, the gospel of Christ is kindness; but those who reject the gospel face the judgment of God. We can rejoice, however, in knowing that the Lord Jesus, our perfect High Priest, had no sin and had complete and permanent acceptance with God. Our reception into the presence of the Lord cannot be jeopardized by the infirmities of our mediator nor by our own weaknesses; our acceptance has been signed, sealed, and delivered. "In him you also, when you heard the word of truth, the gospel of your salvation, and believed in him, were sealed with the promised Holy Spirit, who is the guarantee of our inheritance until we acquire possession of it, to the praise of his glory" (Ephesians 1:13, 14).

*The spiritual priorities of leadership (vv. 3–7).* The reason for the severity of God's judgment was the strategic role that priests played. As we hear in verse 3, they were "near me,"[1] that is, near the Lord. This meant that the priest alone could come near to God in worship and even then most cautiously, bringing sacrificial blood and smoking incense so as to protect him from the fiery glory of the Lord (16:3, 12, 13). By priestly intercession the Lord received his proper respect and due in the eyes of the people; this is what is meant by "sanctified" and "glorified." The impact of the priest's position was felt by the layperson as well. The laity was dependent upon a sanctified and proper priestly mediation. The original language can also be translated, "I will show myself holy" and "I will reveal my glory."[2] This translation indicates a related idea: the people learned the proper attitude of worship toward God through the example of the priest who led the way to right relationship with the Lord.

The silence of Aaron, who "held his peace"[3] though losing his firstborn sons, was striking. We can contrast his response to the typical response of a father such as Jacob who wept over the (apparent) death of his son Joseph (Genesis 37:35). Aaron's silence would have underscored forcefully to the people the gravity of what they had witnessed. As to why he maintained silence, it may have been Aaron's own fear at what happened or the dumbfounding depth of his grief. Perhaps we can attribute to Aaron the discernment that it would have been inappropriate for him to mourn in the sanctuary before the Lord; he received this specific prohibition against mourning rites in verse 6.

Since dead bodies made those who touched them ceremonially unclean, as did even being in the presence of the dead (Numbers 19:11–16), Aaron could not remove the corpses (cf. Leviticus 21:11, 12). The cousins of Aaron who were Levites and thus qualified to care for the holy precincts (Numbers 3:5–10; 18:2–6) carried away the scorched remains by using Nadab and Abihu's burnt garments as stretchers (vv. 4, 5). The bright, beautiful vestments of the priests that symbolized their priestly function (chapter 8) had become ugly gray from incineration. Moses instructed Aaron and his sons not to engage in mourning rites, such as disheveled hair and torn clothing; these were the customary outward signs of deep grief, as is the dark dress of a mourning widow today.[4] Also, they could not leave the sanctuary to attend the funeral, "for the anointing oil of the LORD [was upon them]" (v. 7; cf. 21:10–12). The significance of the "sacred anointing oil" (Exodus 30:25) was its symbolic value, designating Aaron and his sons as especially consecrated servants to the Lord (Leviticus 8:30).[5] God was not coldhearted about Aaron's feelings regarding his sons, nor was he punishing Aaron for his sons' behavior. God was saying that Aaron must put his relationship with him first, above all others. Aaron's spiritual priority was to remain holy in order to carry out his duties for the sake of the community. With his privileges, however, came solemn, even deadly, responsibility.

This incident brings to mind Jesus' instruction about the cost of discipleship. When one person asked to go and bury his father before joining Jesus' travels, the Lord surprisingly said, "Leave the dead to bury their own dead. But as for you, go and proclaim the kingdom of God" (Luke 9:60). He meant let the spiritually dead bury the physically dead. Christian discipleship means sacrificing normal priorities for the greater good of the kingdom of God. Repeatedly I see this in my ministerial students who travel from overseas to complete their education, sometimes leaving a wife and children behind for a year or more. One student, for example, could not return for the funeral of his dear mother because he did not have the funds for an unexpected return trip to Kenya. I have witnessed in my church how laypeople take their precious week or two of vacation time and devote themselves and personal resources to a short-term mission trip in typically difficult places. I have seen Christian youngsters take all of their baby-sitting money and commit it to evangelistic and benevolent causes. We must set aside our own ambitions for the greater purpose of consecrated achievements.

## The Leadership's Mission (vv. 8–11)

*Attentiveness to the mission (vv. 8, 9).* Because of the holy demands that the Lord made on the priest and the community (15:31), it was imperative that Aaron and his sons were at their best in carrying out their duties. Theirs was a life and death ministry. Thus, there was no place for intoxication or they might desecrate the holy things of God and suffer death. Drunkenness for any covenant person was shameful and prohibited (Proverbs 20:1; Habakkuk 2:16) but especially troubling for the consecrated priest. Wine was readily available to the priests since drink offerings accompanied offerings (Exodus 29:40; Numbers 28:14). Presumably the priest could drink alcoholic beverages when off-duty, so to speak, but never when functioning in the tent of the Lord. Today we recognize this principle in precarious situations. Federal laws with prison sentences prohibit airline pilots from consuming alcohol or drugs when on duty. Theirs is a life and death responsibility.

Repeatedly the New Testament warns Christians against drunkenness and licentious behavior that would sully their Christian witness (Ephesians 5:18; 1 Thessalonians 5:7, 8). We can broaden the principle to the general admonition of the Apostle Paul: "Abstain from every form of evil" (1 Thessalonians 5:22). We must give ourselves fully to the service of the kingdom, refusing to become enslaved to addictive behaviors that disable us spiritually (Titus 2:12). A sober, disciplined life is the standard especially required of all in church authority (1 Timothy 3:3, 8).[6]

*The mission of discerning and teaching spiritual truth (vv. 10, 11).* The role of the priests was twofold: to discern what was ritually holy and clean and to teach the congregation the statutes that governed proper behavior (cf. Ezekiel 44:23, 24). The task of discernment explains why sober thinking must be maintained if the priests were to make accurate judgments. The word translated "distinguish" in our passage also describes the separated life that Israel was to live. The people belong to God and must imitate his holiness in all things (Leviticus 20:26). The priests routinely determined between the ceremonially clean and unclean, such as the case of skin disorders (13:6); also they determined the monetary values of votive offerings (27:8–14) and adjudicated court cases (Deuteronomy 17:8–13). Moses taught Aaron and his sons the word of the Lord, and they in turn educated the Israelites (33:10). Teaching the commands of the Lord was essential to the well-being and preservation of the community (4:1, 9, 10, 14). The next level of responsibility was the parents who passed on these teachings to the new generation (6:1–9). The Lord measured the faithfulness of the people by their knowledge of and obedience to the word of God, as the Scripture says: "You shall follow my rules and keep my statutes and walk in them. I am the LORD your God. You shall therefore keep my statutes and my rules; if a person does them, he shall live by them: I am the LORD" (Leviticus 18:4, 5).

The same teaching ministry of the Word of God is necessary for the sanctification of the individual Christian and for the perpetuation of the Christian community today. The Holy Spirit and the Word of God enable Christians to make spiritual judgments: "Do not be conformed to this world, but be transformed by the renewal of your mind, that by testing you may *discern* what is the will of God, what is good and acceptable and perfect" (Romans 12:2; also 1 Corinthians 2:14; Philippians 1:10; 2 Timothy 3:16; 1 John 2:27). God has granted the church some who are endowed with the gift of teaching (Romans 12:7; 1 Timothy 5:17). This is also generational teaching from the older to the younger (Titus 2:1–15). Christian education is essential to the life of the church. There is no substitute for instruction in the Bible, not worship services or even prayer. These must be accompanied with study in the Word, which transforms us when we yield to its precepts and its witness to the Lord Jesus. "And we all, with unveiled face, beholding the glory of the Lord, are being transformed into the same image from one degree of glory to another. For this comes from the Lord who is the Spirit" (2 Corinthians 3:18). As we daily peer into the Word of God, the Spirit changes us; our lives begin to mirror the Word. I remember thinking one time how the way my son walked, who is over thirty years old, resembled the stride of my father, his grandfather. How did he learn this? I wondered. Then it dawned on me that my gait was the same! My son was mimicking *my* swagger, which in turn I had picked up from my father. In a similar way, by living with God's Word daily we will take on the mind of Christ.

## Leadership's Success in Mission (vv. 12–20)

*Command to complete the mission (vv. 12–15).* After offering the blueprint of what the priests must be about, Moses continued his directions for Aaron and "his surviving sons." The mention of "surviving sons" twice (vv. 12, 16) reverberates the severity of divine judgment that befell Nadab and Abihu when the commands of the Lord were neglected. It has been said that when jumping across a chasm, it is better to do so in one leap and not two steps. Better to go all the way and do it right. So it was in fulfilling the instructions of the Lord. No offhand or halfhearted measure was acceptable.

Moses first spoke of the grain offering that was a daily staple for the diet of the priests; it was their stipend for their service in the sanctuary. Moses could have repeated more details already found in chapters 2 and 6, but he chose to emphasize certain aspects of the offering. A memorial portion was burned up unto the Lord on the main altar, and the grain that was "left" was eaten by the priests. The language "is left" in the Hebrew is the same basic root word translated "surviving" when the text refers to Eleazar and Ithamar.[7] This is probably another reminder that the proper treatment of the holy things of God must be carefully fulfilled. The message of the wordplay is probably the following: *Eat the "surviving" portion of the grain offering if you want to continue as Aaron's "surviving" sons!* As a "most holy" offering, it was required of the priests to eat it at the altar in the holy sanctuary area. Its consumption by the priests symbolized on behalf of the worshiper the acceptance of his offering by the Lord. In other words, it was a shared meal with the Lord, symbolically dining together at the Lord's house. That the food was "unleavened" underscored the necessary purity of the offering; yeast is a corrupting ingredient that alters the makeup of the grain and therefore was a useful symbol for impurities and sin.

Thus, the instructions delineate the right person, the right portion, the right mixture, and the right place for consumption. "[F]or so I am commanded" (v. 13) was Moses' acknowledgment that the directives should be followed because they come from the Lord, not from Moses alone. The proper motivation for obedience was the divine character of the commands. The idea of authority in our passage reminds me of the challenge to authority that I witnessed when running with a friend on an indoor track. The posted instructions told us to run on this particular day of the week in a clockwise direction so as to create a uniform flow of runners, avoiding collisions. Some teenagers came onto the track and started some horseplay that included running in a counterclockwise direction. After barely missing a collision, we adults told them the correct direction for the day, but they refused to change directions. Only after we stopped them in the middle of the track and pointed out the posted instructions did they comply. The young people accepted the posted directives because they were written and because they bore the stamp of authenticity. Although we were adults, what we said was, in their mind, our prejudicial preferences, not the law of the gymnasium authorities! Failure to observe Moses' instructions was an offense ultimately against the Lord, not against a man. The same is true of the Word of God that is preached from the pulpit today. The authority rests in the inscripturated Word that comes from the Lord; its precepts are not the high-minded ideas of a pastor or merely a cultural expression of societal norms.

The animal offering followed a different pattern. It was not a matter of "one size fits all." Each act of worship had its own character and message. The peace offering, as the name indicates, was a celebratory feast that was shared with the priests and invited guests. An Israelite presented it as an offering of thanksgiving and praise to God for answering prayer or simply offered it as a freewill gift (7:11–21). This communal meal has its parallel in the new covenant celebration of the Lord's Supper where believers participate symbolically in the body and blood of the Savior (1 Corinthians 10:16–18). The instructions emphasize that the receiving of portions of the offerings were the priests' "due," meaning that they benefited from their service to the Lord. The officiating priest of a peace offering received for his service the right thigh of the sacrificed animal from the Lord; he shared the breast with the other priests, including their families at home (Leviticus 7:30–34). The reference to "a clean place" meant that it was available to those who were ritually clean and in a ritually clean home (22:10–16). As to the details of what constituted the ceremonially clean, the purity laws and holiness code in the subsequent chapters of Leviticus provided them. The eating of the sacrifice outside the sanctuary signaled an extension of the holy to the common domicile. Communion with the Lord was experienced in the ordinary but ritually clean home. The Israelites were to be a holy people at all times, including their homes.

Although they could not avoid uncleanness as human beings, God gave them a ceremonial remedy that restored them to fellowship with him. We have the same obligation to give thanks to God in worship, especially in light of our new citizenship in the kingdom of God: "Therefore let us be grateful for receiving a kingdom that cannot be shaken, and thus let us offer to God acceptable worship, with reverence and awe, for our God is a consuming fire" (Hebrew 12:28, 29).

*Fulfilling the mission (vv. 16–20).* There was yet a different pattern for the sin offering. According to Moses' instructions, the person who offered the sin offering on behalf of the community was to eat its meat in the sanctuary (6:25–30). Its consumption symbolized that the priest achieved reconciliation for the offending party through carrying out the ritual meal. In this way the priest bore the sin of the people. The eating of the meat confirmed the acceptance of the atonement by the Lord and the forgiveness of sin. After the tragedy of Nadab's and Abihu's sudden death, Moses was particularly alert to any infraction and "diligently inquired"[8] about the obedience of the sons (v. 16). The grammatical construction in the original language makes this clear: literally, "inquiring he inquired." Moses was especially disturbed to discover that Aaron's "surviving" two sons, Eleazar and Ithamar, had not followed precisely the divine instructions for the sin offering. They totally burned up the animal and did not partake of it, which meant that the congregation stood in jeopardy before the Lord (6:26).

Aaron's response and Moses' acceptance of his explanation illustrates the discernment that Aaron and his sons were called upon to practice as part of their spiritual assignment (v. 10). Aaron recognized that the special circumstances of the day's offerings by which his older sons had offered unauthorized fire compromised the sin offering. Therefore, he reasoned that it would be unfitting for them to enjoy the meat as a benefit (6:30). What is significant here is that although the detail of the Law was altered, Aaron's decision reflected the purpose of the Law and received divine approval. That Moses "approved" signaled that the Lord had "approved" of the decision (vv. 19b, 20).[9] This is the only occasion when Moses received instruction from Aaron. This signaled to the congregation that Aaron and his sons had a special authority when ruling on ritual matters. Unlike his older two sons, Eleazar and Ithamar carried out their commission properly in accord with the discernment of Aaron.

Spiritual leadership, whether in the home or a Sunday school class or among the congregation, impacts others for their good or their detriment. Christian directives are similar. Spiritual leaders are to meet the highest standard of godly living and stand in peril of chastening if they fail to realize their commission in accord with divine instruction (1 Timothy 3:1–13; 4:16; James 3:1). They are especially to serve as examples to the congregation. Also, they are to avoid the pitfalls of aberrant teachings and theological fads that compromise or distract from the gospel as revealed by the Word of God through the apostles.[10] Paul reserves his sternest warnings against those who distort the gospel: "But even if we or an angel from heaven should preach to you a gospel contrary to the one we preached to you, let him be accursed. As we have said before, so now I say again: If anyone is preaching to you a gospel contrary to the one you received, let him be accursed" (Galatians 1:8, 9).

Christians can have perfect peace in knowing that our Lord Jesus Christ is the High Priest who is our perfect mediator. He was not hindered by sin; his sacrifice and his priesthood were fully pleasing to the Lord. We have no reason to doubt the effectiveness of Jesus' intercession for us and the forgiveness of sin we have received from his death on the cross. Hebrews 4:16 reminds us, "Let us then with confidence draw near to the throne of grace, that we may receive mercy and find grace to help in time of need." The assurance of salvation can be ours when we entrust ourselves to Jesus, his atonement on our behalf, and God's acceptance of his spotless sacrifice. The proof of this is his resurrection from the tomb. He sits now in the heavens, seated at the right hand of God, and we are assured the same position as citizens of Heaven because we are in Christ. Our Christian duty, like the saints (the holy ones) of old, is to live holy lives (1 Peter 1:13–16).

# 10

# Dining with God

LEVITICUS 11:1–47

EVERY CULTURE HAS ITS OWN food taboos. Dogs are not eaten in the West because they are considered "friends"; in China, however, they are accepted without hesitation. Next time you "down" a juicy hamburger, remember that you are eating an animal (cow) considered sacred among Hindus. The nations of the ancient world practiced food taboos related to their worship, too. Pigs, for instance, were widely rejected as a fit offering for the deities, except for the gods of evil and the underworld.[1] Differences in Christian subcultures also occur, reaching back as early as the first inroads of Christianity into Gentile areas where they did not observe Jewish traditions (Acts 15). In the "Bible Belt" where I grew up, alcohol (even a drop of rum for cooking purposes) and cigarette smoking (it was possible to chew on a pipe but not to smoke it) were strictly prohibited. The clash of cultures may be illustrated by this humorous tale. A missionary couple newly arrived from the States paid their first visit to the home of one of their European parishioners. When they arrived at the door for the greeting, the German hostess dropped her wine glass when she saw that the pastor's wife had makeup on her face! Although health concerns sometimes lead to naming certain "vices," the main criterion is tied to the abuse of the body, "a temple of the Holy Spirit" (1 Corinthians 6:19). As the Apostle Paul explained, "You are not your own."

God gave ancient Israel a designated list of foods that were permissible for food consumption. The text says specifically why: "For I am the LORD your God. Consecrate yourselves therefore, and be holy, for I am holy" (v. 44a). This was the assignment God gave Israel at Mount Sinai; they were to be "a holy nation" (Exodus 19:6; cf. 1 Peter 2:9). We will discover that the food laws achieved two purposes for Israel. First, the dietary laws were tied to creation, indicating that the taking of created life was the Creator's province and prerogative. Second, the food laws distinguished Israel from the neighboring nations and made Israel uniquely the Lord's possession. By resisting the foods of the nations, the Israelites had a built-in safeguard against assimilation and taking up the religious life of pagan cultures. That there was religious consideration given to proper food for worship and consumption can be seen even before the Mosaic legislation. God instructed Noah to house in the ark "clean" and "unclean" specimens, and upon disembarking he presented the clean to the Lord in worship (Genesis 7:2, 8; 8:20). Evidently there was an intuitive awareness of what was appropriate for an offering presented to the Lord. Also, one of the universals in human society is a shared meal among its members that heightens a sense of community. The church followed the Old Testament pattern of a fellowship meal. They partook of the Lord's Supper together (Acts 2:42; 1 Corinthians 11:20–34; Galatians 2:12; Jude 12).

What was meant by "unclean" was not the superficial dirt that an animal might bear but a ritual category that had an underlying spiritual message. Commentator Roy Gane tells of a new Christian, a farmer, whose church observed the food laws found in our Leviticus passage. After the farmer had his baptismal service, he hosted the congregation with a meal that included pork! When the pastor asked him if he had learned about "clean" and "unclean" meats, the farmer answered, "Yes, sir . . . so I scrubbed my hogs real good before I slaughtered 'em!"[2] This farmer did not yet understand that the pig was inherently ritually "unclean" and could not be moved to the "clean" category on the basis of a scrubbing.

An important factor we often overlook is the teaching on holy living that governed Israel's every behavior. There was no such thing as a secular versus a religious life in the Law. All was sacred under God's dominion. Paul expressed the same governing principle to his Corinthian readers: "So, whether you eat or drink, or whatever you do, do all to the glory of God" (1 Corinthians 10:31). There is no more common and important feature than family and community meals. By virtue of the holy Tent of Meeting in the midst of Israel's tribal encampment, the people were obligated to be consecrated to God in their daily activities. Thus, the human condition and community practices were deemed either fitting for God (that is "clean") or unfitting (that is "unclean"). Since the people participated in sacred meals, such as the peace offering in their homes, there was recognition that the holiness of the sanctuary was extended to the homes of the people. They and their homes must be ritually clean, and that included their diets.

In order to answer the chief question of what the food laws were designed to do, we must review the chapter to establish the context's structure and basic contents.

## Holy Nourishment (vv. 1–23, 41–45)

That the Lord spoke to *both* Moses and Aaron reflected the important assignment that Aaron and his sons played in applying and instructing the Israelites in the purity laws in chapters 11—15 (10:10, 11; 13:1; 14:33; 15:1). Two listings of creatures occur in our passage (vv. 2b–23, 41–43). The precise identity of several Hebrew terms for the animals listed is uncertain. For this reason the modern English versions show variations in some cases. The categories of the creatures are arranged according to their natural habitat: the land (vv. 2b–8), sea (vv. 9–12), sky (vv. 13–23), and the ground (vv. 41–43). Two negative terms are used to describe the cultic status of the creatures. The more frequent word is "unclean" (vv. 1–8, 24–40). This term describes those creatures that were not only illicit but also polluted through consumption and physical contact. The second is the harsher term "detestable" (vv. 9–23, 41–43); the people who eat these creatures made themselves "defile[d]" (v. 43) in the eyes of God.[3] They include most sea and sky creatures and all reptiles. Sandwiched between the two lists are instructions regarding the touching of dead carcasses (vv. 24–40). The summary conclusion in verses 46, 47 provides the purpose of the food laws, which as we have said is grounded in the holy character and demands of God.

*Land animals (vv. 2b–8).* The land beasts receive more attention than other categories, although meat was not a common feature of the average Israelite household. Land animals were created on the same day as the first humans, the sixth day (Genesis 1:24, 25). The criteria for determining the proper four-footed animal was twofold: completely split hooves *and* chewing the cud (bringing food up from the stomach to be chewed again). The word "and" is significant in verse 3 because the creature must possess both features. These included domesticated livestock—the cattle, sheep, and goats that dominated daily ritual sacrifice and feasts and were the most important of the creatures.[4] Animals that possessed one *or* the other, as we find in verse 4, did not qualify. Special mention is made of four animals commonly known to the Israelites that were prohibited because they possessed only one of the features—the camel, rock badger, hare (or rabbit), and pig.[5] Ritual contagion from the carcasses of the unlawful animals could occur by touch also and therefore were to be avoided when possible.

*Sea creatures (vv. 9–12).* The creatures of the seas and rivers were created on the fifth day. Fish was not a common staple for the ancient Israelite's diet. Fish was typically imported (Nehemiah 13:16; cf. 2 Chronicles 33:14), although some species may have been fished in the fresh waters of the Sea of Galilee. Ezekiel's prophecy portrays an idyllic future in Palestine when fish of all varieties will be abundant (Ezekiel 47:9, 10). At a later time, as in New Testament times, the fishing industry became more important to Palestine. As in the previous category, all fish with two features could be eaten—"fins and scales" (v. 9). Creatures that lacked one or the other had to be viewed as imperfect. Any incomplete creature would not be appropriate for the perfections of the Lord and his people. Moreover, sea creatures that crawled rather than swam appeared out of place as inhabitants of the sea and thus were inappropriate for consumption. A new element in this description is the repeated terms "detestable" and "detest," occurring in total four times in three verses. The usage of this word group usually identifies unfit creatures in food laws but occurs one time (verbal form) designating a religious idol that must be "utterly detest[ed]" (Deuteronomy 7:26). This shows the severity of transgressing this food law.

*Sky creatures (vv. 13–23).* Birds and flying insects are suitable for the air. The birds were created on the same day as the sea creatures. Both birds and fish bore the blessing of God, so that they were numerous and prolific (Genesis 1:22). Birds could be caught for food by snares and nets (Proverbs 1:17; Amos 3:5). No criteria are given for discriminating among the birds; rather, a list of forbidden birds follows. These forbidden birds also received the unfavorable designation "detest[able]" (v. 13). Many of these birds are carnivorous (e.g., hawk, falcon, vulture), feeding on meat killed by hunting or feeding on dead flesh, carrion. Flying insects are treated under the same category of the sky habitat because of their flight or hopping. The kind of mobility that the insect had was probably a factor in determining the approved insects for consumption (see v. 42). Those bound to the ground on all fours were unsuitable, but those with jointed legs that enabled them to jump, such as locusts, were edible (see John the Baptist's diet, Matthew 3:4).

*Ground creatures (vv. 41–45).* The second sustained list names creatures limited to the ground. These are creatures that were the least favorable because of their mode of locomotion and their lowly position in deference to humans, who stand erect. They have unbroken contact with the ground: "swarming things that swarm on the ground" (vv. 29, 41, 42). None of these varmints were accepted for consumption. Snakes, rodents, and creeping things were among these. Eight specific types are mentioned in verses 29, 30 in the context of instruction pertaining to dead carcasses. These were also "detestable" but had the added feature of a person making *himself* equally "detestable" through contact with them (v. 43). The words "make . . . detestable" and "defile" mean "to make one ritually unclean." This level of defilement was to be especially feared. This is probably why only here in the chapter do we have the exhortation to holiness: "Consecrate yourselves therefore, and be holy" (v. 44). Rather than making themselves defiled, the Israelites had to labor to be holy ritually through the careful observance of the purity laws.

The food laws were based on the theology of God's holy character. It was not merely a cultural manifestation of the Israelites but an important relational concept within the unique covenant commitment that God had formed with the nation of Israel at Sinai. That the Lord "brought [them] up out of the land of Egypt to be [their] God" (v. 45) recalled that the people were redeemed and exclusively belonged to him. The Israelites demonstrated their gratefulness and obedience to the Lord through maintaining the purity laws and purification rites. The Apostle Paul expressed a similar sentiment when imploring his Christian readers to live a life worthy of their salvation and namesake, our Lord Jesus Christ (Ephesians 4:1; Philippians 1:27; Colossians 1:10; 1 Thessalonians 2:12; 2 Thessalonians 1:5).

*Why these foods?* Scholars have offered various explanations for why particular creatures were prohibited. The hygienic value of the Hebrews' diet has long been recognized, but this is secondary; some of the prohibited creatures are not unhealthy for human consumption, such as camel and rabbit meat. We must look for another reason. Since the creation account in Genesis reflects distinctions in the animal world and the first created humans distinguished foods in their diets (Genesis 1:26; 9:3), the Hebrew food laws probably echoed the earliest recognition that there was an ordained pattern in creation to be followed. God is a God of order, and creation reflects harmony and symmetry. If the creature in question did not conform to the criteria given by the Creator, the food was disapproved. The food laws taught the Israelites that they too must conform to the holy standards of their Creator and Redeemer. By their very dietary and domestic habits, the Israelites differentiated themselves from the surrounding nations.

In times of exile, for example, the Jews rekindled their distinctive heritage such as observing the dietary laws. Daniel and his friends resisted the foods of Nebuchadnezzar's court and remained true to their Hebrew faith (Daniel 1:8). The Jewish religious leaders became so adamant about adhering to their food practices that those practices became a badge of Jewish identity during the post-exilic era and into Christian times (Colossians 2:16). Observant Jews to this day eat only kosher foods, that is, foods and their preparation that are fit for eating in accordance with Jewish law. The term *kosher* comes from rabbinic literature, not from the Bible. Elaborate Jewish laws after the first century in rabbinic literature expanded the Biblical laws, such as prohibiting the eating of dairy products with meat. This prohibition is not clearly specified in the Biblical food laws.

*Christian application.* What can we learn from these ancient food laws that will help us in our Christian living? We see firsthand the remarkable liberation that Christ has provided for us. The Law's demands have been wonderfully fulfilled in Christ's obedience so that righteousness might be realized. When we come to Christ as Savior, we are the beneficiaries of his perfect obedience and his full acceptance by God the Father. The early Christians recognized that with the coming of Christ, the food laws that once separated the Hebrews and the nations were no longer binding in the same way (Acts 10:11–16; Colossians 2:16). They did observe them, however, when they sought to be a better witness or to promote unity in the body of Christ (Acts 15:1–20; 1 Corinthians 9:19, 20). In a basic way as Christians we still observe the purpose of the purity laws when we take up their underlying principles that remain true in every generation. The Israelites observed the food laws because they were obedient to God's Word by which they brought honor and glory to the Lord, their Redeemer. The same principle directs Christian living; all that we do must be for the glory of God (1 Corinthians 10:31). Christian living that is consecrated to the Lord is derived from the inner witness of the Holy Spirit in the life of the believer; it is not external but from the inner person. Jesus said to his critics, "'Do you not see that whatever goes into a person from outside cannot defile him, since it enters not his heart but his stomach, and is expelled?' (Thus he declared all foods clean)" (Mark 7:18, 19; see Romans 14:17, 18). Observance of food taboos does not in itself bring us closer to the Lord. "Food will not commend us to God. We are no worse off if we do not eat, and no better off if we do" (1 Corinthians 8:8).

Yet Christians must use wisdom and exercise spiritual maturity in choosing food and drink (Romans 14; 1 Corinthians 8; 10:23) and in their associations with non-Christians (1 Corinthians 5:11; 2 Corinthians 6:14). One friend in my seminary days was steadfastly opposed to any drinking of an alcoholic beverage by a Christian. She was the daughter of an alcoholic and saw the destruction of her father's life and the sorrow that her family had endured. For a Christian to treat alcohol cavalierly in her presence would be an injurious gesture against this sister in the Lord. Moreover, the pain associated with drunkenness in our culture, such as drunk driving and physical abuse, would militate against Christian endorsement in the eyes of some non-Christians today. Of course, one could complain that obesity or gluttony is also a growing health problem in the United States, especially among children. There may be medical reasons for this condition, but most suffer from it due to the cultural trend of overindulgence in all areas of life. Addictive behaviors speak to the world of undisciplined lives that we need to address as Christians and give special assistance to in our churches. Our Lord urged his disciples to live a sober and watchful life: "But watch yourselves lest your hearts be weighed down with dissipation and drunkenness and cares of this life, and that day come upon you suddenly like a trap" (Luke 21:34; see Proverbs 23:2).

## Holy Living (vv. 24–40)

There is one more important aspect to the treatment of creatures that makes for holy living. Sandwiched between the listings of the food laws are the directions pertaining to the handling of dead bodies, human and animal. Since God was the God of the living who delivered his people, it was offensive to God that the dead were in his presence. Special steps were needed to remove the offense of a corpse from the sanctuary and from the camp. We remember that the Lord dramatically struck down Nadab and Abihu, Aaron's sons, for unlawful practices in the sanctuary. The removal of their scorched bodies from the sanctuary required Aaron's Levite cousins. As priests who approached God in behalf of the people, Aaron and his two surviving sons could not attend to their dead bodies or even attend their funeral (Leviticus 10:1–7). Holy living meant ridding the camp of anything that pertained to death and disease, the natural imperfections of all creatures. The main point of Moses' instructions was for the people to avoid touching corpses when possible because dead bodies conveyed ritual contagion through contact. This made the person or thing unfit to remain in the camp. Only after the proper ritual cleansing was the person or item reintegrated into the life of the community. Coming into contact with a creature's remains would be inevitable, of course, but the Lord's gift provided a remedy for uncleanness that reunited the offender to the holy camp. The passage addresses three categories of the dead: the four-footed animals forbidden for consumption (vv. 24–28), the swarming creatures on the ground (vv. 29–38), and carcasses of the creatures approved for consumption (vv. 39, 40).

*Carcasses of forbidden creatures (vv. 24–28).* These creatures were already said to be prohibited from consumption, but we learn here that their bodies were also corrupting. All corpses, human or animal, transmitted cultic corruption through touch (Leviticus 22:4; Numbers 5:2), and for consecrated persons, such as priests, just coming into the presence of a dead body resulted in defilement (Leviticus 21:11; Numbers 6:6; Haggai 2:13). The transmission of uncleanness happened through one of two ways: the touching of a dead body or through the disposal of it (vv. 24, 25). The offender was isolated from the community; the duration of pollution lasted until evening (Leviticus 22:6; Joshua 8:29). There was no automatic restoration to the camp at the close of the day. In parallel passages we learn that the offender had to wash his body before returning (Leviticus 17:15, 16; 22:6). A person who transported a cadaver, however, must undergo additional purging since the extent of the contact was longer and more substantial. It was assumed that the clothing of a person carrying off a carcass must have rubbed against the remains, and thus this defilement required laundering the garments as well as washing the person's body.[6]

*The swarming creatures on the ground (vv. 29–38).* The despised vermin that scampered across the ground or household floor deserved more elaborate precautions, especially since they were numerous and contact with them would be inevitable. These creatures, such as insects, conveyed contagion through two means: direct contact (v. 31) or indirectly through secondary contact (vv. 33–38). This latter category reminds us today of tobacco's secondary smoke that is a health risk for bystanders and children in the home. The passage gives everyday scenarios of how this could happen and how to get rid of the uncleanness. Items made of common material, such as wood and cloth, had to be submerged in water until evening (v. 32). Also, generally speaking, any item made of material that absorbed liquid required an extreme response since the corruption could not be removed. A clay pot that was defiled by insects, for example, absorbed polluted water; it had to be smashed since the water could not be completely purged (also 6:28; 15:12). Food or beverages touched by contaminated water was likewise unclean (vv. 33, 34). Cooking fixtures, such as a stove, had to be busted into pieces (v. 35). If, however, the carcass was in a spring or reservoir, the water was not unclean; it was a permanent body of water surrounded by the ground and was not portable (v. 36).[7] Another exception was seed contacted by an insect. If the seed was dry, it remained clean; contact with seed already wet, however, made it unfit. This was because the seed would absorb the contaminated water (vv. 37, 38).

*Carcasses of creatures permitted for eating (vv. 39, 40).* The sole category remaining was the dead body of approved animals. Dead creatures killed by wild animals or by natural means and not slaughtered for food could be eaten, but they still conveyed uncleanness (17:15; this was absolutely prohibited for a priest, 22:8). The purgation rite demanded more of the person who had longer contact with the corpse, involving the laundering of clothes for those who ate or transported the animal.

*Sanctifying the mortal body.* When Jesus was questioned about the resurrection, he responded, "Now [God] is not God of the dead, but of the living, for all live to him" (Luke 20:38). Our God is "the living God" (Jeremiah 10:10), and his plan is to have a living people with whom he can live and love: ". . . as God said, 'I will make my dwelling among them and walk among them, and I will be their God, and they shall be my people'" (2 Corinthians 6:16b; cf. Leviticus 26:12). Jesus was not deterred by death and the dead in bringing salvation to those who recognized him as the Son of the living God (Matthew 16:16). He was willing to touch the ceremonially unclean coffin that held the body of a widow's son and called him from death to life (Luke 7:14). And our Lord touched the corpse of Jairus' daughter:

> And when he had entered, he said to them, "Why are you making a commotion and weeping? The child is not dead but sleeping." And they laughed at him. But he put them all outside and took the child's father and mother and those who were with him and went in where the child was. Taking her by the hand he said to her, "Talitha cumi," which means, "Little girl, I say to you, arise." And immediately the girl got up and began walking (for she was twelve years of age), and they were immediately overcome with amazement. And he strictly charged them that no one should know this, and told them to give her something to eat. (Mark 5:39–43)

But the ultimate salvation of the mortal body is the resurrected and glorified body that God has in store for all who believe. ". . . this mortal body must put on immortality," the Apostle Paul said (1 Corinthians 15:53). All creation equally yearns for its release from death and decay and will join us in the future glory that awaits us at "the redemption of our bodies" (Romans 8:23). As the Lord provided a cleansing of those defiled by death and the dead in the days of Israel, the Lord has now mercifully made possible through the blood and death of our Lord Jesus a permanent and sure purification.

# 11

# Born into the
# Family of Faith

LEVITICUS 12:1–8

IF YOU VISIT A NEW MOTHER in the hospital, your first stop is undoubtedly the hospital nursery to see the new baby. And the first question inevitably from the mother is, "Have you seen the baby?" She is so pleased to learn that you have. The second question put to you is not so easily answered: "Isn't she beautiful?" Of course, this is more of a statement than a genuine question. My home pastor knew how to face the dilemma of being truthful but also pastoral. Actually, the baby is red, bald, shriveled up, and screaming. But to the parents and grandparents, she is the most beautiful baby in the world! How should you respond? My pastor would say to the beaming mother, "That's a baby! That's a baby!"

There is nothing more joyful in our lives than the birth of children. They are given great value in the Bible. The psalmist reflects the viewpoint of the Scriptures toward birthing children: "Behold, children are a heritage from the LORD, the fruit of the womb a reward. . . . Blessed is the man who fills his quiver with them!" (Psalm 127:3–5). Jesus is always depicted in the Gospels as welcoming children and their parents (e.g., Matthew 19:14). We are terribly surprised to learn, however, that the Mosaic law also declares that new mothers are "unclean." New mothers experienced a period of social segregation and afterward were required to bring animal sacrifices to the Tent of the Lord for ceremonial cleansing. How does the Leviticus requirement of purification after childbirth square with the Bible's high view of children and motherhood? We will find that the ritual of cleansing testifies to the sacredness of life and the importance of birth and motherhood and conveys the spiritual message of birth into the family of the Lord. We will come away from this passage with a renewed devotion to God as the source of all life who through his Son Jesus Christ has redeemed fallen humanity.

Our passage divides into two parts: the *sanctity* of life is reflected in verses 1–5, and the *sanctification* of life is reflected in verses 6–8.

## The Sanctity of Life (vv. 1–5)

The message of the Christian faith always celebrates life, life of all kinds, both animal and human. Ours is a God who creates, protects, and provides for life. This important aspect of God's outlook toward life shows itself in many ways, one of which is the way Biblical law instructed the Israelites in matters pertaining to the human body. The connection between the body's power to reproduce life and the various bodily fluids make for a symbolic picture of the power of life and death. Blood is the most natural evidence of life and death. It is indicative of the life-force, and consequently there was special reverence toward the treatment of blood, both of humans and animals. The blood belonged to God because he alone is Sovereign over life. Leviticus tells us that "the life of the flesh is in the blood" (17:11a). This theological rationale explains why the Mosaic law required a new mother to experience a purification ritual after childbirth. There had to be an accounting for the postnatal blood flow of the new mother in the ceremonial life of the people.

*Two clarifications.* Before we continue, however, we should pause to correct two potential misunderstandings of the law for new mothers. First, we must clarify what is meant in the text by a new mother being deemed "unclean" (v. 2b). The word "unclean" is not a term that refers to immorality; rather, it speaks of *ritual* impurity. A ritual is a symbolic act or series of acts designed to convey a message. When a mother gives birth to a child, there is a flow of blood that follows the baby's birth.[1] This is a natural function of the birth cycle. At this critical moment in the life of the mother and child, in the life of the family, and in the life of the community, the passing of blood provided a powerful image of the significance of life and its opposite, the loss of life. The flow of blood conveyed to the parents that life and death are in view. The emission also sent the message that human life is imperfect. The Bible tells us that God is the only true perfect One. He is flawless in his personal attributes, such as his love, moral purity, and faithfulness. Therefore, anything or anyone that had a physical disorder could not be admitted into the house of worship. The thought that a woman giving birth could be viewed as a *disorder* is difficult for us to understand since giving birth was and is considered a divine blessing, a cherished experience valued by Hebrew society. But further reflection on what we mean by the word *disorder* helps us accept this idea. A disorder technically means what is not the normal, regular experience of life, a change whether for good or bad. The stages of conception, pregnancy, and birth require extensive changes in the body and are not the usual daily condition of a woman's body.[2] This means a woman's pregnancy and childbirth reflect an unusual condition, not her typical healthy, whole state.

It is critical to our understanding that we remember that the key to interpreting symbolic ritual is *appearances*, namely, what the events convey, not the acts alone. It would be inappropriate for the symbol of death, in this case the mother's postnatal blood, to be present in the sanctuary where God resided. Only after the cessation of the natal fluids could the woman be accepted fully into the community of worship.[3] The change in the physical condition of the woman appeared to express a disorder.

The second clarification is that Israelite women were not the *only* ones to have a *disorder*. Men, who had physical irregularities such as emissions or skin diseases (chapters 13—15), also were deemed ritually impure. Also, our passage does *not* teach that the newborn child was considered "unclean." There is no instruction given regarding the cleansing of the child. The ritual of circumcision was not a ritual of purification (v. 3); it was a ritual of covenant initiation that declared the child's acceptance into the community of Israel. If it were a purification rite, making the child pure, then females remained in a perpetual state of uncleanness since there was no comparable rite for the daughter. The children then were not considered inherently impure.

After setting aside these potential hindrances to our understanding of the passage, we turn to the message of the text.

*Separation for the mother.* As a consequence of her physical changes, a new mother spent a specified time in seclusion, which meant a cessation of normal domestic activities, although she was permitted to live at home. The seclusion within the home was seven days if the baby was a male child or fourteen days if a female. Seven days were the same length of time in the case of a woman's monthly cycle (v. 2b; 15:19–24). Presumably the two conditions were associated because they both involved the discharge of blood. After this time of domestic segregation, she could again take up her normal household duties. Childbirth, however, required longer ritual separation because the flow of the discharge continued. During this time the mother could not be in the sanctuary, nor could she touch anything holy, such as holy food especially dedicated to the Lord.[4] Her state of ritual uncleanness restricted her from holy things, lest by contact she contaminate the holy by her impurity. The text calls this additional time "the blood of her purifying" (v. 4), meaning that she was in a process of becoming pure but was not yet fully pure.

The duration of the continued restriction was thirty-three days for a male child and sixty-six days for a female. Again, this was not a hygienic issue; rather it had a symbolic function. The point is that men and women are not naturally pure; only God is pure in all his moral perfections. Therefore, there had to be for symbolic reasons an interval of segregation until the woman's body returned to its normal state. The typical time period for the mother to complete her course of emissions was two to six weeks. That the time for a female child was twice that of a male child creates a difficulty for interpreters. The immediate thought by people in our culture today who read this may be reactionary. It can be taken simply that little boys are better than little girls. But this cannot be the case in the context of this passage since the child was not considered unclean. What may be at work here is the presence of two females; the mother and the daughter require twice as many days as the birth of a boy. If this is the case, then the assignment of the additional forty days for the daughter may be explained by the potential she has to be a child-bearer.

One feature of the purity laws in the Bible is the necessity of time as a step toward purification and reintegration into the community. Purification was always a timed process, not an instantaneous event. That the Israelite underwent an extended procedure for restoration communicated the gravity of the person's infirmity and the difficulty of access to the gathered community for worship. The people participated in the process and thereby matured in their perception of a world marred by sin. They also better understood that unaided by God's help the perfections required of them were unattainable. The principle of temporal necessity is similar to Christian experience, too. Sanctification for the believer is both positionally instantaneous and experientially progressive. The New Testament acknowledges that the perfections of Christ that we receive as believers through the Lord result in a relationship with God that cannot be rescinded or surrendered. Hebrews 10:10 declares that "we [believers] have been sanctified through the offering of the body of Jesus Christ once for all." Yet, this relationship provided by Christ must be lived out progressively. Christian maturation means a lifestyle of gradually deepening our spiritual fellowship with the Lord. This is not strange to us because we know that human behavior is shaped by two factors: genetics and our social behavior—the nature and the nurture of the child. Spiritual development also requires spiritual birth and spiritual fellowship. Christians, who are born into the kingdom, by yielding to the Holy Spirit resist the sinful impulses they must master: "For this is the will of God, your sanctification: that you abstain from sexual immorality; that each one of you know how to control his own body in holiness and honor" (1 Thessalonians 4:3, 4).

*Circumcision for the child.* In the case of the birth of a male, the initial seven days of domestic seclusion was followed by the rite of circumcision. On the eighth day after birth, the mother took the child to the sanctuary where the foreskin was surgically removed (v. 3).[5] Circumcision was also practiced by other people groups in the ancient world, such as the Egyptians (Jeremiah 9:25, 26). But the significance of circumcision in other cultures was typically a rite of male puberty, when a boy begins a transformation physically into a mature adult. Hebrew circumcision was commanded of Abraham and his descendants as the sign of the covenant that God had made with the patriarch and all his descendants (Genesis 17:11–14, 23–27; 21:4). This mark in the body indicated that the child was a member of the covenant community. A resident alien, for example, could only celebrate the Passover memorial if he and his household had chosen circumcision (Exodus 12:48). The Passover meal itself was a sign of the salvation that God had given his people in delivering them from the slavery of Egyptian bondage (chapter 12). Both rites, circumcision and the annual Passover meal, declared that the participants were members of the community of Israel.

That the new mother could enter the Tent of Meeting on the day of her son's circumcision, despite her continued postnatal flow, shows that the custom of circumcision took priority (vv. 3, 4). The ceremony of circumcision, however, was always recognized in the Scriptures as only an external sign of identification with the people of God. It was intended to be an expression of the inner person's devotion to God and belief in the word of promise. Leviticus 26:41 describes disobedient Israel as having "uncircumcised heart[s]." There were two levels of circumcision: physical circumcision and spiritual circumcision. These two are reflected in Jeremiah's condemnation of disobedient Judah: "Behold, the days are coming, declares the LORD, when I will punish all those who are circumcised merely in the flesh—Egypt, Judah, Edom, the sons of Ammon, Moab . . . for all these nations are uncircumcised, and all the house of Israel is uncircumcised in heart" (Jeremiah 9:25, 26). In other words, the surrounding nations were circumcised physically but were not covenant believers, and the Jews whose circumcision was solely in the flesh were also not covenant believers and thus no better off than the godless nations who practiced circumcision. What God had always demanded of his people was spiritual commitment, a spiritual relationship with God symbolized by the rite of circumcision. Thus Moses could say, "Circumcise therefore the foreskin of your heart, and be no longer stubborn" (Deuteronomy 10:16).

The New Testament writers interpreted circumcision in the same way, understanding that physical circumcision is valuable as a sign but is not sufficient for spiritual regeneration. There must be personal repentance and trust in the Word of God, whether one is circumcised or not (Colossians 3:11). The Apostle Paul observed, "But a Jew is one inwardly, and circumcision is a matter of the heart, by the Spirit, not by the letter. His praise is not from man but from God" (Romans 2:29). The parallel in the New Testament church to circumcision is the ordinance of water baptism, which provides an *outward* sign of the believer's identification with Christ and his church.[6] Again we turn to the apostle who shows the parallel: "In [Christ] also you were circumcised with a circumcision made without hands, by putting off the body of the flesh, by the circumcision of Christ, having been buried with him in baptism, in which you were also raised with him through faith in the powerful working of God, who raised him from the dead" (Colossians 2:11, 12).

Some church traditions see water baptism as "the door of the church," meaning that it is the first ritual whereby the new member is admitted into the church of Christ. This is true to the extent that it is the first *public* act of the believer's affiliation with the gathered church of local believers. The New Testament, however, makes a distinction between water baptism and spiritual baptism, understanding that spiritual baptism is the spiritual regeneration of a believer who enters into relationship with Christ and the Universal Church, the Body of Christ (Romans 6:4; Ephesians 4:5; Colossians 2:12). Water baptism symbolizes the suffering and resurrection of Jesus and the identification of the baptismal candidate with the sufferings of Christ, the believer who has experienced new life in the Lord. Water baptism does not impart saving grace any more than circumcision for the Jew assured acceptance by God. Yet, it is also not less imperative than circumcision was for the faithful Jew. Water baptism is a Christian imperative and stands as the first formal evidence of one's new spiritual place in the family of faith (e.g., Matthew 28:18–20; Acts 10:47).

### Sanctification of Life (vv. 6–8)

*Purification provided (vv. 6, 7).* Although it was inevitable that men and women would experience times of separation from normal social relationships due to physical impurities, there was gracious provision offered by God for restoration. The procedure of purification included water on some occasions (e.g., 14:8), but the prolonged cases of uncleanness required the application of blood to the sanctuary altar. Physical impurities meant that the altar had been polluted. Animal and bird sacrifices involved the spilling of blood, and it was by this ritual that the new mother could be accepted again at the sanctuary.

The two offerings were a burnt offering and a sin offering. The burnt offering was a young lamb; this was usually an expression of gratitude and renewed dedication to the Lord. This would be a fitting offering as an expression of thanksgiving for the birth of the child. The sin offering was either a pigeon or turtledove; the blood of the bird was drained out at the side of the altar (1:14, 15). The sin offering, however, did not address some specific sin in the life of the mother. No sin had been committed by the mother. Rather, the sin offering was a *purification* offering, a shedding of blood whereby the ritual impurity that had compromised the purity of the altar in the sanctuary might be removed. The new mother's physical discharge of blood had brought impurity to the sanctuary and required purgation. This is what the text means by "atonement" (v. 7).[7] The Hebrew word for "atone" can have various meanings, depending on the context. In the case of sin, the word means to "expiate," that is, to make amends for sin. The outcome is that the Israelite was "forgiven" by God (e.g., 4:20). For physical impurities, however, there was no sin involved (chapters 12—15); the blood in such cases wiped away ceremonial corruption. By carrying out the ritual, the mother had full acceptance once again in the sanctuary and had the freedom to touch holy things, such as food dedicated to the Lord (e.g., Deuteronomy 26:14).

*Provision for the poor (v. 8).* Repeatedly the Mosaic law provides for the poor whose financial means cannot support the more costly animal offerings. The covenant with God included all of the people. A special provision is given for the mother who was poor. Two turtledoves or pigeons could be substituted. One bird was for the burnt offering and the other for the sin offering. These offerings were also said to achieve the same desired effect—atonement for the mother and her purification. Purification was not based ultimately on the value of the gift but on the proper motivation of the giver.

## Jesus and Our Purification

The message of the passage for us today speaks to the purification that Jesus has provided.

*Ritual purification.* Our Leviticus passage is of special interest for Christians because of the birth story of Jesus in Luke's Gospel. The passage contributes to understanding the incarnation of Jesus, when the Son of God became a human being. The New Testament's account of Jesus' infancy tells of his presentation at the temple in Jerusalem by his parents where he underwent circumcision and where his mother Mary offered birds as her sacrificial gifts (Luke 2:21–24). That Mary and Joseph presented Jesus at the temple shows that they diligently obeyed the law of their Jewish heritage. Three times in the

Luke passage "the Law of Moses" or "the Law of the Lord" is noted so as to emphasize the parents' adherence to God's Word. Jesus was reared in a household that honored the Word of God and observed the teaching of Scripture (Luke 2:41–51).

We also learn from this incident in the life of the infant Jesus that the family had a meager income since Mary's offerings were birds (Luke 2:24). The Scriptures as a whole do not dwell on Jesus' economic status. Jesus is not depicted as wealthy or destitute.[8] Paul refers, however, to the Lord's spiritual poverty when he came into the world: "For you know the grace of our Lord Jesus Christ, that though he was rich, yet for your sake he became poor, so that you by his poverty might become rich" (2 Corinthians 8:9). Jesus who left the glory of Heaven at his incarnation exchanged it for the lowly conditions of humanity. So the exhortation by the Apostle Paul to his audience was to follow the example of the Lord by expressing their faith (i.e., their being spiritually "rich") through giving their material possessions to assist the poor.[9]

*Spiritual purification.* The account of Jesus' circumcision in the temple as an infant brings us back to the point of the purification ritual in the Leviticus mandate we have explained. The birth ritual speaks of the sanctification of God's people, the purging of sin, and the gift of new life—a spiritual and communal life that enjoys fellowship with the Lord God. God has given life and has made a people for his very own. The purification ritual in Israel acknowledged the miracle of birth as God's gift but also the necessity of reconciliation, for God in his perfections cannot tolerate anything less among his people. The initiation of the child into the covenant people of God through the rite of circumcision fosters the hope of a spiritually living people who are obedient to the Word of God. The perfection of Christ and the atoning sacrifice of Christ on Calvary's cross removes the obstacles to fellowship with the heavenly Father that the sinful human condition has erected. As the Apostle John makes clear, "But if we walk in the light, as [Jesus] is in the light, we have fellowship with one another, and the blood of Jesus his Son *cleanses* us from all sin" (1 John 1:7).

The incident of Jesus' circumcision and of the purification of Mary reflects what the Biblical writers teach regarding our Lord's mission. His circumcision was evidence of the humanity and humility of Jesus (cf. "but emptied himself, by taking the form of a servant, being born in the likeness of men," Philippians 2:7). He was submissive to the Law of God, humbling himself by becoming a human being. Galatians says, "But when the fullness of time had come, God sent forth his Son, *born of woman, born under the law*, to redeem those who were *under the law*, so that we might receive adoption as sons" (Galatians 4:4, 5).

Jesus' coming into the world was by human birth, by his mother Mary, a young Jewish girl who had exhibited a pious life of devotion to God. The expression "born of a woman" was used of any human person born (Job 14:1; 15:14; 25:4). Jesus was not only fully human—he was a Jewish baby by ancestry. Yet, unlike all of us, Jesus was a human being without sin (2 Corinthians 5:21). What the Apostle Paul points out in Galatians is that Jesus, by virtue of being a Jew, was born "under the law" and therefore was subject to the demands of the Law. The Law in his case, however, was not a curse because he was not disobedient; he was not a slave to the Law as were all others who were subject to the Law of God. By his obedience and voluntary subjection to the Law, the Lord Jesus liberated those who were enslaved to the Law because of their sin.[10] Jesus took upon himself at the cross the curse of the Law for us who have repented and believed.

A child born into the community of ancient Israel reminds us of the new birth, the spiritual birth, that the Spirit of God achieved for us through the death and resurrection of our Lord (James 1:18; 1 Peter 1:3). We too can enter the family of God through faith in the Lord by whose blood we can receive redemption. By the work of the Spirit we are united forever with God. The child of God's family is born both of the flesh and of the Spirit (John 3:5, 6). We have been made "members of the household of God" (Ephesians 2:19b).

# 12

# Holy to the Core

## LEVITICUS 13:1—15:33

TREASURE HUNTERS IN THE FLORIDA KEYS reported discovering thousands of pearls buried beneath the ocean floor. Salvagers were combing through the wreckage of a Spanish galleon that had sunk in 1622. The rare and old pearls were contained in a small lead box. The first estimation was that the pearls were worth as much as a million dollars. This account of hidden treasure reminds me of Solomon's advice for obtaining wisdom: "[S]eek it like silver and search for it as for hidden treasures" (Proverbs 2:4). Our passage contains hidden treasure buried within the many ritual details described in the text. If we are industrious in our search, we can hear the Word of God and receive blessings from its teachings.[1]

The overarching lesson is the importance of proper worship in the presence of God made possible through the gracious relationship God has with his people. Chapters 12—15, known as the purity laws in the book of Leviticus, recognize what we all know is true: We live in a world that is marred by death and decay in every aspect of life. Theologians speak of our world as a fallen world because sin committed by our first parents in the garden of Eden brought God's judgment on humanity and on the physical world.[2] The predicament we all face is summed up in this question: How can a people devoted to God live with God in a fallen world in which decay and death are the normal experience of human existence? It is inappropriate for men and women to enter into the presence of God when they exhibit the signs of decay and death. The purity laws acknowledge the challenge that humans face and provide a gracious answer that enables the people whose lives have been impacted by decay and death to be restored to the proper worship of God. Through their healing, God has made them whole again, alleviating them of the visual signs of decay and death. He has made the unfit fit again.

The purity laws also show us that the matter of the holiness of God is pervasive in the life of a believer. Holiness is considered by many people today as no more than good behavior, conforming to an established moral code in the context of religious practice. But the concept of holiness is fundamentally a description of a person's *relationship* with the only and truly Holy One, the Lord God. This relationship with God was the result of the redemption God provided for his people, liberating them from Egyptian slavery. Thus the teaching on the believer's holy living must begin with a right relationship with God. From this commitment to the Lord comes the desire to live in accordance with the redeemed life that God has given. This is the commandment of the Scriptures for Christians today: "[S]exual immorality and all impurity or covetousness must not even be named among you, as is proper among saints" (Ephesians 5:3).

The message of the passage further tells us what God is like—a God of life and a God of perfections. It also tells us what all humanity is like. Our lives are marked by birth but also death, by wellness but also sickness. The disparity between the character of God and the limitations of human living meant the need for a bridge whereby the people could cross over into the holy presence of their saving God. God himself built that bridge through his gracious redemption and maintained that bridge through his law. He is a God who provides a means of relationship by atonement. He is a God of mercy and forgiveness. We will see as Christian readers how the provision of salvation for all men and women was secured through Jesus Christ, whose life and death ensured the relationship between God and the repentant person who trusts the Lord. Paul comments, "[Christ] gave himself for us to redeem us from all lawlessness and to purify for himself a people for his own possession who are zealous for good works" (Titus 2:14).

Our three chapters, although a very wide slice of Scripture, are taken together because they concern essentially the same issue. How can a people whose lives and possessions are marred by decay and death come into the presence of God for worship? Our passage presents evidence of human frailties by noting the routine features of human life. These defects show the imperfections and mortality of all humanity. The passage first describes the diseases of body and of house in Leviticus 13, 14. Second, it describes in chapter 15 the body's fluid discharges, primarily male semen and female blood.

## Disease (13:1—14:32)

This passage describes human infirmities of two kinds: an individual's skin disorders and moldy defects in garments and houses. Clothing and houses are the trappings of daily human existence. That these two kinds of irregularities should disqualify a person from worshiping at the Tent of Meeting is surprising to us since in our world today these are relatively benign problems that can be easily remedied. To understand the severity of the diseases, however, we must recognize the ceremonial significance of the conditions, not the hygienic aspect. The symptoms of skin decay and the discoloration of the garments and of stone walls were external signals of the inherent problem all of us face—the decay of human bodies and the decay of the things of this world.

As we look at the text, we see a discernible pattern in the arrangement of the topics that will be helpful. The subject matter intersperses descriptions of the skin disorders and the domestic disorders. Perhaps we can simplify by thinking of the two categories as dermatological disorders and domestic disorders. Chapter 13 gives the procedure for diagnosis, distinguishing routine inflammations from the chronic. Chapter 14 entails the course of action addressing the routine and chronic kinds of skin disorders.

*Dermatological (13:1–46).* The passage first concerns one of the most obvious signs of disease—skin disorders. Anyone who suffers from such diseases as eczema and psoriasis, symptoms of which include reddish blotches and scaly skin, will tell you how difficult it is to mask such problems. The first task of the priest was discerning the severity of the malady, whether it was a passing condition or one that was unending.[3] Traditionally, ancient and modern translations have translated the Hebrew word in our passage (*tsaraath*) as the skin disease "leprosy."[4] But the description of the illnesses in the Leviticus text does not correspond at every point to the symptoms of leprosy. Leprosy today is known as Hansen's disease, a disease that is due to a bacterium. If left untreated it results in facial and other physical deformities. Although the Hebrew term can refer to a severe skin disorder that does not heal, the word has a broad usage, referring in our passage to a wide range of skin pathologies. That the Hebrew word is not a technical term for one kind of disease, such as leprosy, is shown by its use in describing the patches of mildew in garments (13:47–49) and in the stones and timber of houses (14:34, 35). For this reason modern versions sometimes choose another expression to translate the word in our passage, such as "infectious skin disease" (NIV). The passage indicates, however, that there must have been some form of contagious skin disease that was a notorious and greatly feared ailment.

The priest decided whether the blemish was contagious or benign based on the *appearance* of the malady (13:1–46). There were two symptoms of the disease under consideration. The first was a discoloration of the hair at the spot of the blemish, and the second was a spot in the skin that was deeper than normal. If this were the case, the priest declared the person unfit for normal activities, and that person was quarantined for a period of two weeks. If after that time of observation the symptoms had not spread, the priest declared the malady only an "eruption." The person washed his clothes and returned to his normal life. If the spot had spread, however, the diseased area was declared acute, and the person was quarantined indefinitely until the symptoms disappeared. When a person suffered a chronic condition, the criterion for discerning healing was the growth of new skin. The affected skin, identified in the text as "raw flesh," had healed when new skin had grown over the blemish. Additional instructions dealt with diseased skin that developed secondarily as a complication to a prior condition. These prior pathologies included a boil on the skin, burned skin, scaly skin on the head and beard, white patches of skin,[5] and discolored skin on a person's bald head or forehead.

But, we ask, what became of the person who continued to suffer the symptoms of the disease and was declared "unclean" indefinitely? Verses 45, 46 describe the steps taken to segregate the afflicted person from any social contact. The person wore torn clothes, untied his hair, and covered his mouth as he shouted out, "Unclean, unclean," warning others to beware his presence (v. 46). Wearing tattered clothes and leaving hair unkempt were symbolic acts of mourning. The diseased person lived "alone," remaining outside the camp. He could, however, join others of the same disease and was free to move about in the countryside (Numbers 5:2; 2 Kings 7:3; Luke 17:12). The prospects for such a person were dim, and he faced the possibility that he would be banished forever (cf. Uzziah, 2 Kings 15:5). He became dependent upon his family or the benevolence of others in the community to provide his material needs.

The severity of the isolation is by our standards today thought cruel, but this was not intended to be punitive. There was no *necessary* connection between sin committed by the affected person and his disease, although it was possible (cf. Miriam, Numbers 12:10–15). This is an important point to recall. The diseases described here are not the result of specific sins committed by the person. Rather, the diseases were part and parcel of the fallen world in which we live. It was and is a faulty conclusion to believe that every disease suffered by someone is the result of God's wrath against a sinner (cf. John 9:3). The stringent requirements of the Law protected the welfare of the community as a whole. The congregation was put in jeopardy since the disorder had implications for the survival of the camp.[6] Apart from any medical considerations, the ritual implications were staggering enough. Neither imperfect animals nor blemished priests were permitted to approach the holy altar in the sanctuary (Leviticus 21:17–23; 22:4). Such a transgression ceremonially polluted the

Tent of Meeting, nullifying the effects of the ritual offerings presented by worshipers. For a similar reason, an individual with a skin disease was prohibited from attending the sanctuary until the priest had declared the person ritually fit for acceptance at the Tent of Meeting. The key to understanding the message of the passage is that disease made a person unfit to enter into the presence of God who was the God of life and of holy perfections. Since the earthly Tent of Meeting was a copy of the spiritual heavenly sanctuary (Hebrews 8:5; 9:1; 10:1), it would be wrong to expose the symbols of death and decay in the place of worship.[7] Although we live in a fallen world, the world for which Christians are destined, Heaven, will not have decay, disease, and death. Our place will be secure.

*Clothing (vv. 47–59).* The text turns next to abnormalities in the clothing of a person. Eruptions in fabric or leatherwork were suspect because they showed an outward appearance like the skin diseases. The same Hebrew term was used to describe the scaly patches in garments as was used for describing a person's scaly skin diseases. The correlation between the two was the appearance of the blemishes—both were scaly and rough in texture. Traditionally commentators identified the disorder in garments as a fungus growth, such as mildew. The blemish was viewed as a potential threat and required a priestly ruling as to the damage the abnormality might cause. The precise nature of the threat is not clear from the description in the text. The procedure for detection was similar to the skin diseases. The priest's goal was to differentiate between a non-contagious growth and an infectious one, which is termed here a "persistent" disease (vv. 51, 52). The priest relied on the extent that the spot spread and whether the color of the blotch faded. If the diseased spot was permanent, the garment had to be incinerated immediately; but if the spot was not contagious it could be laundered and returned for normal use.

*Purification ritual for skin disease (14:1–32).* Chapter 14 continues the discussion of dealing with skin and garment abnormalities. The rituals described in this chapter were purification rites that provided ceremonial cleansing, restoring the affected person or item to ceremonial normalcy. It is important to observe that the ritual was not a therapeutic remedy for the disease. The ritual always followed *after* the diseased person or item had experienced "healing." The priest was not a doctor who prescribed a medical procedure. Any healing that occurred was the result of God's activity. The ritual only enabled the once unclean person or item to undergo a *ceremonial* reinstatement so the person could once again enter the sanctuary or the restored piece of clothing could be used again.

In the case of an affected person, the priest went outside the camp to examine the affliction. Once it was acknowledged that the disease had been healed, the priest initiated one of the most elaborate rites in the Law. We can summarize the procedure by noticing the progression of reintegrating the individual. There were three concentric circles: The infected person was outside the camp (vv. 3–9), the person was permitted inside the camp (vv. 8, 9), and finally he was permitted to enter the Tent of Meeting (vv. 10–20). The first ritual step occurred outside the camp and involved two birds, cedarwood, scarlet yarn, and a hyssop branch. The same procedure occurred for a person who became ritually unclean through touching a corpse (Numbers 19). Perhaps this was the way the person with skin disease was viewed. The shedding of the scaly skin suggested the wasting away of the body as in death.[8] This would be reason for the person to be denied access to the sanctuary, since God as the God of life would not tolerate death or symbols of death in his presence. After this step, the diseased person could enter into the camp, but he could not reside in his home. There was an observation period of seven days. On the eighth day, the healed person entered the Tent of Meeting, presenting animal and grain offerings. In the case of a poor person, birds could be substituted for the costly animals (vv. 21–32). The result of the offerings was "atonement" (vv. 18–21, 29, 31), which meant the successful removal of the person's ceremonial uncleanness. The individual was then fully restored to his God and to his family and community.

*Purification ritual for houses (vv. 33–57).* The subject turns to the outbreak of the disease in affected houses. The best estimation by scholars is that the outbreak was the fungal growth of mildew. The priest employed the same measurement for determining the severity of skin disease—discoloration of the stone and the depth of the patch below the surface of the stone (vv. 35–38). As in the case of the skin disease, examinations at seven-day intervals revealed to what extent the affliction had spread in the walls of the house. In the most severe case, the whole structure was dismantled and carried outside the camp. The residents washed themselves and their clothing (vv. 39–47). The best outcome was the cessation of the outbreak, which would be repaired by replacing stones and plaster. After the repair of the structure, the priest performed the same elaborate ritual of the two birds called for in the case of a person healed of skin disease (vv. 48–53). The same result too occurred; the priest made "atonement" for the house (v. 53), meaning that the ritual uncleanness had been removed and the house had been restored to its full acceptance in the community. The ritual for the house differed from the case of a diseased person at one significant point—the absence of animal sacrifices at the sanctuary's altar. This was because a house did not have a covenant relationship with God.[9] What was it about mildew that could be so important to the community? The scaly discoloration of the stonework indicated that the house was deteriorating, which meant the house was in decay. Because the people as members of a holy community lived in these dwellings, they could be ritually contaminated by the mildew, making them unfit to enter the Lord's sanctuary.

## Discharges (15:1–33)

As in the earlier descriptions, the text provides a detailed depiction of typical human excretions. That the people experienced bodily discharges was expected merely by virtue of their being human. The instructions in the passage occur according to gender, male discharges first, followed by the female ones.

*Male discharges (vv. 1–18).* Male genital discharges were diagnosed according to whether they were chronic (vv. 2–15) or temporary discharges (vv. 16–18). The language translated "discharge" (*zab*) is the Hebrew word for "flow, issue." The diagnosis of the chronic condition is broad enough to include any persistent uncommon flow. The passage focuses on the contagious nature of the affected person. Any person's *direct* contact with the diseased person resulted in that person's own ritual contamination. Also, the contagion can be passed to another person *indirectly*, such as by the clean person touching the bed or chair of a contaminated person. Conversely, the contaminated person can transmit uncleanness through initiating contact, such as spitting on a clean person or riding on a saddle (vv. 8, 9).[10] The Law instructed that contaminated persons or things be washed with water, and the infected persons remain unclean until the close of the day. When the man with the flow had experienced healing from his discharge, he waited one week and then on the eighth day presented himself to the priest at the Tent of Meeting. He made two bird offerings for his "atonement." The passage does not say that the persons who were contaminated through contact had to undergo the same ritual procedure. The implication of this omission may be that the contagion was not a medical disease but a ritual impurity. The persons and things infected secondarily could be cleansed through water ritual, whereas the man who had the flow had to wait until its cessation could be certified.

The instructions regarding the temporary condition pertained exclusively to the normal emission of semen. Sexual relations because of the passing of semen made the man and woman ceremonially unclean. Since normal semen flow was not as pernicious as the chronic condition, the ritual cleansing was bathing, and the state of uncleanness lasted only until evening. No animal sacrifice was required.

*Female discharges (vv. 19–30).* The laws for female discharges address the discharge of blood. The nature of contamination and the procedure for restoration paralleled a man's obligations for temporary (vv. 19–24) and chronic discharges (vv. 25–30). The temporary discharge was the monthly period of a woman. During the week of her ritual impurity, anything that she touched was unclean, and secondarily those who came into contact with those same items became unclean. Persons who contracted the corruption had to bathe and wash their clothes, remaining unclean only until evening. For the chronic discharge of blood that exceeded a week, the same rules of contagion applied as long as the condition persisted. If her blood discharge ceased, she was considered healed. After a week of assessment and if the flow had not continued, the woman on the eighth day presented two birds as sacrifices at the Tent of Meeting. The parallel between the male and female conditions and their ritual purifications show that the woman's discharges were not viewed as any more unclean than that of the man.[11]

## Preserving Life (v. 31)

The challenge for the community was to remain ceremonially pure in order to continue under the protective benevolence of God. Impurity resulting from the various conditions described in the purity laws (chapters 12—15) put the members of the community in jeopardy, individually and collectively. These impure conditions contaminated the altar of sacrifice at the Tent of Meeting. Offerings presented at the altar were therefore unacceptable to God since they were presented on a contaminated altar. This pollution of God's dwelling-place meant that the people were subject to the penalty of death. This was a matter of life and death for the affected individuals but also for the whole community. The purpose of the laws was to maintain the people's "separation" (*nazar*) from the uncleanness that inevitably occurred as a regular part of human experience. The word "separate" also can mean "dedicate, consecrate" when used of persons or things separated *unto* God. In this case, the idea is that the people having once been unfit by ritual uncleanness were now separated *from* their ritual impurities. They were fit for worship again because God made them fit.

## Christian Purity

We are probably puzzled by what these purity laws can possibly mean for us as Christians. In our Christian lives we do not practice these laws for good reasons, the chief of which is that these laws have been realized in the complete and perfect obedience of our Lord Jesus Christ. They are not directly applicable to us as Christians. Nevertheless, these laws too are the Word of

God and are profitable for our Christian living when we recognize their correspondence to Christian teaching. What are their hidden pearls of teaching? Among the many pearls we will comment on just two, Christian compassion and Christian devotion.

*Christian compassion.* The Lord God showed compassion for his covenant people by providing a means through ceremonial cleansing to restore them to the house of God. We noted in our exposition of the Leviticus passage that the ceremonial rituals of cleansing only occurred *after* healing had happened. The washings and the sacrifices were not magical incantations or medicinal remedies. The people were dependent upon the healing that God alone could give them. That Jesus healed the infirm when on earth was a testimony to his deity as Lord. The evangelist Matthew recognized that the healing ministry of Jesus showed that the era of the kingdom had arrived: Jesus "took our illnesses and bore our diseases" (Matthew 8:17, quoting Isaiah 53:4).

Jesus exhibited his compassionate lordship over the Law and over disease when he healed lepers, even sympathetically touching one leper, which would have made Jesus ceremonially unclean (Matthew 8:3). But our Lord initiated the new era of the kingdom at his coming as his life completed and superseded the instruction of the Law. The commentator Derek Tidball highlighted the difference between the two covenants, the old and the new, when he summed up the old by the saying "Keep out! You are unfit" and the new message of Jesus as "Draw near! Let me make you clean!"[12] Jesus also healed a ritually unclean woman who had suffered twelve years of continuous blood flow. The physician Luke noted that the woman had spent all her resources seeking a cure from physicians. She risked offending Jesus by touching the hem of his robe, but the Lord's mercy again fulfilled and superseded the Law. She received healing when touching the Savior's garment because she did so as an expression of faith in the Lord as the Great Physician (Luke 8:43–48). The opposite result occurred from that expected in the Law: Jesus was not made unclean by her touch, and she was restored because she *did* touch.

The Bible repeatedly calls upon God's people to visit and minister to the sick. Mercy for the sick has always characterized the Christian message, as evidenced by the many Christian philanthropists, physicians, and nurses whose work has founded hospitals and clinics around the world. The ministry that many laypeople, typically working in anonymity, carry on for the ill and their families is an important witness to the love of the Lord—both his love for the sick and the helper's love for Christ. Such acts of mercy and healing declare that the Lord has come and has overcome the human dilemma that we all must admit.

*Christian devotion*. Our last observation brings us full circle, back to the title of this message, "Holy to the Core." The passage shows above all that the people in the covenant community had committed themselves to the Lord in all aspects of their lives. There was nothing in their daily life that the Word of God did not impact. The modern idea of two separate lives, a religious one and a secular one, was foreign to their outlook. Holy living began with a relationship with God, and from it came the lifestyle for which the Word of God called. In other words, relationship preceded and served as the seedbed for the fruit of holy living. *Relationship* comes before *regulation*. Today many people think that *holy living* is a synonym for morality. Holy living for them is practicing values that fit with the moral legislation of the Ten Commandments and the Sermon on the Mount. Indeed, there is a correlation between authentic devotion to God and Christian virtues, for Peter quotes Leviticus when he exhorts his readers to holy conduct: "You shall be holy, for I [the Lord] am holy" (1 Peter 1:15, 16). But moral conduct is not necessarily connected with love for God and commitment to Christ. We all have come across people who were of another religious tradition or of no religious tradition at all whose lives were morally impeccable. They exhibited integrity, courage, and sacrifice and closely controlled their sensual desires. Sometimes such moral people show better behavior than Christians do! But holy living is at its most fundamental level the *relationship* we have with God (Colossians 1:19–23). This relationship with God is secured for us through Jesus Christ, by whose blood atonement we have been cleansed of our sins and reconciled to God. Christ's death for our sins and the gift of his righteousness has made us fit for the kingdom. The Scriptures tells us, "If we walk in the light, as he [God] is in the light, we have fellowship with one another, and the blood of Jesus his Son cleanses us from all sin" (1 John 1:7). Our loving devotion to the Lord spurs us on to live obediently. Jesus said as much: "If you love me, you will keep my commandments" (John 14:15).

# 13

# Day of Atonement

## LEVITICUS 16:1–34

JULY 4, 1776, is the most important date in American history. Although American citizens today may be foggy about the date of the constitutional founding of the United States when Congress first met (March 4, 1789) or the date for the first American presidency (April 30, 1789), they are clear on the date that sounded the American colonies' independence from British rule. Usually the birth of a movement receives such special attention. In the Christian calendar, Christmas is the chief day of remembrance. In the Jewish calendar, Passover remains the most important festal day, a memorial to the beginnings of Israel as a people when they were liberated from Egyptian bondage. But if Passover is the most important festal day, the most solemn day in the Jewish calendar is the Day of Atonement, known in Hebrew as *Yom Kippur*. This sacred day is the subject of our passage.

The Day of Atonement was a day on which the people afflicted themselves[1] (vv. 29, 31) by acts of penance, such as fasting. As in the Christian remembrance of Good Friday, the Day of Atonement elicited from the people both remorse for their sins and a sense of relief at receiving the forgiveness that the day provided. Good Friday produces in us deep sorrow at our sins that Jesus bore on the cross, and yet the "good" that the cross achieved in our behalf kindles in us a deeper devotion to the Lord.

This chapter's message is critically important for three reasons. First, the chapter occurs in the center of the book of Leviticus. Like a bridge it connects the two halves of the book. Chapters 1—15 describe the rituals of sacrifice and the purity regulations. Chapters 17—27 describe the characteristics of holy living by the covenant community. The effect of the Day of Atonement made sacrifice, purity, and holy living a possibility for another year. Second, the Day of Atonement is the ritual that on the whole best illustrates the theological teaching of Israel's worship of its covenant Lord. It teaches the essentials for appropriate worship, which are what God demands of worshipers, the steps that God instructs the Israelites to perform so their worship is acceptable, and the spiritual benefits that worship brings to the people. Third, the theological message portrayed through the rites performed on this most sacred day serve as a template for understanding the message of Christianity. The centerpiece of Christianity is the cross where Jesus' death resulted in the forgiveness of sins through the shedding of his blood for all who repent and express faith in Christ as Savior. The rituals that happened on the Day of Atonement provided an explanation through "moving pictures" of what happened in God's eyes when Jesus died at Mount Calvary. Remember, three men died on crosses that first Good Friday. Why is it that the man who died on the middle cross took away sins and not the other two men? The New Testament writers provide the answer.

The contents of chapter 16 entail the most elaborate and complex ritual recorded in the book of Leviticus. We should not be surprised that such a detailed ceremony is mandated in the Law. Ceremony is important at moments of special national attention. It gives the people as a whole community opportunity to reflect upon the meaning of the event, forming a nationwide bond. Probably the most significant ceremony for the United States is the inauguration of the president every four years as called for in the US Constitution. The US Code, Title 36, Subtitle 1, Part A, Chapter 5 specifies that the Congress will form an inaugural committee to oversee the planning and implementation of the inauguration. In 1933, to ensure a specific time of transition, the states ratified Amendment XX of the Constitution that stipulates that the president-elect must be sworn into office on January 20 at noon when the term of the previous officeholder expires. The specific oath of office is mandated also in the Constitution, Article II, Section 1, which reads, "I do solemnly swear that I will faithfully execute the Office of President of the United States, and will, to the best of my ability, preserve, protect and defend the Constitution of the United States." This detailed instruction with the day's pomp and ceremony shows the significance of the transfer of power in the nation. Likewise, the meticulous description of the ritual on the Day of Atonement signifies its central importance to the life of the nation.

The chapter's thirty-four verses give (1) the preparations for the ritual (vv. 1–10), (2) the ritual procedures themselves (vv. 11–28), and (3) instructions for the Day of Atonement as an annual memorial (vv. 29–34). Embedded in the chapter is a summary paragraph in verses 6–10 that conveniently captures the main features of the ritual—a microcosm of the whole chapter's account. We will turn to it as our focal passage and will draw on related verses elsewhere in the chapter when helpful.

Verses 6–10 encapsulate the core activities of that day. What makes the Day of Atonement unique is the special role of the high priest. This is the only day of the year that the high priest, and only the high priest, could enter into the most sacred room in the Tent of Meeting. This cubical enclosure, set off by curtains, was the Most Holy Place (the Holy of Holies) where God was present. Inside the room, the priest sprinkled blood from animal sacrifices at the sacred ark of the covenant, the piece of tabernacle furniture that represented the dwelling-place of God. A second part of the ceremony that was unique was the encompassing effect of the sacrifices. Whereas the sin and guilt sacrifices described in 4:1—6:7 addressed offenses by individuals, the Day of Atonement dealt with the accumulated sins of the whole nation that had been committed in the previous year. Another part of the ceremony that distinguished the day was the riddance of a living goat, traditionally translated "scapegoat," which carried the sins of the nation away from the camp.

## Atonement for the High Priest (v. 6)

*Sin offering.* The ritual purging of the high priest and his sons initiated the chief activities of the Day of Atonement. Verses 11–14 detail the procedure carried out by the high priest. A bull was slain as a sin offering by the high priest so that the priests were purged first of their sins. This was necessary since the priest could not perform the purity ceremonies on behalf of the people if he remained in his own sin and guilt. Sins committed by the priests resulted in ceremonial corruption of the Tent of Meeting. If the high priest were impure, then the sacrifices he offered and the altar where they would be presented would be contaminated by sin and rendered unacceptable. The result of the purging ritual was "atonement" on behalf of Aaron and his priestly family. The Hebrew word translated "make atonement" is the word from which *Kippur* in the name *Yom Kippur* derives. You can hear the similarity in sound in the two words—*kippur*, meaning "atonement" and *kipper*, meaning "to make atonement." Atonement has different aspects. One is the idea of "pacify, reconcile." In the context of the purgation rituals, the word more properly means "to wipe clean," especially when the Tent of Meeting and the altar are the objects (vv. 20, 33). The ritual involved not only making atonement for the repentant but also purging the physical tabernacle by removing its corruption.

*Inside the Most Holy Place.* The high priest took a censer of burning coals from the bronze altar and added two handfuls of fragrant incense, which produced a cloudy veil. With it he entered the Most Holy Place, and the perfumed smoke filled the room, protecting the priest from gazing upon the holy "mercy seat" of the ark. The "mercy seat" was the gold plate or slab that lay on top of the ark. At each end of the top was fashioned an angelic figure with wings whose eyes were cast downward, looking on the "mercy seat" under their wings. The notion of a "seat" probably derived from the imagery of God enthroned on or above the cherubim (e.g., 1 Samuel 4:4; Psalm 99:1).[2] The ark is identified as "the footstool" of God, according to 1 Chronicles 28:2. The better translation is "the place of atonement"[3]; in other words, it was the location where the rite of atonement occurred. It was the place where "[God] will meet with you" (Exodus 30:6). When Moses met with the Lord, it was from above the mercy seat that the voice of God could be heard (Numbers 7:89).

This golden slab is said in verse 13 to be set "over the testimony." The word "testimony" refers to the contents of the sacred ark, which was the sole piece of furniture in the Most Holy room. The ark was a rectangular box made of acacia wood and overlaid with gold. It is called "the testimony" because it contained the copy of the stone tablets of the covenant agreement (Exodus 40:20). The Ten Commandments are called "the . . . tablets of the testimony" in Exodus 32:15; 34:29. The description of the Most Holy Place in the Old Testament paints God as a King who resides in his throne room. This, of course, was only symbolic language since the Law did not permit the making of a physical idol or image of God. Our passage explains in verse 2 that God appeared in a cloud in which was his glory. The cloud hovered over the Most Holy Place in the Tent of Meeting.

If the priest saw the ark, he would be struck dead by God's wrath (v. 13). This was not an empty warning. Aaron had witnessed the destruction of his two sons, Nadab and Abihu, because of their sin against the Lord in the Tent of Meeting (10:1–5). This tragic incident was in the foreground of the text as evidenced by the mention of his deceased sons in verse 1. The disobedience of the two brothers polluted the sanctuary and became a notorious example of the need to purge the Tent of Meeting and purify the priests. The same protective step was called for when the Lord's anger sent a plague against the rebellious members of Israel in the wilderness (Numbers 16:46–48). Aaron stood with his smoking fire pan "between the dead and the living, and the plague was stopped." This danger was especially true of Aaron in the Most Holy Place since he was at that time the closest a mortal could be to the presence of God.

A Jewish legend, not found in the Bible or in Jewish interpretation, says that Aaron was fitted with a rope around his waist or legs when he went inside the curtain. If the wrath of God flared against the high priest and he died on the spot, the priests from the outer room could pull the body out of the Most Holy Place. What this legend shows is the Jewish understanding of the peril that the Day of Atonement caused. After igniting the incense, the priest returned to the altar from which he retrieved some blood of the butchered bull. Once again inside the curtain, he sprinkled the atoning blood on the east side of the mercy seat, meaning the front side that faced the entrance to the room. Next he took some of the blood and sprinkled it seven times with his finger in front of the mercy seat.

## Atonement for the People (vv. 7–10)

The high priest next turned to the offerings on behalf of the people. Two male goats were brought before the high priest. Aaron cast lots to determine which goat was "for the LORD" and which was "for Azazel" (v. 8). The text says that the lots were cast "before the LORD at the entrance of the tent of meeting." This description implies that it was the Lord who decided the outcome of the cast lots, not a matter of human ingenuity or just blind luck. The high priest's lots were probably small stones with the inscribed name "Urim" on one and "Thummim" on the other. The stones were safeguarded in the pouch of the garment worn by the high priest (Exodus 28:30; Leviticus 8:8). Precisely how this procedure worked we are not told in Scripture. We can theorize that the word Urim, from the word "curse" (*arar*), expressed a negative response, and Thummim, from the word "perfect, complete" (*tamam*), expressed a positive one. This meant that yes/no kinds of questions must have been asked. There was no magical incantation spoken by the high priest in concert with the casting of the lots.

The casting of lots was a legitimate way in ancient Israel and in the early church to discern the will of God for his people. The procedure was rare, judging by the sole occasion of its use by the church in Acts 1:26 when God appointed Matthias to take the place of Judas the Betrayer. Even in this case there is no indication that the high priestly lots, the Urim and Thummim, were available to the apostles.[4]

*Sacrificed goat.* The goat identified "for the LORD" was the one chosen to serve as a blood offering, sacrificed at the altar (v. 9). The priest, as he had with the prior bull offering, took some blood of the slain goat and entered the Most Holy Place again where he sprinkled the blood (v. 15). The ritual atonement had two effects: The people's ritual impurities were removed from the holy place, and the sins of the people were forgiven. The imagery of ritual "uncleanness" depicted the spiritual impurities of their sins that the people had committed against the Lord. Now that the inner sanctum had been cleansed, attention turned toward the remaining features of the Tent of Meeting. The furniture in the Holy Place and the various hangings of the tent were cleansed, presumably by the sprinkling of blood. Afterward the high priest focused on the altar, the place where the people daily worshiped the Lord through sacrifice. Taking blood from both the slaughtered bull and goat, he smeared their blood on the four corners of the altar, identified here as "the horns of the altar" (cf. Exodus 38:1, 2) and also sprinkled blood on the altar. The result was the ceremonial removing of all the impurities accumulated through the year by the people. Now the whole sanctuary was purified and available again for another year. The progression of the cleansing ritual moved from inside to outside— from the most holy location at the mercy seat to the Holy Place to the altar in the courtyard.

*Scapegoat.* The remaining live goat was the one designated "for Azazel" (vv. 8, 10). The word "Azazel" is not a translation but a transliteration of the Hebrew word. The meaning of the Hebrew has been a subject of much speculation by scholars and Bible students. We see this reflected in the various ways modern versions have translated the Hebrew. There are three main interpretations. The traditional translation in the King James Version and others is "scapegoat." This word is familiar to us because we use the term in a similar sense to refer to someone who bears the blame for others. Another way we express this is by the saying "the fall guy," meaning a person who is stuck with the blame for an infraction without cause. The reasoning behind the translation "scapegoat" is that the Hebrew can be interpreted as consisting of two words, namely, "the goat that departs." A second interpretation is that the word is the name of a specific location in the desert. The third view is that Azazel is the name of a goat-demon that inhabited the wilderness. This view reflects the idea that ancient peoples believed that goat-demons ruled the desolate, remote wilderness. This last option is the least plausible since in Leviticus 17:7 there is a specific prohibition against making an offering to goat idols. Moreover, the notion of making an offering to a demon simply does not harmonize well with what we know is the theology of Leviticus. Probably the best solution is "the scapegoat" (e.g., NIV, NASB).

The priest placed both hands on the head of the scapegoat and confessed "all" the sins of the people (vv. 20–22). The priest stood in for the people, acknowledging the community's need for forgiveness. The gesture of resting his hands on the animal's head indicated that the sins of the people had been symbolically transferred from the people to the innocent goat.[5] Verses 10 and 22 state that the scapegoat bore the sins of the people, making atonement for the people. That the scapegoat must be brought into the sanctuary before its release shows that the role of the scapegoat was necessary to complete the ritual of cleansing.[6] The emphasis of the scapegoat ritual is the removal of the sins of Israel from the Tent of Meeting and the camp. The scapegoat was led out of the camp by a designated man and was driven into the wilderness, symbolically carrying away the sins of the people. Later Jewish tradition, not recorded in the Bible, described how the scapegoat was pushed over a cliff to its death. This act ensured that the goat burdened with Israel's guilt would never wander back into the camp.[7]

The final acts of the day were several. The priest sacrificed two rams as burnt offerings, one for the priest and the other for the people (vv. 3, 5, 24). The burnt offerings expressed the rekindled commitment of the priest and people to the Lord. The designated man returned to the camp, but only after undergoing ritual washings of his clothes and body. The remaining carcasses of the bull and goat on the altar whose blood was taken into the tent were removed to outside the camp where they were fully burned up. Last, the person who carried out this final task washed his clothes and bathed his body, after which he was permitted to return. These last steps continued to reflect the substitutionary feature of the Day of Atonement. The animals that bore the sin and the two persons who handled their remains were ritually contaminated by the sins of the priest and of the people. By doing away with the carcasses outside the camp and by the ritual cleansing of the men also outside the camp, the community was freed from any residual effects of the purification process.

## Atonement Forever

The writer to the Hebrews recognized that the Day of Atonement was a picture of the death of Christ, whose shed blood provided complete purging and eternal forgiveness for Christian believers.[8] We might say that the Old Testament's Day of Atonement provided the sketch, and the New Testament filled in the color. The author of Hebrews feared that his Christian readers, who were suffering persecution, might abandon their Christian faith and return to the Jewish traditions that were more acceptable to political authorities. To encourage his readers, the author demonstrated that the gospel was not only better than the previous system, but that the message of the Old Testament was fully realized in the person and work of Christ. This message is for us today as we contemplate the meaning of Christ's death.

The author of Hebrews compared the old ritual system of sacrifice and the perfect sacrifice of Jesus. In chapter 10 he showed that the Day of Atonement supplied only temporary success, since it was necessary to perform the ritual every year. The people would not need to experience cleansing and forgiveness if they had been fully and finally forgiven. This was not true of the gospel, for the atonement of Christ was final. It came about not by animal sacrifices but by the Lord Jesus who gave his body to crucifixion. The writer says, "And by that will [of God] we have been sanctified [that is, purified] through the offering of the body of Jesus Christ once for all" (10:10).⁹ This *one-time* offering made all who believe perfect in the eyes of God for *all time* (10:14).

The basis for this assurance was the role that Jesus as the eternal High Priest played in the sacrificial offering. He was not only the perfect sacrifice, but he also was the perfect, eternal High Priest, for he did not make atonement for himself as the high priest in Israel was obligated to do. Jesus had no sin. Thus he was free to bear our sin and guilt. Our problem was not his problem, but he chose to make our problem his problem. As the eternal, perfect High Priest he was given eternal access to the heavenly throne room of God. The author of Hebrews observed that the earthly tabernacle was a copy, a model for the authentic realities of the heavenly tabernacle where God resides. By the blood of the perfect sacrifice, Jesus as the perfect priestly intercessor achieved the purging and atonement that the animals of the old system could never accomplish. Aaron's arena was earthbound, a replica that was designed to point to eternal realities. Jesus' arena was the eternal, heavenly Most Holy Place (9:1–14). In the heavenly throne room, the Lord transported his blood and made intercession for us entirely and finally, after which he took up residence in the throne room, sitting at the right hand of the Father. Whereas Aaron's proper place was outside the Most Holy Place, never to dwell there, the Lord Jesus is at home in the presence of the Father.

What this means for us today can be summed up in two of the ways that the author of Hebrews exhorted his readers. Religious performance has "made nothing perfect"; but on the other hand, a better hope is introduced, through which we draw near to God" (7:19). We are not to add to the finished atonement that Christ has already accomplished. There is no deficiency in the death and resurrection of our Lord. There is no way that the salvation Christ declares can be improved upon or altered in any way. It is a temptation for us as human beings to think we must contribute in some way to our own salvation. Our labors are not useless, but as the basis for our forgiveness and acceptance with God, they are woefully inadequate. They are rather the fruit of our faith in the completed salvation God has achieved for us through Christ. Religious symbols and traditions of worship and of instruction cannot replace or supplement the realities of our Lord's death.

My grandson at seven years of age loved cars, especially NASCAR racing. On one occasion as a treat I bought a NASCAR race car for him. Now I didn't buy him an actual authentic NASCAR race car for obvious reasons. He couldn't do anything with it other than admire it because he couldn't meet the requirements for driving it. Also, I couldn't buy it anyway since I didn't have the money or the desire to get the real thing. All I did was buy him a *model car*, just two or three inches long, made of plastic, that cost me two dollars or so. He was competent to "drive" the toy car, and I was financially able and willing to provide it. Now, it would be silly for us to confuse the two items. One is merely an expendable copy of the reality. Yet, when we come to the salvation that Christ has for us, we sometimes confuse the symbols for the realties. The church's celebration of the ordinances and its various religious activities are meaningful and useful, but they do not make us closer to God. We are "brought near [to God]," the Apostle Paul says, "by the blood of Christ" (Ephesians 2:13). Don't think a rigorous adherence to morals or a vibrant religious life can substitute for the costly blood of the Son of God.

Second, the writer of Hebrews exhorts his readers to act on this precious gift of Christ's sacrifice by entering into the heavenly throne room. "Let us then with confidence draw near to the throne of grace, that we may receive mercy and find grace to help in time of need" (Hebrews 4:16; also 10:22). Since we have the perfect High Priest who has made this assured acceptance with God in our behalf, we can confidently pray, knowing that our Lord hears our prayers and supplies his mercy and grace without end. We too often neglect the rich unfathomable blessing of prayer though we, through the shed blood of Christ, can enter the very presence of the Father and make our supplications known and our praises heard. We dare not be frivolous in our prayers, either by neglect or by presumption, but we can pray with confidence without timidity. As James told his readers, "Draw near to God, and he will draw near to you" (James 4:8). If we do not pray, it is because we do not fully grasp what it means for us to have this irrevocable access to the heavenly Most Holy Place. Nothing can ever rob us of this wonderful privilege; no one can charge us with uncleanness and expel us from the Father's presence. This awe-inspiring gift incites us to praise God the Father, offer sacrifices of thanksgiving to the Lord Jesus, and rely on the power of the Holy Spirit.

A story is told of a hunter in the frozen Canadian frontier who came to a frozen pond that he had to cross. He was unfamiliar with the depth of its ice at that time of year, and he only gingerly went forward on hands and feet. He did not know if the ice could bear the weight of his body, and with great caution he moved forward as a child does on all fours. About midway he heard a tremendous crashing sound in the woods behind him. Coming at breakneck speed across the ice was a carriage full of people, drawn by pounding horses. He watched from his childlike stance as the carriage raced to the far edge of the pond and disappeared into the woods ahead. Here we have two pictures of what it means to understand what God has done for us through the atoning grace of our Lord Jesus. The people of the Old Testament could not have confidence in the priest or the temporary offerings made each year. Each year brought a new challenge as to whether God would accept their offerings. Was Aaron cleansed of his own sins? Did he carry out the ritual properly? Did the man who led the scapegoat to the wilderness area act as he should? On and on the people would have been laboring under a guilty conscience as another year progressed. But with Christ all the tentativeness of the old system was set aside by the perfect means of forgiveness and acceptance. Because of what Christ has done we can live confidently, receiving the promise of God for us, not living in fearful uncertainty. God wants us to be emboldened to serve and to persevere in our Christian living. Don't look back, says the author of Hebrews. Press ahead, knowing that the ice will not give way.

# 14

# Honoring God at Table

## LEVITICUS 17:1–16

THE FIFTH VESSEL of a new class of warship has been named the USS *New York* in honor of the heroes who died in the attack on the World Trade Center on September 11, 2001. The bow stem of the ship was made of recovered steel from the World Trade Center and was erected into the main hull on August 4, 2005. The bow stem will lead the ship wherever it travels. The motto of the ship is "Never Forget." One of the navy captains who watched the mangled steel as it was melted and poured into the molds for the ship said, "Those big rough steel workers treated it with total reverence."[1] I was struck by the reference "total reverence." We don't much hear today about reverence for respected things. That these workers showed unusual deference to the tortured steel reflected their recognition of the importance of the events on that dreadful day. This is the genesis of reverence, recognition of what deserves honor. Our passage calls for God's people to express their worship of God as Creator and Redeemer through reverencing the holy things of the Lord.

 Our passage is strategically located in the development of the book of Leviticus. It leads the way for the second half of the book, chapters 17—27, which scholars call "the Holiness Code." The Holiness Code focuses on the lives of the people who are living in communion with the Lord. Since he is most holy, the people must reflect his holiness in all aspects of their own lives. Chapter 17 also includes the explanation for why the sacrifices described in the preceding chapters, 1—16, are effective for making atonement for the sins of the people. The key verse that explains why sacrifice provides the avenue for continued life with God is 17:11: "For the life of the flesh is in the blood, and I have given it for you on the altar to make atonement for your souls, for it is the blood that makes atonement by the life." The blood represents the life that God has created, has protected, and now has delivered up on behalf of his beloved people. The community is called upon as a result to honor God and his gifts by its special reverence for the blood of animal and human life. The three ways the people must honor the Lord as Creator and Redeemer were (1) by the worship of the Lord exclusively, (2) by the acknowledgment of his gifts, and (3) by cherishing life whether human or animal. These admonitions arise from the instructions in this chapter regarding the proper handling of blood given for the forgiveness of the people's sins.

## Honor God by Worshiping Only at His Altar (vv. 1–9)

The most fundamental way that the community honored the Lord God as Savior was by offering worship to him alone. This imperative reflects the first two commandments given to Israel at Sinai: to worship only the Lord and to resist any form of idolatry (Exodus 20:3–6).

*Worship the Lord where he may be found (vv. 3, 4).* A major hurdle to our understanding the message of this passage is the difference in the locations of worship between the life of Israel and the worship we as Christians enjoy. In the ancient world the *place* of worship was bound to the identity of the deity who was believed to live in the sacred shrine. The revelation given to Israel offered the people a similar understanding of location and worship by giving to them the Tent of Meeting (also translated "tabernacle" in the text). The earthly tent was a representation of the heavenly throne, a kind of emblematic clone of the real thing. The wars between Coca-Cola and Pepsi Cola have become legendary. In the mid-1980s the historic formula of Coca-Cola was set aside for a new taste that more closely imitated the Pepsi flavor. Public howls protested New Coke, as it was named. Within the year the company returned to the old formula, entitling it Coca-Cola Classic. New Coke quietly fell away. The slogan in 1985 for the new flavor was "We've got a taste for you," which by 1990 was supplanted by the slogan "You can't beat the real thing." Clones are useful but not altogether satisfactory. The Tent of Meeting was a temporary provision where the Lord *symbolically* lived among his covenant people, but it was useful for temporary service.

All of the instructions of Leviticus 1—16 presupposed that legitimate worship of God would only occur at the authorized place of worship. Our passage commands the people of Israel to bring their animals for offerings to the Tent of Meeting. The text's use of the word "kills" in verse 3 clarifies that the killing in mind is sacrifice for worship, not hunting for meat. The word in the original language is the most common Hebrew term for ritual sacrifice.[2] Here the animals specified were domesticated animals named as the proper beasts for sacrifice—ox, lamb, or goat (cf. chapters 1—7, 11). If a person wanted to eat meat from these animals, he brought his animal to the tabernacle as a peace offering made to the Lord (chapter 3). The peace offering provided meat for the priest and for the offerer. One's family and the poor were also invited to enjoy the feast of thanksgiving. Eating meat had a special connotation of blessing because it was not a common part of the Israelite's diet. It was a delicacy that was available to the upper class.

Our passage focuses on the site of the slaughter, leaving aside the details of the ritual that were explained in Leviticus 1—7. *Where* the sacrifice occurred was the measure of the legitimacy of the individual's worship. At the Tent of Meeting the offerer killed his beast, and the officiating priest handled the carcass and the blood at the altar. If the person did not follow the ritual instruction, it was tantamount to denying the claims of God as the Savior of his people. This is reflected in our text where it reads "gift to the Lord" and "tabernacle of the Lord." To make an offering anywhere else would be considered a tribute to another god. The penalty for this apostasy was to be "cut off from among his people" (v. 4). This expression could refer to capital punishment but not necessarily. "Put to death" is the common expression for execution of a criminal. It may be that the meaning of "cut off" was expulsion of the transgressor (22:3), exile from the protection of the Lord's community. The reason for the severity of the penalty was the severity of the crime. The guilty party, the text says, bore "bloodguilt" for killing the animal. The expression "shed blood" (*shaphak dam*) many times in the Old Testament describes murder or warfare (e.g., "murder" as a capital crime in Genesis 9:6).[3]

The reasoning behind this condemnation arose from acknowledging the ownership of the life of the animal. The life of the animal belonged to God, and he had given its blood to the Israelite as a means for securing the person's atonement. The unlawful taking of the animal's life, that is, using its blood, meant that the Israelite had illicitly killed the beast.[4] The guilty person had taken the blood for his own purposes, usurping God's right to the life of the animal. In the ceremony of atonement, the blood of the animal was returned symbolically to the Lord by pouring or tossing the blood at the altar in the tabernacle courtyard (Leviticus 1—7). Failure to return to God his due meant that the guilty person had seized from God control over the life of the animal.

How might we as Christians offer worship in the proper *place*? Here we face a quandary because the New Testament does not designate a particular building for Christian worship today. There is, however, only one proper place for Christian worship. The episode of Jesus encountering the Samaritan woman at Jacob's well, recorded in John's Gospel (John 4), instructs us in the only legitimate place for Christian worship. The question the woman raised with Jesus pertained to the theological debate between the Samaritans, who worshiped at Mount Gerizim, located north of Jerusalem, and the Jews who worshiped at the Jerusalem temple. The Samaritans had abandoned the temple and practiced their worship at Nablus, the location of Mount Gerizim. Jesus announced that neither place would command the people's attendance because of the new way of coming before God. "But the hour is coming, and is now here, when the true worshipers will worship the Father in spirit and truth, for the Father is seeking such people to worship him" (John 4:23).

*Worship only the Lord (vv. 5–7).* Verses 5–7 provide the rationale for the necessity of bringing the animal for sacrifice to the tabernacle. Sacrifice anywhere other than the Tent of Meeting was considered in essence worship of other deities. Ancient peoples were not atheists. A person either worshiped the Lord God or the pagan deities. The passage indicates by the parallel language in verses 5 and 7 that the offerings made in "the open field" were understood as "sacrifices to goat demons." The worship of other gods was a constant threat. A sacrifice in an unauthorized place, even if offered in the name of the Lord, was tantamount to the worship of the gods. God, centuries later, by the prophet Jeremiah condemned the people of Judah for their "abominations [of false worship] . . . on the hills in the field" (Jeremiah 13:27).

"Goat demons" in the original language is only one word, the common word for a male goat. The same word also means "hairy," used of a hairy person like Esau or of a hairy male goat. The English words "demons" or "idols" in our translations, although not in the original language, bring forward the idea that the goats were believed by the nations to be gods. False deities are sometimes referred to as "demons" in the Bible (Deuteronomy 32:16, 17; 1 Corinthians 10:20). Goat deities were revered in many places among other peoples. Their habitat was in the wilderness where danger lurked. Carved idols of these deities were made alongside calf idols in the time of Jeroboam, king of Israel (2 Chronicles 11:15). A fertility connection is implied by the further description in our text, "after whom they [the worshipers] whore." The word for prostitution commonly occurs in the prophets for the pagan worship of false deities, especially for the male deity Baal. Fertility cults were the centerpiece of ancient religions who believed that the deities through sexual unions generated seasonal prosperity for the land and family. Through ritual prostitution the worshipers expressed their request for the deities to do the same and provide prosperity to the nation. Idol worship and the fertility practices associated with it were abhorrent to God. By requiring the Israelites to bring their sacrifices to the sanctuary of the Lord God, the intention was to prevent worship of other gods.

In our modern Western world, we just can't conceive of how a person could worship a lifeless idol. We sometimes think that was a practice only in ancient times and is not known today. But this is not the case. Idolatry occurs in many locations in the world. We skip over the reality of idolatry in a heartbeat, but idolatry and things associated with demonic cults are very real for millions of people. As the world shrinks in size, opportunities for false worship will become ordinary in Europe and North America. For example, Hindu temples and homes with their private shrines of gods and goddesses are common in all regions of the United States, including the stronghold of the South's Bible Belt.

The threat of apostasy for us today, however, is more likely from the allurement of wealth and pleasures. Although first-century Christians faced idol worship, there was an idolatry that was subtle but just as menacing in their lives. The Apostle Paul admonished his readers, "Put to death therefore what is earthly in you: sexual immorality, impurity, passion, evil desire, and covetousness, which is idolatry" (Colossians 3:5). The vices in this exhortation move from the sensual life to the inner life of a Christian. Only covetousness, however, is identified as idolatry here because "Gain" can become one's god.[5] In the identification of "idolatry" in the New Testament, other than literal worship of gods, the sin of idolatry is greed (Ephesians 5:5).[6] When we make earthly acquisitions our aim, we lose sight of our heavenly commitment. We have died with Christ, the Apostle Paul says, and have been raised to the new life of Christ. Peter O'Brien in his commentary on Paul's equation of covetousness with idolatry remarked, "Perhaps it [covetousness] is . . . more dangerous [than sensuality] because it may assume so many respectable forms."[7] Under the guise of the good, such as practicing a commendable work ethic, providing for our families, and Christian philanthropy, we can really be greed-grubbers. We honor God when we recognize him alone as worthy of our full undivided loyalty. As Jesus instructed us, "You cannot serve God and money" (Matthew 6:24). The rationale that greed is idolatry is that service to money means worship of money as a person's god. The Christian ethic is to sacrifice, not to take and hoard.

*All who worship must worship the Lord (vv. 8, 9).* The passage also ensures that *every* person in the community who offers *any* form of worship must do so to the Lord God at his altar. Further instructions in verses 8, 9 expand in two ways on the basic teaching of verses 3, 4. The Law includes all sacrifices that are made, not just the peace offering. The text reads, "a burnt offering or sacrifice" (v. 8), which refers to the whole system of worship described in chapters 1—7. Burnt offerings were common and congregational, and the general term "sacrifice" probably refers to the remaining kinds of sacrifice.[8] The second expansion is the inclusion of the resident "strangers." These were foreigners who had migrated to Israel. They were not necessarily converts to the God of Israel. The aliens had no obligation to worship God; they could slay their meat at home. They could not under any circumstances, however, ingest blood (v. 10). The strangers were not required to worship the Lord, but they were required to observe the principal religious practices of Israel, such as the Day of Atonement, Sabbath observance, and Passover.[9] If they chose to offer worship to the Lord, they had to follow the same worship laws as the native Israelites (22:18), which meant they too had to bring their offering to the tent for slaughter.

There were other restrictions for the alien too, such as prohibition against practicing idolatrous religion (Deuteronomy 17:2–5). This was simply because importing the religions of the nations would prove to be a snare for the Israelites. This later became the pitfall that brought so much trouble to the people in their history. They assimilated elements of false religions into their assembly, especially idolatry and polytheism. Also, permission of false religious practices contradicted Israel's purpose as a chosen nation. Israel was commissioned to be "a kingdom of priests" (Exodus 19:6) who instructed the nations in the revelation of the true and living God.

The church too has always faced the problem of aberrant teachings and practices that have threatened the authentic gospel. Paul was zealous for the original teachings of Jesus and the apostles as the sole orthodox teaching of the church (2 Corinthians 11:12–15). He set in motion safeguards against false teachings and teachers in the churches he founded. These false ideas were typically syncretistic in theology and immoral in lifestyle. They were a constant threat to the perseverance of new Christian congregations. Today some alleged Christians are ecclesial "Lone Rangers." They develop aberrant doctrine and heretical worship practices. These are teachers who have little or no accountability to a local church or ecclesial authority. Also, because of many media outlets today, Christians are tempted to rely on local and national broadcasts of religious services as their "home church." In this case, we mean "home" literally. They stay at home observing services on TV or through the Internet. They do not formally associate and assimilate with Christians in a church body. Even if the church services are theologically orthodox, *willful* neglect or resistance to congregating with the church is prohibited in the New Testament.[10] The writer to the Hebrews recognized the need to assemble regularly so that the members might be encouraged in faithful Christian living: "Let us hold fast the confession of our hope without wavering, for he who promised is faithful. And let us consider how to stir up one another to love and good works, not neglecting to meet together, as is the habit of some, but encouraging one another, and all the more as you see the Day drawing near" (Hebrews 10:23–25). Just as "'do-it-yourself spirituality' was to have no place in Israel,"[11] it is not to have a place in the Christian's life today.

## Honor God by Acknowledging His Gift (vv. 10–12)

We also honor God by recognizing that the Lord God is the source of the many blessings we have received. Verses 10–12 describe the prohibition against eating blood by extending its application. These verses use the sternest language of the entire passage. First, the prohibition is not limited to the Israelites, as in verses 3, 4, who were commanded to bring their animal offerings to the sanctuary. The passage specifically includes "strangers [foreigners] who sojourn among you," repeating the phrase twice (vv. 10, 12). Second, the penalty was severe for the transgressor. Unlike the earlier verses that speak of "cutting off" the offender from his community, the penalty is spoken by God in the first-person voice: "I will set my face against that person" (v. 10). God appears to take this personally, as we sometimes say today. Only five times in Leviticus does the Lord speak of "setting his face" against the criminal. Four of the five pertain to idolatry, including our context (17:10; 20:3, 5, 6), and the other to the refusal to obey the Lord's commands (26:17).[12] Idolatry is the epitome of breaking covenant with God. It is the denial of the Lord's claims as the sole living God and his unique relationship with his people. The offense meant that the culprit was exiled from the community. In this case, the penalty included the possibility of death, for idolaters were the objects of God's wrath (Deuteronomy 29:18–22; Leviticus 26:27–33).

Third, the prohibition in verse 12 is absolute, translated here, "No person among you shall eat blood." The same grammatical form occurs in the Ten Commandments: "you shall not . . . ," meaning that the crime is *never* to be practiced (Exodus 20).[13] Foreigners whose culture included idolatrous religions would be the most likely to fall into idolatry. They did not have the option of creating a haven of false worship in the community. The same absolute restriction is imposed on Christians by the teaching of the New Testament Scriptures. From the perspective of the authors, like their Jewish ancestors, the practice of idolatry was reprehensible. It was utterly contradictory to the central claim of the gospel and the essence of who God is.

If the people ate the blood of sacrifice, it was a denial of the blood as God's gift for their atonement. Verse 11 is central to the passage since it presents the clearest statement of the theological reason for proscribing the ingestion of blood. Superstition regarding blood was rampant in the ancient world. It has its counterparts today too in various cults, especially those associated with the occult. Blood was thought to possess power inherently; by eating the blood, the person appropriated the spiritual power of the blood. Drinking or eating blood was a part of ancient rituals. The Bible adamantly opposes this understanding and prohibits the eating of blood in any form, whether directly or in meat not properly drained (Deuteronomy 12:23; 1 Samuel 14:32–34). The blood is a gift from God that had to be presented to the altar in worship if it was to have the effect of atonement.[14] "I have given it for you" announces that the blood is God's to give, and by that gift forgiveness is achieved. The gift must be honored by the recipients by proper handling of the blood. To drink the blood would be tantamount to spurning the Giver and using the blood for the individual's own purpose.

Blood, however, is not *inherently* the spiritual life of a creature. "For the life of the flesh is in the blood" in verse 11 does not mean, as the ancient nations thought, that the blood possessed the spiritual life-force of the victim that was released when eaten. The point of the passage is that the life of the victim was *represented* by its blood, and the shedding of its blood meant its death. It is obvious that life depends on blood. One does not have to be a rocket scientist to see that blood is an appropriate figure of speech for the life of a person or animal. This is reflected in Genesis 9 when God established the penalty for murder: "Whoever sheds the blood of man, by man shall his blood be shed" (Genesis 9:6). The reason for the prohibition against murder is theologically stated: "for God made man in his own image." Human life is the gift of God who has bestowed it and consequently requires the proper handling of it. Animals too have "the breath of life" (Genesis 6:17). Although not created in the image of God, animals must be recognized and honored as God's creatures. The blood, then, that God gives to the worshiper is to be returned to the Lord at his altar. It is sacred and cannot be profaned. To do so would cut across the central feature of God as Creator and as Sovereign Lord over his people. It is by this blood, this gift of life, that the sins of the people are removed.

*God's gift.* The church is also commanded to honor the gift that God has bestowed on us. As C. H. Spurgeon observed, Jesus is "the Gift of gifts."[15] God expects us to honor the Lord Jesus Christ. Peter in his first letter speaks of our redemption as purchased by "the precious blood of Christ, like that of a lamb without blemish or spot" (1 Peter 1:19; cf. Acts 20:28). The blood of Christ signals the sacrificed life of the Lord. Jesus' life has infinite value because he is the infinite Son of God who lived in complete obedience and whose life was pure without stain of sin or sins. Christian hymnody commonly refers to the power of the blood of Christ, such as "There Is Power in the Blood" (by Lewis E. Jones, 1899) and "There Is a Fountain Filled with Blood" (William Cowper, ca. 1772). Contemporary Christian artists, too, such as Del Way's "Only the Blood" proclaim the message of our passage. When we sing these songs, we must not confuse the power of the blood itself for the sinless life that it represents. Jesus' blood was human blood. It did not possess a mystical magical property. The power was in the shedding of the blood, the giving of the life of Jesus. God has given us the life of Jesus, and we must cherish it.

How might we dishonor the blood of the Lord Jesus? Anyone who neglects the blood of Christ by rejecting or ignoring the saving work of Christ is subject to the wrath of God. The writer to the Hebrews spoke of this threat. He argued that if breaking the law of Moses resulted in death for the criminal, then "How much worse punishment, do you think, will be deserved by the one who has trampled underfoot the Son of God, and has profaned the blood of the covenant by which he was sanctified, and has outraged the Spirit of grace?" (Hebrews 10:29). There is simply no hope for the person who snubs the shed blood of Christ, for there is no other means for salvation. Solely by the blood of Christ, the perfectly obedient Savior, is forgiveness of sin realized. If we properly understand the decadence of our sin and the foul stench of our wickedness, we appreciate the necessity of the power of the blood of the only fully Righteous One in God's eyes, our Lord Jesus.

*The Lord's Table.* Another way in which we can dishonor the blood of Christ is the trivializing of the Christian Table, the altar where we remember the Lord's death by the communal taking of the bread and cup. Because of some misguided interpretations, many church traditions have tended to minimize the Table. There has been, however, a resurgence of interest in the liturgy of the church, and people are increasingly interested in the practice of the two Christian ordinances, baptism and the Lord's Supper. The eating of the bread and drinking of the cup must be observed with utmost seriousness. Participation in the Table is a witness to our faith in Christ and his atoning death, but also to his future return when he shall gather his church. When we commemorate the Table, we must be clear in our presentation of the elements as to who can offer them, to whom they can be offered, and in what way they are to be received, especially emphasizing the meaning that the Table portrays. The Table's elements are only for Christians and can be administered only by the gathered church. The procedure for the rite is described by the Apostle Paul in 1 Corinthians 11, following the model of our Lord's Last Supper with his disciples (Matthew 26:26–30).

Paul addressed the troubling practices of the Lord's Supper at Corinth.[16] Paul recognized that these irreverent practices contributed to the failing health of the Christians at Corinth. He warned, "Whoever, therefore, eats the bread or drinks the cup of the Lord in an unworthy manner will be guilty concerning the body and blood of the Lord. Let a person examine himself, then, and so eat of the bread and drink of the cup" (1 Corinthians 11:27, 28). Paul complained that the sacredness of the service was disrespected by the wealthy members of the church. We do not know the precise details of the infraction, but the following scenario is possible. A common meal preceded the formal celebration of the Lord's Supper. The behavior of the prosperous at this common meal was not consistent with the meaning of the Lord's Supper. The well-to-do ate and drank to satiation, while the poor and others had little or nothing to eat. This division between the wealthy and poor was a cultural feature of Greek society.[17] It was not the *Lord's* Supper any longer but the *people's* supper because the Lord's Supper proclaimed the equal status of each Christian in the partaking of Christ's death and life. All people are unworthy for sure, but each is given equal access to God through Jesus by his imputed grace. To maintain the divisions that Corinth practiced was a denial of what the Lord had accomplished through his sacrifice. The people who defamed the Lord's mission then were held accountable for the death of Christ, subjecting them to the discipline of the Lord.

Today the tradition of how the church receives the Lord's Table differs, since many congregations do not couple the Table with a feast. Nevertheless, the principle abides. We, too, run the risk of profaning the Lord's blood when we eat and drink as though the Lord's death has made no difference. If we come to the Lord's Table without regard for the redemption he has provided and the unity of the body that he has secured, we deny by our attitude the reality of Jesus' death. Any form of schism, harboring sinful resentment toward another, or an offense against other members of the church subjects us to the Lord's discipline. We should add that one purpose of Jesus' shed blood was to purify believers, making us fit for God as his treasured possession. If we exhibit brazen lives of sin, we make Christ's atoning actions as if of no effect (Titus 2:14).

*Eating the blood.* Before we move forward to the final verses, we should address a common question among Bible believers about the prohibition of eating blood and the Christian's dietary habits. Are Christians required to drain the blood of butchered meat before consumption? This is the prescribed preparation in the rabbinic tradition, known as kosher eating, practiced in Orthodox Judaism to this day. Even if not, we might ask, is the Christian prohibited from consuming raw or undercooked meat and fish that contain blood? The answer to both questions can be answered in a word: No! We do not observe a matter pertaining to sacrificial ritual since the sacrificial system of the Old Testament has been realized in the death of Christ. The Old Testament law in its ancient form is no longer obligatory for the church today. In the earliest days of the church, the Gentile Christians were instructed by the Jerusalem church to observe certain Jewish customs such as refusing to eat blood. This achieved the practical purpose of Gentile believers' unity with Jewish Christians whose conscience was offended by the consumption of blood (Acts 15:20; Romans 14:21).[18] But the general principle that pervaded broad Christian behavior was the recognition that the food laws and those things that marked Jewish identity, such as circumcision, were not required of Christians (1 Corinthians 8:8; 10:31).

## Honor God by Valuing Life (vv. 13–16)

Up to this point the instructions for handling blood have all concerned the role of blood in sacrificial worship. Moses now addressed the handling of blood that came from animals not intended for worship. There are two situations named in the text. First, hunting animals was common, and the question probably arose as to how to deal with the blood of an animal in the open field but not meant for worship. Second, persons sometimes came across animals that had died a natural death or had been killed by another animal. Two different procedures for handling the blood were called for.

In the case of hunted animals, the hunters had to drain the blood of the beast or bird before consumption. The blood had to be drained from the corpse, presumably on the ground, which then was covered over with dirt. Deuteronomy 14:5 names animals that were ceremonially clean and were permitted foods for consumption, including deer and other wild species (cf. Deuteronomy 12:13–28 for further provisions[19]). The covering of the blood with dirt expressed respect for the life of the animal. When the blood was poured into the soil and covered over, the blood could not be used for any additional purpose, such as for a pagan ritual. In the case of animals that the person found already dead, the blood had not been drained and had probably coagulated, making it impossible to rid the blood fully from the meat. Deuteronomy 14:21 clarifies that an Israelite must not eat the fallen animal. It may be eaten, however, by a foreigner among them, although he became ritually unclean (cf. Leviticus 11:39, 40). If the Israelite were unaware that he ate such an animal,[20] his ceremonial uncleanness was not so severe that a sacrifice was required. The contaminated person remained unclean until evening and washed his clothes and bathed himself. Obviously, domesticated animals, which otherwise were acceptable for offerings at the Tent of Meeting, were unlawful if found dead since the blood of a living animal was demanded for the altar.

These provisions restricted the killing and handling of animals for human consumption. The instructions reflected the teaching in the Law that presupposes that all life, whether human or animal, was sacred and deserved special treatment. When we say that life is sacred, we mean that all life comes from God and that all life, whether to give or to take, is his exclusive prerogative. Human life and animal life as creations of God must be respected and cherished according to their place in God's created order. Murder of a human being is the most horrific crime committed by a person because he murders one made in the "image" of God (Genesis 9:6). As for the lower creatures, the underlying teaching of our passage is that people must not engage in wanton killing of animals and birds by taking life savagely and disposing of them ruthlessly. Such treatment of life, whether human or animal, actually dehumanizes mankind because as creations in God's image, our humanity includes the stewardship of caring for the created order (Genesis 1:28).

And, finally, our passage that points to the sacredness of human life also points us to the supreme gift of God, his Son, Jesus Christ. Jesus Christ yielded his life; it was not taken from him by human force. Rather, it was the force of divine love for us that compelled Christ to suffer for our sins and to deliver us from sin and impurity. "And walk in love, as Christ loved us and gave himself up for us, a fragrant offering and sacrifice to God" (Ephesians 5:2).

# 15

# The Sanctity of the Family

LEVITICUS 18:1–30; 20:1–27

WHEN I WAS WORKING my way through seminary years ago, I had a part-time job as a sales representative for a private security company. The company emphasized home security in the suburbs, which were subject to break-ins. By drawing one-square-mile boundaries, the company formed patrol zones in which an armed officer on duty patrolled in a marked vehicle. Typically the residents who subscribed to the service were parents who wanted to shield their loved ones from harm. When we thought of a protection service in those days, we focused on criminal theft and violence. Today we see that there are also insidious dangers in our culture that threaten the very definition and soundness of families. The moral boundaries that once circumscribed behavior have been compromised in our popular culture. These changing ways of life have even made significant inroads into Christian communities. The notion that boundaries are hindrances to a person's freedom and well-being has won an audience, to our detriment. Any child psychologist or observant grandparent will tell us that boundaries are essential in the life of a child. Child-rearing without behavioral boundaries will create a frustrated child and eventually an aimless adult. Disciplined restraint nourishes life, producing a more meaningful life. God gave his people moral boundaries so they would thrive under his approval and blessing.

Our passage gives us a look at the moral boundaries that establish proper sexual relationships in families and in society. Chapters 18—20 make up a section that instructed the people in conduct devoted to God. We will examine chapters 18 and 20 together since they are the bookends of the section. This pair of chapters largely addresses the same issue of sexual behavior: Chapter

18 gives the specific commandments, and chapter 20 names the corresponding penalties when those commandments are not obeyed. The sociological setting helps us understand the need for such boundaries. Typically an Israelite's home housed father and mother and children. Closely situated were the homes of extended family members, involving as many as twenty or more persons.[1] This proximity of family members provided opportunities for unlawful sexual behavior. Also, the marriage of persons within the same family lineage was a practice known among the Hebrew patriarchs.[2]

### The Covenant Lord of God's People (18:1–5, 24–30)

Repeatedly chapter 18 declares, "I am the LORD your God" and "I am the LORD." "I am the LORD your God" begins the chapter (v. 2) and ends the chapter (v. 30). The passage therefore repeatedly asserts the authoritative source of the instructions. When it comes to evaluating the social mores commanded by the Bible, it is tempting to rely on secular sources of authority that complement the Biblical standards. We are technocrats in our culture, making social science studies with their graphs and statistics a compelling argument. Coupled with anecdotal stories, we have all known and seen in the media horrific sexual deviations of our day that persuade many that the moral precepts of Scripture are the right way to go in order to avoid a society that drifts into social chaos. But the Bible does not rely on such external data or on the polling of public opinion. Our passage declares that these commandments have their source in the ultimate authority of God. The phrase "the LORD *your* God" is shorthand for the most important core teaching in all of Scripture. "Your" God declares that the Lord has redeemed a people for himself. This is language that reflects the historic liberation of the Hebrews from Egyptian bondage. For the people to neglect this teaching would be a rejection of the lordship of God.

One reason for the emphasis on the lordship of the Covenant-Giver is the nature of the teaching in Leviticus 18. It is remarkably countercultural and counterintuitive. In the ancient world, especially in Canaanite theology, the prism for understanding reality was through the act of cohabitation. The gods and goddesses produced through relations the good ordered world in which people live. The idea that God was not sexual, that is he is neither male nor female, was unique. That the Lord God of Israel had no wives or consorts distinguished the religion of Israel from all others. This feature gave the instructions on sexual behaviors a different perspective than was commonly accepted. The nations generally confused creation and the Creator, deifying creatures and denying the one true God his sole place as Sovereign Lord. The Apostle Paul addressed the chief sins and guilt of the Gentiles in the book of

Romans, in which he showed that idolatry and polytheism were fundamentally denials of the Lord as Creator-God (Romans 1:22–25). He coupled with this sin the wickedness of sexual aberrations that characterized Greco-Roman culture (1:26–28).

There is a tie between understanding the nature of God and sexual passions because the two speak directly to the authority of the Creator. He made the world with its boundaries in six days, and he has established the sexual identities and roles of men and women. To confuse or reject the Creator's design is to deny the lordship of God. The new vernacular for gender confusion is *gender construction* and *gender blending*. These terms speak of looking beyond biological differences between men and women and focusing on how social settings such as family, church, and workplace create gendered identity. There is a remarkable openness today to creating one's gendered role instead of accepting the assignment of one's gender at birth.

What the history of Israel tells us is that the people, once they had entered the land of promise, fell into the sinful practices of the indigenous nations. The result was turning the Lord God as Redeemer into a Baal-like figure who was the chief god of fertility among the Canaanites. As in the case with the nations, the Hebrews practiced fertility rituals and adopted the sexual mores of the nations (e.g., Judges 3:5–7). We face a similar challenge today as God's people, foreigners in this troubled world. The underpinning of our culture that for many decades relied on the Judeo-Christian teaching is slowly eroding before our eyes. Regardless of what may come, the people of God must observe the teachings of the one true Lord. The authority for the teaching on right family relationships is rooted in the transcendent God. Verses 24–30 are explicit on the matter. They explain that the failure to observe the Lord's instructions will make the people subject to God's judgment, as is the case with the nations who inhabit the land. The Lord will "vomit" them out of the land, too. The verses that conclude Leviticus 20 set the issue in the broadest framework. The failure to abide by the Lord's instructions meant that the people would no longer be a holy people, separated from the nations (20:22–27). The chief purpose of God's redemption of Israel is that they might be a holy instrument to bring saving knowledge to the nations. As the Lord instructed his prophet Jeremiah regarding the wicked of his day, "You must influence them; do not let them influence you!" (Jeremiah 15:19, NLT).

The basis for our moral teachings and lifestyle is the commandments of our Lord. It is not because of social-economic studies or the findings of genetic studies.[3] We worship God, and this means submitting ourselves to his ways. God is Creator, and he has chosen to run the world as he sees fit. To deny him that in our lives is the most violent act of disobedience. The New Testament recognizes that sexual immorality as a lifestyle is a characteristic of a person who is not fit for the kingdom of God. In the book of Galatians, we read this warning:

> Now the works of the flesh are evident: sexual immorality, impurity, sensuality, idolatry, sorcery, enmity, strife, jealousy, fits of anger, rivalries, dissensions, divisions, envy, drunkenness, orgies, and things like these. I warn you, as I warned you before, that those who do such things will not inherit the kingdom of God. (Galatians 5:19–21; cf. Jesus' remarks in Mark 7:21–23)

This does not mean that those who have committed any of these sins are not true believers, for we all have continued to struggle with these vices. Rather, the passage teaches that those who *persist* in these sins are not submissive to the transforming work of the Spirit. The warning leads to repentance, or if ignored, these sins serve as a testimony to one's rejection of the gospel.[4] The rationale given in Leviticus 20:26 captures the motivation of the holiness laws as a whole: "You shall be holy to me, for I the LORD am holy and have separated you from the peoples, that you should be mine." We must live our lives in such a way that we show through our holy devotion that we belong to God and not to another.

### The Sanctity of God's People (18:6–23; 20:1–22)

The regulations are many in chapters 18 and 20, but they can be cataloged to show that there was rhyme and reason for their inclusion and arrangement. I have already mentioned that the emphasis of the two chapters is the effect of sexual aberrations on the fitness of the people to live in the land as God's holy people. There are regulations concerning other practices in the two chapters, such as offering up children to pagan deities. But these laws can be shown to be related to the sexual prohibitions that dominate the two chapters. The prohibitions in 18:6–23 can be gathered into two groups. Verses 6–16 describe the range of kinship connections between a man and a woman whose cohabitation was outlawed. Verses 17–23 focus on the illicit acts that they perform.[5]

*Forbidden sexual relations (18:6–23).* The prohibitions in verses 6–23 concern sexual relationships with close relatives and sexual relations that are not exclusively between a man and a woman. Beginning in verse 7 and occurring throughout chapter 18 is the idiomatic expression "uncover the nakedness." This is a polite way of saying sexual relations. Not all the possible family relationships are named, such as uncle and niece or first cousins.[6] Also, homosexuality is condemned (v. 22), but there is no mention of lesbianism in our text, not because it was permitted, but because the passage is told from a man's sexual perspective (except v. 23b). This list therefore is probably representative, not exhaustive.

Verses 6–11 name the closest blood relatives: mother, stepmother, half-sister, granddaughter, and stepsister. The explanation for the restriction on the stepsister in verse 11 gives us insight into the reasoning behind the prohibitions in this group. Although she is a stepsister, she is treated as a blood sister because she was reared in the same household. Marriage among relatives closely connected as *blood* relations was outlawed.

Verses 12–14 prohibit a man's aunts by blood for marriage. Verses 15, 16 list relatives by marriage, a daughter-in-law and sister-in-law.[7] Verses 17, 18 mention the man's wife's closest relatives—the wife's daughter and granddaughter and her sister.

The last paragraph, verses 19–23, names unlawful sexual liaisons that are *not* family-related. These prohibitions were included because they fit in with the general topic of sexual violations. The first prohibition, however, denounces sacrificing a child to the pagan god Molech (v. 21).[8] The inclusion of idolatry in this context is logical, however, since the passage as a whole deals with sexual relationships, including those that produce children.[9] Worship of Molech as a Canaanite deity may have also involved cultic prostitution, although this is not certain.

The listing of prohibitions includes homosexuality and bestiality (vv. 22, 23). Human sacrifice and bestiality are so repugnant to us, it is hard to conceive of these practices actually occurring. Although probably rare, it was a reality that the Israelites had to face. More acceptable in our culture is the sexual lifestyle of the gay community. Nevertheless, the Scriptures are clear that such sexual relationships were unacceptable. The language that condemned it is strongly worded; it is deemed "an abomination" (v. 22). Although some may want to argue that this is an Old Testament phobia that is not consistent with Christian grace, the New Testament confirms the Old Testament teaching that approves only of heterosexual unions within marriage (1 Corinthians 6:9; 1 Timothy 1:10). We have the reasoning of why homosexuality is unlawful provided in Romans 1 when the Apostle Paul addressed the universality of human sin and guilt (Romans 1:18–30, esp. 26, 27). The Gentiles had rejected the testimony of nature and chose sinful idolatry and sexual perversions to honor their gods. The sexual practices of the Gentiles were a great affront to God because they were a rejection of God as Creator. He made men and women to play their appropriate sexual roles whereby they would propagate and dominate the world as stewards of the Lord's creation (Genesis 1:28). Heterosexuality outside the bounds of marriage is no less a sin, but the nature of homosexuality has more serious repercussions since it is a repudiation of the Lord's claim on his created order.

We should recognize that there is a difference between homosexual *desires* and homosexual *practices*. By this I mean that people who have homosexual desires are not necessarily slaves to their desires. A person can resist sinful impulses. This ability to resist sinful temptations is available to the Christian by virtue of the Holy Spirit who lives in the life of a Christian man or woman (Romans 6:17). Moreover, those who engage in homosexuality are *not* outside the realm of God's loving forgiveness. Members of the Corinthian church had practiced homosexuality before receiving the gospel (1 Corinthians 6:9–11). Christians can be forgiven of sexual immorality and receive the new life of Christ. We are admonished to live a life consecrated to God, lives worthy of the new life that Christ has given us (Colossians 3:5–10; Titus 3:3–7). Christians above all others, having received the compassion of Christ's loving forgiveness, must show the same compassion toward those who have become ensnared in the gay lifestyle.[10]

*Penalties for disobedience (20:1–21).* The penalties for sexual transgressions are given in chapter 20. (1) The severest penalty is execution of the offender by the people of the community. (2) Lesser offenses merited expulsion from the community, being "cut off" from among their people (vv. 17, 18). That a lawbreaker "bear his iniquity" (v. 17) means that once expelled, such persons are subject to the punishment that God may choose to inflict on them, including infertility (vv. 20, 21). (3) Another penalty was barrenness. Childlessness was viewed as a "reproach" by God since children were a blessing that he alone could give (e.g., Genesis 20:18; Deuteronomy 7:13, 14; Luke 1:25).[11] Children were prized since they were vital for perpetuating a family's legacy and property.

As a necessary aside, we should comment on the question of God's blessing and the infertility that many couples experience today. It is wrongheaded to reason backwards that since a couple does not become pregnant, they must be under the curse of God for some unknown sin. This is a mistaken notion that can be answered by remembering that there are a number of different reasons why the sorrows and disappointments in life may be ours. We live in an imperfect world marred by human sin that has impacted every aspect of life. Also there are times when God uses human sorrow as a means of achieving a higher purpose. When Jesus was asked if a blind man was born blind because of his sin or his parents', the Lord answered, "It was not that this man sinned, or his parents, but that the works of God might be displayed in him" (John 9:3). We are called upon to weep with those who weep and to bear one another's burdens, not to sit in judgment against a person, ascribing to him a sin, for such was the error of Job's friends.

The reason for the stern penalties in our passage is related to the Ten Commandments. These ten stipulations were the heart of the covenant under which Israel lived as the people of God. The covenant was stated succinctly to Moses when God assured him of Israel's deliverance from Egyptian bondage: "I will take you to be my people, and I will be your God" (Exodus 6:7a; cf. Leviticus 26:12; Hosea 1:10; 2:23; Romans 9:26). These Ten Commandments were the obligations that Israel was to live by under the rule of the Lord. The Lord in turn promised to prosper and protect Israel, bringing the people into the land of promise. If Israel failed in their obligations, the penalty for their disobedience was national calamites of war, pestilence, and drought (Deuteronomy 28). Therefore, it was of utmost seriousness when a person committed infractions against the Lord, especially the Ten Commandments. Such transgressions risked bringing the wrath of God against the nation. The crimes cited in Leviticus 20 are related in one way or another to the Ten Commandments. If the people did not deal with criminals in their midst, then the whole nation was subjected to the wrath of God.

It was for this reason that sexual infractions were not considered merely private matters. Every person's religious and moral behavior impacted the lives and well-being of their neighbors and fellow citizens. The community as a whole was responsible for carrying out the death penalty. It was not an act of personal vengeance but of covenant necessity for national survival. Our culture contends that sexual matters are private, and we should not be in the business of legislating morality. Although we can understand the fear of too much government intrusion, a person's sexual practices tend to spill out into the mainstream of civic life. Sexual addictions, sexually transmitted diseases, pornography, and child abuse have a societal cost that we all end up paying. The same is true for the church. Personal behavior for members of a church impacts the life and witness of that church.

Verses 1–5 describe the death penalty for the person who commits idolatry by worshiping the god Molech. The sensual language used to describe the crime, "whoring after Molech," shows the connection between pagan worship and sexual deviance. The evil of idolatry is so deplorable that the Lord says in the first person, "I myself will set my face against that man" (v. 3). This refers to the wrath of God's covenant curses if the people fail to carry out the execution. The passage reflects the principle of community solidarity. Although individuality was recognized in the Law, there was also an emphasis on community identity and responsibility. "No man is an island" (John Donne) is an apt description of the Law's perspective on accountability. The assumption is that the idolater will influence others, leading his own family and clan into false worship and sexual sin. The community will suffer because of its failure to stop the practice of idolatry and for its eventual adoption of the practice.

This crime led to naming a related one in verses 6–8, the evil of sorcery. Sorcery is the use of evil powers and spirits. This too is defined by the sexual term "whoring." False religion typically relied on "mediums and necromancers" because their magic and occult rituals were important means of discovering the will of the gods and of manipulating nature by securing the favor of the gods. The penalty for sorcery was expulsion of the person who turned to sorcery instead of relying on the word of God for instruction. Deuteronomy 18 includes sorcery in its list of the "abominable practices" of the nations that had to be avoided if the people were to remain under God's covenant care (vv. 9–14). God gave his word through his law, his priests, and his prophets. In our case today, the faithful will resist any alternative spirituality to the Word of God, such as Scientology or eastern mysticism. The admonition in verses 7, 8 to "consecrate" themselves by conforming to the holy instructions of the Lord draws the lines of right and wrong behavior brightly. Holiness required the people to eschew sorcery and to depend solely on God's appointed means of instruction. When you obtain your boarding pass for a flight, you must give it to the gate attendant when you board the plane. Not just any ticket or boarding pass will do. God has provided one authorized means whereby we can come into his presence and learn of him—our Lord Jesus Christ. First Timothy 2:5 declares, "There is one God, and there is one mediator between God and men, the man Christ Jesus."

Verse 9 introduces a new direction. It announces the death penalty for the person who "curses his father or his mother." This is an explicit allusion to the Fifth Commandment that required the people to "honor [their] father and [their] mother" (Exodus 20:12). The reason for its mention in this context is because some of the following sexual sins enumerated in verses 10–21 involve dishonoring parents. In giving the Fifth Commandment, God specifically tied it to the nation's future perseverance in the land. Because the Lord delegated parents' authority to teach their children the word of God, rebellion against their teaching was in essence rebellion against the authority of the Lord. When young people despise the moral teaching of their parents, they commit two serious blunders. First, young people need the advantage of experience, and the only way to get it is through parental instruction and modeling. Parents have walked in the avenues where youth have yet to travel. Foolish people don't listen to others. Second, to repudiate one's parents is to repudiate the Lord God himself. No one can afford to run that risk!

Now we read the catalog of prohibited sexual practices. Verse 10's prohibition against adultery stands at the head of the list of infractions. It differs from those that follow in verses 11–21, which all pertain to incest. The prohibition against adultery is another specific reference to one of the Ten Commandments (Exodus 20:14). Adultery was so grave in the eyes of God that the man and woman suffered execution. The reason for the severity of the penalty was because the crime cut to the core of the concept of covenant loyalty. The Lord required loyalty from his subjects, not only loyalty to him but also to one another. When a spouse committed sexual disloyalty, the man and woman broke their loyalties to their spouses, transgressing the sacred bonds of marital union. Hebrews 13:4 describes God's great displeasure at marital infidelity: "Let marriage be held in honor among all, and let the marriage bed be undefiled, for God will judge the sexually immoral and adulterous." The epitome of the whole law was captured in this admonition: "You shall love your neighbor as yourself" (Leviticus 19:18; Romans 13:9). To take another person's spouse was challenging the authority of the covenant's commandments given by God.

*Enjoying the land of blessing (vv. 22–25a).* What was at stake in keeping the Law was the favor of God upon the nation. He promised to bring them into "a land flowing with milk and honey" (20:24; Deuteronomy 6:3). The picture of an arable land flowing with rivers and streams would have been a welcome sight for a people who were living in a frightening wilderness. But the promise describes an idyllic land, characterized by streams of "milk and honey." The reason for the expulsion of the Canaanites was the moral decadence of their society (Genesis 15:16; Leviticus 18:27, 28; Deuteronomy 12:29–31). The imagery used in our text to describe expulsion is "vomit"; the land "vomits" out the former residents (v. 28). The motivation for the expulsion of the inhabitants was not Israel's fear of foreigners or an ethnic bigotry against people unlike them. God held his own people Israel to the same standard, if not more so. The gauge was the moral purity of the people. If Israel acted wickedly, they became in effect a pagan nation sold out to other gods and guilty of immoral perversions. The Israelites, too, would be "vomited" out, so that the land might be relieved of its uncleanness. That is exactly what happened to the Israelites who centuries later suffered exile for their sins.

But the blessing God has for his disciples today cannot be lost. This blessing is the *spiritual* blessings that God has bestowed on his church through his Son, Jesus Christ. The New Testament tells us that God "has blessed us in Christ with every spiritual blessing in the heavenly places" (Ephesians 1:3b; cf. Romans 10:12). The Lord provides material blessings for his people to meet their needs, but even so we must seek the kingdom of God, not the things of this world (Matthew 6:31–33; Philippians 4:18). The wealth that God promises each of us, regardless of our material poverty or riches, is the vast storehouse of spiritual treasures that the Lord has bequeathed to us as our inheritance (1 Timothy 6:17; 1 Peter 1:3, 4). The gift of the Holy Spirit, the assurance of forgiveness and eternal salvation, and the blessing of prayer are but a few of the riches we have received. These were given to Christians through the sacrifice of our Lord Jesus who became poor that we might receive the riches of Christ (2 Corinthians 8:9).

### The Witness of God's People (20:25b–27)

We come to the final paragraph of the passage, which clarifies the ultimate purpose for these laws: "I [the Lord] have separated you from the peoples" (vv. 24b, 26a). The sexual restrictions in chapters 18 and 20, the food laws (cf. 11:44–47), and any appeal to sorcery are named as criteria for determining the sacred state of the people of God. This goes to the reason for the election of Israel from the outset. Israel is to be "a kingdom of priests and a holy nation" (Exodus 19:6) and thus to represent the Lord to the nations. The church has inherited that assignment, as Peter says, so that we might "proclaim the excellencies of [Christ] who called you out of darkness into his marvelous light" (1 Peter 2:9b). Whereas Israel distinguished itself from its neighbors by obedience to the ceremonial and holiness laws, we distinguish ourselves by our adherence to righteous living. We please God by practicing purity in our sexual thoughts and actions (1 Thessalonians 4:1–9).

### "You Shall . . . Live by Them" (18:5)

But who, we ask, can possibly maintain the laws that God has commanded? The message that the passage as a whole gives us can be summarized in the charge that God gave Israel in 18:5: "You shall therefore keep my statutes and my rules; if a person does them, he shall live by them: I am the LORD." Herein is the central demand of the Law: "*If* a person does them," that is, obeys them. That little two-letter word "if" is crucial to a person's eternal destiny. The Law was "good" and "holy" (Romans 7:12). Keeping its commandments provided Israel a righteousness that secured their life in the land (10:5).[12] But as Israel proved by its expulsion from the land, and as each of us knows in our own heart, we as human beings cannot "keep [God's] statutes" because we are self-centered sinners. Our disobedience often rivals our measure of obedience. But we might say in our hearts, "I have not committed any of these horrible sins— these obscene perversions!" Like the rich young ruler we may think, "All these [commandments] I have kept. What do I still lack?" (Matthew 19:20). But Jesus' reply exposed the sinful heart of the man who was unwilling to give up his old life for the new life the Lord called him to undertake. We fool ourselves if we think that God is satisfied with actions and not our hearts. Adultery is not only a matter of sin of the body but also of the heart. Jesus taught that there is an internal law in each one of us: The person who lusts in his heart has committed adultery already, Jesus taught (5:28). Honesty compels us to admit that we have not escaped disobedience to God's demands for upright living.

The New Testament in Romans 10:5 picks up Leviticus 18:5 and interprets it in the light of the gospel of Jesus Christ. Since the Law cooperating as it does with sinful humanity cannot grant life, there is another avenue of salvation. That means of receiving righteousness is the word of grace that God had long ago promised and that the new age in Christ has brought. Faith was not new, of course. God had announced that he would "circumcise" *spiritually* the hearts of his people (Deuteronomy 10:16; 30:6). A day would come when they repented and experienced life anew in the land. Faith is the means by which God always intended for the regeneration of his people. In our days, the faith that Christians have in the death and resurrected life of Christ secures that reconciliation with God. Jesus alone has perfectly obeyed the laws of God. Anyone who attempts to follow a code of conduct as the basis for meriting Heaven will be disappointed. The result in doing so will be death without any hope since the only means of salvation by faith has been rejected. The plea of God for us is to repent and recognize that our salvation rests with Jesus Christ and him alone.

# 16

# Daily Christian Living

## LEVITICUS 19:1-37

CHRISTIANITY DOES MORE THAN prepare us for "the sweet by and by." It is also meant for "the nasty now and now," as Bob Harrington, "the chaplain of Bourbon Street," put it. The extensive listing of exhortations to holy living in chapter 19 touches almost every aspect of life and life's decisions. The chapter corrects the mistaken notion that religious relationships and social relationships are two separate worlds. Religious prayers and rites are not all there is to religion in the Old Testament or the New. *Holy living* before God and *honest living* before our neighbors are the two pillars upon which the whole of God's demands rest. By *holy living* I mean our fidelity to God, and by *honest living* I mean our integrity toward other persons. Jesus captured the two pillars best when he answered the question regarding which is the greatest commandment in the Law: "You shall love the Lord your God with all your heart and with all your soul and with all your mind. . . . And a second is like it: You shall love your neighbor as yourself. On these two commandments depend all the Law and the Prophets" (Matthew 22:37–40). Are we surprised that when Jesus describes the core of God's revelation he quoted from the books of Deuteronomy and Leviticus? "You shall love your neighbor as yourself," says Leviticus 19:18. For Jesus and the apostles, this commandment was part and parcel of the authentic gospel. The vertical axis and the horizontal axis are not at cross-purposes or even strangers; they are mother and father that give birth to genuine godly living.

Chapter 19 addresses both dimensions—holy living and honest living. The chapter entails admonitions that teach we must love and obey God and admonitions that teach we must love others. There is an important connection between holiness and love. We see it reflected here in our chapter but also in the New Testament (1 Timothy 6:11). Love for one's brother in the Lord is a part of godly behavior (2 Peter 1:7).[1] The centerpiece of the chapter is verse 18: "You shall love your neighbor as yourself." Around this pivotal verse are collections of commandments that emphasize holy living or honest living. We will briefly describe each and then look carefully at what this chapter's key message of verse 18 says to us. However, there is a fundamental claim undergirding each pillar that requires our observation first.

### "I the Lord Your God Am Holy" (vv. 1, 2)

Sixteen times in this chapter the expressions "I am the Lord" or "I am the Lord your God" appear. This title for God identifies him as the Covenant Lord of his people, Israel. The chapter's beginning and end reflect the cardinal event of Israel's past—the formation of God's people at Sinai after their deliverance from Egyptian bondage. Exodus 20:2 begins the covenant, the Ten Commandments, revealed at Mount Sinai: "I am the Lord your God, who brought you out of the land of Egypt, out of the house of slavery." The first part of this verse occurs in Leviticus 19:2b: "I the Lord your God . . ." The concluding portion of the verse, referencing the Egyptian exodus, occurs in verse 36b of our chapter: "who brought you out of the land of Egypt."[2] These two echoes of the covenant at Sinai form the literary "bookends" of Leviticus 19. The arrangement of beginning and ending with allusions to the Sinai covenant emphasizes the basis for the commands that are cataloged in this chapter. The grounds for the demands of holy living and honest living detailed in Leviticus 19 are the historic redemption and formation of the people of God. In other words, the Lord and Israel had a history, a relationship based on God's gracious salvation of the nation. Together the Lord and people entered into agreements of mutual commitment. The Lord was Savior, and the people accepted obligations of loyalty in thanksgiving to the Sovereign Lord. Also, in the Leviticus chapter there are several references to the Ten Commandments, which we will comment on later.

The chapter's preamble gives a variation of the title, "I am the Lord." It reads, "You shall be holy, for I the Lord your God am holy" (v. 2). This sets the tone for the whole chapter and is repeatedly brought to the reader's attention. The passage declares that the exhortations in this chapter are rooted in the very character of God. God is holy in two senses. First, he is inherently distinctive in line with the very definition of what *holy* means. In other words, if a person wants to define *holy*, he must look to God as the standard. Second, the Lord is morally pure. In every way he is inherently pure without sin or corruption. He is complete in all his perfections. For Christians the incarnation of

Jesus provides us with a living portrait of a "holy servant" (Acts 4:27, 30). We can look to Jesus as the standard of holy living.

Although Moses is the one who addressed the congregation, it is not he but the Lord who originated the Law. The Law is not a human creation by itself. Because it is given by the Covenant Lord, the exhortations were to be obeyed, not questioned. Moreover, the very fact that it was God who gave the Law means that the Law, although ancient and delivered in a different culture, contains a message that transcends a particular time and people. Therein are important underlying principles that are relevant to any generation of believers, including ours.

The preamble, "You shall be holy," is for all believers. Peter instructs his readers to follow the Leviticus command to "be holy": "As obedient children, do not be conformed to the passions of your former ignorance, but as he who called you is holy, you also be holy in all your conduct, since it is written, 'You shall be holy, for I am holy'" (1 Peter 1:14–16; cf. Leviticus 11:44, 45). Peter understood that the Church of Jesus Christ, as the people of God made up of Jewish and Gentile Christians, undertook the commission that God gave his covenant people at Sinai: "you shall be to me . . . a holy nation" (Exodus 19:6; cf. 1 Peter 2:9). Since the Lord was holy, the people of God are charged to imitate his holiness. Day-to-day choices should reflect the essence of who the Lord is and his claim on us as his unique special possession. By exhibiting the holiness of God through Israel's conduct, the nation functioned as a witness to the nations. Christian conduct serves the same purpose to the unbelieving world. By the sanctifying presence of the Holy Spirit in the life of the individual Christian and in the church collectively, we are enabled to devote ourselves to the Lord and to serve others.

I read of a coin dealer, John Feigenbaum, who purchased a rare 1894 dime for 1.9 million dollars in 2007. In transporting it by plane cross-country from Oakland to New York City, he carried the rare coin in his pants pocket. After he wondered if the dime might fall out of his pocket, he stuck it in his briefcase. Repeatedly through the flight, he checked the briefcase to ensure that the coin had not vanished. We, too, have a precious possession that travels with us. We must be aware of and obedient to the precious gift of the Holy Spirit, purchased by a price far greater than gold and silver—the blood of the Savior. We show our allegiance to our Master when we commit to a holy lifestyle, living daily as Christians who are worthy of the Lord. For the Apostle Paul the Christian life meant imitating God and walking in the love of Christ. Self-sacrifice and the absence of self-indulgence show us to be worthy of membership in the family of God (Ephesians 4:1; 5:1–14).[3]

### Holy Living (vv. 3–8, 19–32)

What then are the characteristics of a person devoted to the Lord? Two collections of instructions in Leviticus 19 profile a person who is loyal to God. The commands concern a wide range of religious activities. The people were to honor the Lord's special days, they were to offer proper worship at the sanctuary, and they were to obey the Ten Commandments, which required worship of the one true God only.

*Worship the Lord (vv. 3–8).* The first collection of exhortations in verses 3–8 begins with a command to obey parents. At first glance we might scratch our heads, wondering why this command would be at the head of the chapter, coming even before the demand to worship only the Lord, avoiding idolatry (vv. 3, 4). The nature of parental authority, "revere [your] mother and [your] father," is an ordinance that reflects a person's loyalty to God. Parents have received delegated authority from the Lord, and when we rebel against their moral instruction, we rebel against the authority that the Lord has over the family. When we are loyal to God, we will be respectful of our parents' teaching. The flip side of this is that parents must be ever-conscientious in their instruction and modeling of godly living, since they shoulder the responsibility that God has committed to them.

With the line of authority established, the text now turns to specific traits. A loyal member of the household of faith carries out the demands of God for proper worship (vv. 5–8). The example in our text is a special provision in the eating of the peace sacrifice (cf. chapter 3). Worship in Israel involved two aspects—individual acts of piety and community worship. The peace offering brought both together since it was an offering by an individual who rejoiced at God's goodness and who invited the community to participate in the fellowship meal. Christian living, too, means proper conduct in our worship, privately and publicly. The epistles in the New Testament are replete with general instructions on how to carry out proper worship with the proper attitude (e.g., 1 Corinthians 11; 14:26; Colossians 3:16; 1 Timothy 2, 3). Worship and obedience come more easily to us when we have a true picture of the One whom we worship, God the Father (1 Peter 1:17).

I am reminded of the astonishment that some parents experience when they discover that their children are disruptive "monsters" when away from home in day-care centers or in school. It is as though aliens from distant worlds have taken over the bodies of their children! But when the children are picked up by parents, they become well-behaved children in an instant. What is the difference? Children know when they are in the presence of parental authority. The children show more respect for Mom and Dad because there is more accountability for their behavior. Our heavenly Father has called us to "a holy calling" (2 Timothy 1:9), and we are accountable for the decisions we make. If we properly value the Sovereign God before whom we stand, we will be incited to worship with "holy hands" and "pure heart" (Psalm 24:4; Matthew 5:8; 1 Timothy 2:8).

*Obey the Lord (vv. 19–32).* "You shall keep my statutes" headlines the longest section of the chapter, addressing the same subjects as verses 3–8. "You shall keep my Sabbaths" appears in both verses 3 and 30. Therefore, we can think of this section as focusing on obedience. This section weaves together two strands of admonitions—laws governing animal sacrifice in worship and laws that concern personal conduct. Linking the two sets of admonitions is the assumption that the Israelite's conduct must be consistent with the worship of God.

The way this coordination works is this: The believer's life must differentiate itself from the conduct of unbelievers, those who practice pagan worship. The passage uses the language of difference: "different kind[s]," "two kinds," "distinction" (vv. 19, 20). Distinction from those who worship false gods is explicit and implicit. The *explicit* commands regulate the worship practices of Israel. (1) False religions regularly relied on magic for understanding the will of the gods. These involved several methods, including fortune-telling and consulting mediums. The Israelite must rely solely upon God's word as it had been revealed through Moses. (2) The neighboring peoples practiced forms of self-mutilation through cutting their hair and bodies, so as to show their devotion to their gods or to participate in rituals for the dead. The Israelites were prohibited from such practices. (3) Since fertility cults dominated Canaanite religion, prostitution was a common feature of its worship. An Israelite father was prohibited from forcing his daughter into prostitution. Although the text does not specify that the prostitution was for religious purposes, the same principle undergirded street prostitution. Both were designed to enhance the financial gain or interests of the father at the expense of the daughter. Such immoral practices polluted the land morally, making the people subject to God's expulsion of the nation.

Also, the people showed the principle of distinction through *implicit* means. Cattle, clothing, crops, and treatment of sexual offenders must be treated with distinctions. In other words, there was a constant reminder that the people of God showed their worship of the one true God, the Covenant Lord, by their conduct in worship and in life's daily settings. (1) Refusal to mix cattle breeds, seed crops, and fabrics illustrated the people's exclusive worship. (2) The people also recognized distinctions in sexual behavior. In the case of a female slave who was owned by a man but was forced to engage in sex with another man, it was not considered adultery demanding death of the two people. Rather, the man offered a guilt offering and received forgiveness. This assumed that the man in accordance with the directions for the guilt offering had compensated the defrauded man when he lost the value of the slave woman who had been sexually compromised. (3) There was a distinction made in the harvest of the land upon entering the land of Canaan. The early years functioned like a period of purging, since the harvests were not considered edible. The harvest of the fourth year was devoted to God as a gift to the Lord. Eating the fifth year's harvest was permissible. This procedure showed that the harvest given to his people came from their Covenant Lord, not through the fertility rituals offered to Baal and his consorts. (4) Last, the admonition to "honor the face of an old man" (v. 32) implied exclusive devotion to God. The recognition that the elderly received greater respect than the young reflected the Bible's theology of leadership. God had ordained certain institutions to administer his rule over the community. This chain of command involved parents and elders who exercised teaching and adjudicating functions. To give them priority was tantamount to honoring God.

The import of this for us as Christians is coming now into focus. We do not imitate all these ancient customs today, but the principle that they teach is still applicable for us. We are to live a life that shows our devotion to Christ and his moral expectations. As kingdom citizens we are commissioned to live holy lives, conducting ourselves in conformity with God's moral standard (Ephesians 4:22–24; Colossians 3:9, 10; 1 Thessalonians 5:23, 24; 1 John 3:3). The quality of the fruit of our choices in life will reveal the nature of the tree that produced it. "Thus you will recognize them by their fruits" (Matthew 7:20). For God's people not to live holy lives is as incongruous as a husband who bears a wedding ring but only occasionally acts like a married man. His public profession has not stamped his identity.

### Honest Living (vv. 9–18, 33–36)

Holiness is not limited to the setting of worship. Holiness involves how we live with others. Godliness must also be manifested outside the walls of the church or house. The instructions in verses 9–18 begin with a call to assist the poor and closes with our key verse for the chapter: "you shall love your neighbor as yourself" (v. 18). Verses 33–36 round out the chapter by illustrating ways in which we show love toward others. The key instruction reappears in verse 34: "You shall love him as yourself."

*Treat others with integrity (vv. 9–16).* Verses 9, 10 describe how the land-owner can provide some of his produce for the poor. Poverty was not acceptable for the family of God. Steps are found in the Law to help the poor rise above their difficult circumstances. By leaving the edges of the grain harvest and the fallen fruit of the vineyards for the poor to obtain, the community sustained the impoverished (cf. Leviticus 23:22; 25:25–48). The Lord promised to grant prosperity to the nation if the people were faithful to the covenant. This would mean that there would be ample resources to share with others. Inevitably, however, the ideal was not met, and poverty was a regular feature in society (Deuteronomy 15:4, 5, 11). Jesus had this in mind when he observed, "For you always have the poor with you, and whenever you want, you can do good for them" (Mark 14:7). The agrarian economy of ancient Israel made the ownership of land critical to financial livelihood. Bereavement, natural disasters, and bandits could result in indebtedness that meant loss of family lands. If poverty came upon a person due to natural disasters or by marauding bandits, the community was expected to help families in poverty. Assisting the poor was always an option and is for the godly person today in the household of faith. Generosity is characteristic of Christ and is our Master's economic axiom: "it is more blessed to give than to receive" (Acts 20:35). Christians who do not consider the needs of the poor are betraying their Christian profession. We do not alleviate our responsibility by contending that our obligations are met through income taxes conscripted by the government to fund entitlement programs. That money is required of us and is not given out of a spirit of benevolence.

Verses 11, 12 restate the section of the Ten Commandments that pertains to how a person must treat his neighbor. Integrity in all dealings with fellow members of the community was demanded by the Lord. Since God had a relationship with each person under the covenant, the members of the community should treat one another as fellow members. To injure another person was an offense against God. Theft, lying, and giving false testimony in court were obviously *not* expressions of loving one's neighbor. The bonds of covenant unity were more important than personal gain, especially at the expense of others. "Am I my brother's keeper?" asked Cain. The answer is yes. Each of us has a responsibility toward others before God. Holiness impacts our personal relationships and our societal obligations.

Verses 13–16 describe offenses against a vulnerable person by taking advantage of him. A person who is a hired worker, a handicapped person, or a poor person does not have the social status to withstand the power of land-owners, merchants, and government officials. Verse 16 sets the matter in a court setting where the weak are slandered, placing them at a disadvantage in court. A corrupt court system can give priority to the claims of the strong, putting the life of the weak at risk.[4]

*Treat others with love (vv. 17, 18).* The guiding principle for the ethical treatment of others follows in verses 17, 18: "You shall love your neighbor as yourself" (v. 18). The beginning and end of the two verses use the contrasting words "hate" and "love" to express the same idea. The two verses show parallel parts that will help us understand the fuller significance of what the Lord was commanding. "You shall not hate your brother in your heart" parallels "You shall not take vengeance or bear a grudge." The passage immediately emphasizes the solidarity of the community by using terms like "brother" and "sons of your own people." This does not mean outsiders could be hated and mistreated. The Law provides many safeguards for caring for foreigners. And Jesus answered the question, "Who is my neighbor?" by showing in the Parable of the Good Samaritan that a neighbor is anyone in need and is not limited to ethnic or economic lines (Luke 10:29–37). What it means to "hate" a brother is to hold "a grudge" and act it out by "vengeance." Notice also that the passage refers to the internal attitude, "in your heart" and "bear a grudge." The word translated "grudge" means "to keep, to reserve" (*natar*); the sense here is that a person sustains his anger. The impression from the passage is that the anger festers and results in vengeance, perhaps murder.

Tribal feuds nurtured anger and promoted recurring vengeance. There was a provision for justified retaliation between men, but it was limited to special circumstances (Numbers 35; Deuteronomy 19). The Bible prohibits personal vengeance (Deuteronomy 32:35; Romans 12:19; Hebrews 10:30), seeing revenge as the domain of God who as righteous Judge can alone exact the proper measure of wrath against evildoers.[5] The threat of this law is that the lawbreaker will be judged guilty of sin. Although the person may have been initially wronged by another, if he holds a grudge he will have exchanged his innocence for sin. The irony is clear here: the offended person becomes the offender.

"You shall love your neighbor as yourself" is preceded by the parallel directive, "you shall reason frankly with your neighbor." To love one's neighbor also means or at least includes correcting your neighbor. The words rendered "reason frankly" reflect a Hebrew term that means "to judge, correct, convince" another person. Other English versions have stronger language, "rebuke" or "reprove." The motivation for correcting a brother was the threat of committing sin. The sense of the passage is that by discussing the offense, the wrongdoer will come to see his sin and will repent. In turn this will defuse the anger of the offended party. Of course, the person who confronts his enemy must be justified in taking this step and must do so out of the highest motivation. Confrontation is not meant to humiliate or exact vengeance through ridicule but to resolve the conflict without any lingering resentment. An example of Abraham and a neighboring king named Abimelech shows how misunderstanding can be resolved through honest discussion. King Abimelech's servants seized a well belonging to Abraham, and the patriarch brought this to the king's attention. Since both parties wanted to resolve their differences and enter into a pact of friendship, the king and Abraham came to a mutual agreement of returning ownership to the patriarch (Genesis 21:25–27). Too often we permit resentment to be stored away, like garbage in a dumpster. Unless we deal with it honestly and humbly, the trash eventually spills out into our lives.

One of the more perplexing aspects of the command to love one's neighbor is the phrase "as yourself." This idea of self-love sounds diametrically opposite to the general tenor of Scripture, which puts loving others above oneself (Romans 12:3, 10; Philippians 2:3). Yet, to love another person by honoring him and giving him precedence does not mean self-loathing. The assumption is that a person will think *too much* of himself, not too little, and therefore will be resistant to putting the interests of another above himself. This verse is the underlying idea of the "Golden Rule" that Jesus taught: "So whatever you wish that others would do to you, do also to them, for this is the Law and the Prophets" (Matthew 7:12). We cannot substitute acts of religious piety for social justice, Jesus says (Mark 12:33b). James brings this out most clearly in the New Testament when he condemns prejudice against the poor within churches (James 2:1–13). Loving another person is, James says, the fulfillment of "the royal law" (2:8; cf. Romans 13:9, 10; Galatians 5:14). This is the context for the most-quoted verse in the book of James: "faith apart from works is dead" (James 2:26b). We prove that our faith is real if we live by the great commandment to care for the interests of others.

*Treat others with justice (vv. 33–37).* Special concern over the treatment of aliens dominates the closing verses of the ethical instructions collected in this chapter. The reasons for the presence of foreigners were many, including the immigration of slaves fleeing neighboring countries and the practice of intermarriage, often in the aftermath of war. Since aliens were not a natural constituency, it was easy for the native Israelites to take advantage of them. Many laws in the Mosaic legislation give aliens special protections (e.g., Exodus 20:10; 22:21). The distinction between an alien and a native Israelite, however, was not papered over in the Mosaic law as though no differences existed (e.g., Deuteronomy 14:21). Yet, these differences did not override the basic humane treatment reserved for all created in the image of God. What these verses were calling for was the equitable treatment of the foreign population who had taken up residence in the land. They were to be treated with the same dignity as the native-born (Numbers 15:15–29). Aliens could especially be defrauded in court through prejudiced rulings and bribes (Deuteronomy 10:17–19). Another means of stealing from the alien as well as from the poor was through dishonest scales. Merchants could rig the scales or alter the packaging so that the customer paid more than what the weight of the commodity deserved. So notorious was later Israel for these practices that the prophets announced the destruction of the country because of such injustices (e.g., Amos 8:5; Micah 6:11). Proverbs says, "A false balance is an abomination to the LORD, but a just weight is his delight" (Proverbs 11:1). Jesus, too, scolded the religious elite for their neglect of justice (Matthew 23:23, 24; Mark 12:40). James declares that authentic religion must include care for the oppressed and troubled (James 1:27).

These concluding verses return to the ethical dimension of what holy living is. The chapter ends in this way to repeat the important message of the chapter. The call to holy living in the Bible always involves our obligations toward others. It is not a matter of just *avoiding harm*, however; it is a matter of *seeking justice* for others. We must be proactive in bringing our Christian commitments into play when we consider what is just both in the church community and in society at large (Isaiah 1:17). There are many ways we can promote social equity. In addition to giving to relief agencies sponsored by our church and denomination, there are hands-on opportunities through building reclamation, business opportunities for small-business entrepreneurs, and education in literacy and technology. Our Lord taught that generosity toward others is a trait of kingdom citizenship. When our Lord returns, he will receive only those who gave to the destitute and visited the sick and the imprisoned: "Truly, I say to you, as you did it to one of the least of these my brothers, you did it to me" (Matthew 25:35–40).

# 17

# Raising the "Holy" Bar

### LEVITICUS 21:1—22:33

MOST ARE FAMILIAR WITH the expression *raising the bar*. The expression is derived from athletics, specifically the high jump or pole vault. The athlete must clear the bar with his jump in order to continue in the next round of attempts. At each new round the bar is raised, making the level of difficulty greater and greater. *Raising the bar* means raising the standard of conduct or achievement to a more demanding expectation. Leviticus 21, 22 effectively does this for Christian ministry. The standard for a Christian leader is higher than for others. The reasons for this are evident since the leader sets a pattern that influences others. Also, a leader can only qualify as a successful leader if he shows he is worthy of the position.

This is not strange to us because we hold our leaders in all phases of life to higher standards. In the home, parents and older children perform in a more responsible way. In public life, politicians, athletes, and educators as well as ministers are expected to lead the way in achievements and in professional integrity. A leader may not want to take on the obligation of a role model, but it comes inevitably with leadership. The basketball star Charles Barkley commented in a 1993 commercial for Nike, "I am not a role model . . . parents should be role models." He was right that parents should be role models, but public figures and leaders do not have the luxury of escaping role model status.

The message of chapters 21, 22 addresses formal leadership but also informal leaders. Each one of us in some way has a leadership function. It may be at home, school, work, or in the neighborhood. There is always someone looking to us for direction, either by word or deed. This is especially true of all who affirm faith in Jesus Christ. People in general expect more of Christians, and when we hang out our shingle, identifying ourselves as Christians or at least as church members, the people who know us immediately raise the bar. These two chapters then speak to each of us even if we don't have a public leadership position in the church.

What holds these two chapters together is the same sentence that begins each chapter: "Speak to the priests, the sons of Aaron" (21:1) and "Speak to Aaron and his sons" (22:2). Unlike the other chapters of Leviticus, these two are directed to the priests. Although many think of Leviticus as a book about religious leaders, it says more to the laity about proper worship practices than to the clergy. These two chapters are the exception and therefore require our special attention.

What does God say to the religious leaders of the community? In essence in both chapters he commands the priestly leadership to maintain ritual and moral purity. Since they represent the Lord as the intermediaries between God and the people, they must avoid any compromise in their conduct in religious and social matters as well as in personal moral purity. Although in these two chapters a number of the instructions sound strange to us, they have a logical explanation when we remember that the main issue is the adequacy of the priests to function in their assigned roles. What was at stake was nothing less than the spiritual survival of the people they served. If the priests failed to obey the Lord and to represent God to the people or failed to represent the people to God in the proper manner, the ongoing spiritual vitality of the relationship between the Lord and his redeemed people was threatened. A holy God cannot be misrepresented to his people, and the people cannot depend on a priesthood that is ritually unclean and morally compromised.

Both chapters also have in common the subject of sacrificial offerings. These offerings were the staple of the worship that Israel offered up to God. It was as central to the public worship in Israel as Sunday services are to us today. Imagine how crucial church services become when we lose the opportunity due to some natural disaster or the failure of church leaders to fulfill their tasks on a weekly basis. The congregation's spiritual health is clearly affected when leadership morally or otherwise stumbles. The repercussions usually are far-reaching. Consider the Lord Jesus himself. His Father gave him a special assignment that he fully embraced. But what if the Lord in the midst of his assignment had changed his mind, compromised his integrity, or had simply become a deadbeat? The whole world would remain in sin and would be without hope. But the Scriptures make it clear that Jesus maintained his focus on the call to obedience: "Although [Jesus] was a son, he learned obedience through what he suffered" (Hebrews 5:8). This submission to the

Father's charge crystallized in his Gethsemane prayer, "My Father, if it be possible, let this cup pass from me; nevertheless, not as I will, but as you will" (Matthew 26:39).

The challenge was to the priests to officiate at the holy altar where the laity brought offerings as "food offerings" to the Lord. These offerings were the layperson's act of worship, whether in the case of dedication, thanksgiving, or forgiveness of sin. If the priest failed to render the proper procedure, the sacrifice was not acceptable because the offering had been polluted ritually. The prescriptions for the priests in our passage are of two kinds: first, instructions regarding the person and character of the priest, and second, the nature of the offerings that they oversaw at the altar. The passage can be viewed from the negative and the positive emphasis of the two chapters. The emphasis in chapter 21 is the negative message: avoid sacrilege! The positive side is expressed in chapter 22: advocate holiness!

## Avoid Sacrilege (21:1–24)

The word *sacrilege* does not occur in the passage, but I have chosen it as a heading for our first section because it conveys the outrageous nature of the violations described in chapter 21. The etymology for the word *sacrilege* can be traced back to Latin, where it means "to rob sacred property." A person who takes for his private enhancement those things that are devoted to God is a *sacrilegus*, a robber or unlawful collector of holy things. In our world today, we are repulsed by the desecration of the dead by vandals, or worse, grave robbers. Such crimes are considered the lowest of the low in our thinking. The text uses the word "profane" to describe sacrilege, nine times in chapter 21 and four times in chapter 22.[1] Our contemporary word *profane* may not convey adequately the thought of the passage since we tend to think of *profane* as ugly profanity. The Hebrew word, however, exceeds coarse language or even taking God's holy name in vain. "Profane" can be used of soiling the reputation of God or the holy things associated with him, such as sanctuary or Sabbath, or polluting the reputation and status of other persons.[2] These various uses occur in our chapter: profaning the name of God (21:6), profaning oneself and one's father (v. 9), profaning the sanctuary of God (vv. 12, 23), and profaning the priest's children (v. 15). Committing desecration was tied to covenant transgressions. A person's disobeying the commandments of God meant a diminishing of the respect due to the Lord, whether it was in the moral or ritual realm.

*Avoiding religious pluralism (vv. 1–9).* One of the tempting challenges faced by God's people in the past as well as today is that of accommodating other religious worldviews. An example from the past and from the present will show this. The Israelites faced a formidable challenge to their faith by the Canaanites who worshiped a fertility god named Baal. The word *baal* means "lord, husband" and can refer to a person or be used as a proper noun for the false deity Baal. The Bible usually avoids speaking of God as *baal* when referring to him as husband or lord of Israel. Hosea made a wordplay on the name Baal when God condemned the Israelites for their worship of Baal instead of the Lord. "And in that day, declares the LORD, you will call me 'My Husband,' and no longer will you call me 'My Baal.' For I will remove the names of the Baals from her mouth, and they shall be remembered by name no more" (Hosea 2:16, 17). Baal will no longer be recognized as Israel's husband or lord; rather, the people will return to the Lord God (*Yahweh*) as their rightful husband. The reason for this avoidance of the word *baal* and things pertaining to the worship of the god Baal was the theological confusion that might have created in the minds of the people. The people were at times so apostate in their history that the Lord God was regarded virtually the same as a fertility baal. He was called the "LORD God" in name only.

A contemporary example is similar. The Roman Catholic bishop of Breda in the Netherlands publicly encouraged his Dutch parishioners to pray using the word Allah rather than the traditional names for God.[3] The word *Allah* is the Arabic word for "God." His rationale was well-meaning but flawed. He hoped by using the Arabic name for God that Jews, Christians, and Muslims could come closer together since all three look to the same God, the God of Abraham. Various Islamic organizations in the United States supported the idea, agreeing that this would be a bridge for strengthening each one's faith without being tied to man-made language. We are told it is the belief in God and the moral life that he calls for that is the real substance of a person's religious faith. The bishop rightly recognized that historically Jews and Christians in Arabic-speaking countries have used the term Allah in their Arabic language. The problem lies in the theological content that each name conveys to the listener today. Timothy George in his book *Is the Father of Jesus the God of Muhammad?*[4] comments that in one sense the answer is yes since the God of Abraham is the only true God and therefore is the God of all peoples and persons, including Muhammad. Yet it is wrong, he says, to equate the God of Islam with the God of Christian profession because of the importance of the character of God as the *triune* God. Only by the Son's incarnation, sacrificial death, and ultimate resurrection does a person receive God's imputed righteousness and salvation. The use of the name Allah for the God of the Bible is not wise since it minimizes the differences and creates potential confusion for people, both Christians and Jews. Who is the God of Jesus? "The God and Father of our Lord Jesus Christ" (Romans 15:6; 1 Peter 1:3–5).

The various regulations for the priests in Leviticus 21:1–9 were designed to restrain the people of God from diluting their sole allegiance to God. The temptation was to accommodate the religious life of their Canaanite neighbors whose religion was polytheistic and immoral. Since the priests were leaders of the people, their practices were especially scrutinized. They were called to instruct the people in the way of the Lord and to model the proper way to approach God in worship.

Among the instructions for the priests was a prohibition concerning their association with the dead. Contact with the dead, whether layperson or priest, resulted in ceremonial uncleanness (Numbers 19:11–22). The priests were restricted from attending funeral services except for their closest relatives, what we would call the nuclear family (vv. 1b–3). Why? The people of the ancient Near East regularly promoted family shrines where religious cults of the dead flourished. The cults of the dead involved celebratory meals following the formal funeral in which the family maintained their connection with the dead by keeping them alive, so to speak, by providing them food, drink, and sex. Orthodox Biblical religion condemned the cults of the dead because they denied the gulf between the living and the dead. There is no co-equal power or deity with the Lord God in the realm of the dead. And God is the God of the living. Some mourning rites were permissible for the people and the priests, such as weeping, tearing of garments, wearing sackcloth, and loosening the hair. But any trimming of the hair's edges on the head or mutilating the body was strictly outlawed, probably due to their association with pagan cult practices (19:27, 28; 21:5).[5] The high priest was prohibited from *any* association with the dead, including his parents (v. 11).[6] The reason for this extreme measure was because of the ritual status of the high priest who had been especially consecrated to God's service in the eyes of the people.

Our God is the living God. Life, not death, is celebrated by God's people. As Jesus commented, "[God] is not God of the dead, but of the living" (Mark 12:27). The Christian Church has always viewed death as the beginning of new life, the door to the blessed life of the believer with Christ and the family of God. Although Christians mourn, rightly so, for the loss of loved ones and the loss of life, there is a qualitative chasm between those who mourn *with* hope and those who have "no hope." I read of a staunch bachelor who grumbled about his elderly aunts who used to come to him and annoy him at weddings by poking him and laughing as they said, "You're next, sonny." The meddlesome ladies stopped, however, when he started doing the same thing to them at funerals! Some have hope, but others do not. Paul noted this when he said to his Thessalonian readers, "But we do not want you to be uninformed, brothers, about those who are asleep, that you may not grieve as others do who have no hope. For since we believe that Jesus died and rose again, even so, through Jesus, God will bring with him those who have fallen asleep" (1 Thessalonians 4:13, 14). It is not that non-Christians have no hope in an afterlife, but theirs is an afterlife without the comforting joy of being with Jesus (cf. Ephesians 2:12).[7]

*Avoiding moral impurity (vv. 10–24).* Especially important to the religious life of Israel was the role of the high priest. He was special as the chief mediator between God and his people, Israel. The standards for the high priest even excelled those of the priests. Before the Lord continued addressing the priests in general, the Lord focused in verses 10–15 on the requirements demanded of the high priest. The high priest had to be discriminating in making choices pertaining to the crucial times of life—the death of loved ones and marriage to a loved one, his wife. We said above that the high priest under no circumstances could be associated with the dead, lest he become unfit to carry out his duties in the worship of God. The explanation for this uncompromising prohibition is implied by the text's acknowledgment that he bore "the anointing oil of his God" (v. 12). This refers to the rite of Aaron's investiture as high priest and of his sons in which they received the oil of consecration (8:30). These servants of the Lord stood out from the people because of the special anointing that they received. This was the gracious act of God that chose Aaron and his descendants to lead the congregation in the worship of God. In the event of a death in his family or of anyone else for that matter, Aaron was not to venture from the sanctuary to attend the funeral or its mourning rituals. For him to be in the presence of death while specially bearing the oil of holiness would profane the house of God. This shows that the behavior of the priestly leadership had an impact on the life of the community at large. Disobedience by the priests brought impurity upon the whole people.

The second prohibition noted in our text for the high priest is restrictions on his choice of a marriage partner. We are told that he was to marry "a virgin" and one who was descended from Israelite parents (vv. 13–15). So there would be no confusion, the Lord specified that the woman was not to have been married before and certainly was not to have practiced the sinful occupation of a prostitute. We can reason that the restrictions again are related to the symbolic role that the high priest played in the life of the congregation. The idea of a virgin woman was a symbol of purity in the ancient world. This tradition was carried over in our own times by the symbolic gesture of the new bride whose gown is flowing white. The mention of prostitution shows that the issue was not marriage so much as the sexual purity of the woman. It would be possible for a prostitute to have not been married before and thus could technically be available to the high priest. But the practice of prostitution, whether it was street or temple prostitution, defaced the picture that the high priest was to portray to the people. The conduct of the high priest and the character of his family life conveyed by symbolic portraits the holy character of God. If he were to have a child by a non-virgin it would have implications for his descendants who were to follow him in the priestly vocation.

The expectation of a holy life consecrated to the service of God is required for church leaders as well. Church leaders must be blameless and pure in their conduct, for they set examples before the children of God (1 Timothy 3:1–13; 4:12; Titus 1:6–9). The qualifications are high—a godly home life, personal integrity, and a moderate lifestyle. The apostles at the outset of the church's history instructed the congregation to select deacon-servants who were "men of good repute" (Acts 6:3).

But although the priests in Israel were held to the higher bar of expectation, we know that the priests did not live up to the calling that God had placed upon them. As early as the first occasion of public worship, the sons of Aaron, Nadab and Abihu, offered inappropriate offerings and were struck dead by God in the Tent of Meeting for their sin (Leviticus 10:1–5). The sons of the priest Eli committed grievous moral sins at the door of the Tent of Meeting, engaging in promiscuous behavior and robbing people of their offerings destined for the Lord. Eli's sons too met with their demise (1 Samuel 4). The most egregious example was Aaron himself who led Israel into idolatry during the wilderness journey (Exodus 32). Three thousand of the offenders were executed, and a plague sent by the Lord fell on the community. The consequences of the illicit teaching and behavior of the priestly leaders were severe. We too stand in peril when our church leaders promote heterodox teaching and mislead the flock into aberrant activities. That the church must hold its leaders to such a high bar of ethical behavior is for its own good, for its own survival. We do ourselves no favor when we compromise God's standard out of moral laxness or procedural convenience. It is not a commendable act of grace toward a fallen leader if it results in jeopardizing the spiritual life of the flock.

The last set of instructions in this section (vv. 16–24) regards the avoidance of ritual impurity. Although the text describes ritual limitations, not directly moral ones, I have set them under the heading "Avoiding moral impurity." This is because the ritual statement conveyed the weightier teaching of moral purity that is required of all God's servants. The priests were responsible for the altar and the sacrifices that were conducted before the Lord. The animal and grain offerings were offered by the worshipers as "food offerings" to the Lord at his house, that is, the Tent of Meeting. Since God is complete and perfect in all his attributes and actions, it would be unfitting to approach God through anyone or with anything that would manifestly appear imperfect or incomplete. Therefore, the priests who served the Lord were to be whole in appearance, not having any obvious physical disorder. The word "blemish"[8] repeatedly occurs in the passage, describing the disqualification of the priest. The word can refer also to unsuitable animal offerings that cannot be presented to the Lord. The word also has a figurative meaning. It describes spiritual and moral defects (Deuteronomy 32:5). The text provides illustrations of such defects, including blindness, lameness, skin diseases, and disfigurement. The priest who exhibited any of these physical disorders was not completely banned from the service of God. Also, infirm priests could receive their appropriate portion of the sacrifices for their livelihood.

In today's world we are rightly sensitive to the status and needs of the handicapped in our society. This passage does not teach that persons who have handicaps are any less valuable to God; they have the same access to the Lord and are a welcomed part of the church and community. If anything, the Bible teaches the importance of care for the infirmed, who were typically poor and neglected in ancient societies. The book of Leviticus specifically condemns anyone who exploits the deaf and blind (19:14). When Job defended his faithfulness to God, he commented that he was "eyes to the blind and feet to the lame" (Job 29:15). The admonition in Leviticus to love one's neighbor (e.g., Leviticus 19:18) applied to all people. When Jeremiah described the joyful return of the exiles to the land of plenty, he specifically named among them the blind and the lame (Jeremiah 31:8). Especially when we look at the healing and caring ministry of Jesus we remember how he was sought out by the handicapped and their families (e.g., Luke 14:12–15). With the passing away of the old covenant with its temporary places of worship and its regulating laws, the Christian message declares that all people are accepted in God's sight. How is this possible? Unlike the priests of Aaron's lineage whose lives were marred by sin and imperfections, the perfect and sinless high priest, Jesus Christ our Lord, sits at the right hand of the Father, where he intervenes on our behalf. We must not worry or be troubled that the priesthood of Jesus could ever be soiled or foiled. The security of every Christian is certain since we are relying upon the Lord Jesus' perfect and complete mediation, forgiving our sinful imperfections and assuring us a place forevermore in the family of God. The writer to the Hebrews declared the efficacy of Jesus' priesthood:

For if the blood of goats and bulls, and the sprinkling of defiled persons [i.e., the priests] with the ashes of a heifer, sanctify for the purification of the flesh, how much more will the blood of Christ, who through the eternal Spirit offered himself without blemish to God, purify our conscience from dead works to serve the living God. (Hebrews 9:13, 14)

## Advocate Holiness (22:1–33)

After admonitions against immorality, the subsequent chapter emphasizes the holiness that the priests were to practice and advocate through their example.

*Holy service (vv. 1–9).* Verses 2–9 repeatedly implore the priests to be ceremonially "clean" in carrying out their duties. Again, the passage speaks of the priests' relationship to "the holy things" of worship (v. 3). The priests were the recipients of portions of the offerings, their income for serving at the house of God. Since the offerings were dedicated to God, the offerings were the Lord's to share with his appointed ministers. They, however, had to maintain the proper relationship to the food offerings by keeping themselves ritually and morally pure. The purity laws in Leviticus 11—15 detail the kinds of things that would make a person unclean. These are gathered again here for stressing those things that the priests were to avoid. These included skin diseases (chapters 13, 14), bodily emissions (chapter 15), and contact with unclean animals and the dead (chapter 11). Only after undergoing the proper rituals of purification could the priests participate in the partaking of the offerings. Failure to render their holy service, however, came with the sternest penalty. The priests had to obey the Lord in the handling of holy things or they faced the penalty of death: "[The priests] shall therefore keep my charge, lest they bear sin for it and die thereby when they profane it" (v. 9a).

With the joy of special service, which meant living in the presence of God, the priests bore a special burden of responsibility. If they sinned against the Lord, they were disqualified from representing the people to God. "Bear[ing] [their] sin" (v. 9) meant they were guilty of transgression and must receive the just deserts of their actions—namely, death! The picture of the priests burdened by their sin is a graphic portrayal of their approaching the altar of God in an unclean condition. I am reminded of the prophet Isaiah whose vision of God in the temple resulted in his confession of his sinfulness: "Woe is me! For I am lost; for I am a man of unclean lips, and I dwell in the midst of a people of unclean lips; for my eyes have seen the King, the LORD of hosts!" (Isaiah 6:5). At hearing Isaiah's confession, however, the Lord sent one of the attending angels to purge Isaiah's lips with burning coals retrieved from the temple altar. Isaiah was spared by the grace of God, and similarly the Lord had provided through ritual the means for the priests to experience cleansing. The symbolism of ritual cleansing and restoration to service pictured the forgiveness that the Lord graciously had for them. The priests were not expected to be perfect, since ritual cleansing for them is described in our passage. But they could so profane the sanctuary of God that they deserved the most grievous penalty for their disobedience.

Such a stern warning to the servants of God is heard in the New Testament also. Paul cautioned Timothy to be reserved in commissioning people to church leadership: "Do not be hasty in the laying on of hands, nor take part in the sins of others; keep yourself pure" (1 Timothy 5:22). The sobering implication of this admonition is that those who commission a person to service are responsible for any future misconduct of the commissioned person.[9] Appointing a person who has not proven himself runs the risk of too hastily placing that person in a leadership position. A person whose life does not measure up to purity of service will show his colors soon and will injure the witness of the local church and the spiritual condition of the church members under his care.

*Benefits of holy service (vv. 10–16).* Although the responsibilities of Christian leadership and service are demanding, the benefits of service are great too. In the setting of the tabernacle and priesthood, the priests whose livelihood depended on tabernacle offerings received portions of the sacrifices presented for worship. This had theological significance as well as the practical aspect of supporting the priests in their ministry. By partaking of the holy sacrifices, the priests showed that the sacrifices of worship had been accepted by God. When we as the church eat the Lord's Supper, there is a symbolic message of partaking in the suffering of Christ on our behalf. In the case of the ancient offerings, only the priest and those who were dependent upon him for their economic needs, such as an unmarried daughter, could eat the holy gifts.[10] No layperson had the right to eat the food set aside for the priestly workers. The priests did not have land to work or a professional trade. The Lord instructed the Israelites to provide from their own income a living for the servants who ministered in the Tent of Meeting. Since someone who was unqualified might unintentionally eat a sacred portion, the Law provided a path of reconciliation. An offender had to compensate for the defrauding of God's offerings. The theological teaching is that transgressors had robbed God of his rightful due. He must return the gift (if available, or its equivalent) and add a fifth as a surcharge to the value of the confiscated goods.[11]

This leads us to ask, should a person seek the call to leadership in the church? The gifts of spiritual leadership are just that—*gifts* bestowed by the Spirit of God. We cannot earn or achieve these endowments, but there is ample evidence that seeking the gifts of teaching and proclamation is approved. Paul in his first letter to the Corinthians advised the Corinthians who were so infatuated with spiritual gifts to "earnestly desire the higher gifts" (1 Corinthians 12:31). And 14:1 reads, "Pursue love, and earnestly desire the spiritual gifts, especially that you may prophesy." The motivation for this was not self-aggrandizement or competition but that the gift might contribute further to the good of the members of Christ's body. Before we leave the subject of spiritual gifts, we must remember the sentiment of Paul's admonitions to seek the better gifts of service. He decidedly wanted his parishioners to accept whatever gifts the Lord gave them, yet with deep humility, not considering themselves better than others. So he reinforced this when he instructed the saints in a better way, a better means of contributing to the kingdom than any of the gifts. First Corinthians 13, known as "the love chapter," exhorts us to practice love. Love is vastly superior to any gift, for it will endure for all eternity and will accrue unending benefits for the giver and the receiver. All of us can exercise love toward others. We might not be gifted to preach or teach or practice any of the more public, celebrated gifts, but all of us must commit to Christian love. Our eyes of leadership should be cast first at leading by the example of love.

*The cost of holy service (vv. 17–33).* We have spoken of the *benefits* of holy service for those in Christian ministry and church leadership. But there is also a *cost* that is inherent in proper worship and Christian service. Our passage concludes by making this point. Anyone in the family of Israel, including the priests and foreigners living among the Israelites, could bring to the Lord only the finest specimens of animal sacrifice.[12] The text describes the animals as "without blemish."[13] The word "unblemished" means that the animals were whole and sound, not bearing any physical defect. The significance of this trait was the animal's pleasing appearance. This requirement matches the earlier instruction of the priests who had to exhibit physical wholeness. So, at the Lord's holy altar perfect offerings were administered by perfect priests. The Lord God who alone is perfect deserves the best that the worshiper can offer. These better animals were costlier to the giver. The priests who ministered at the tabernacle's altar were attentive to the gifts that were brought. It would have been a travesty for the priests to present to the Lord inferior offerings.

Other limitations imposed in the Law ensured that the sacrificial animals were of the best quality. The animals could only be offered if older than seven days, but never on the same day as their mother (vv. 27, 28; Exodus 22:30). These seven days were to be spent with the mother.[14] The eighth day in the Bible symbolically indicated the maturity of a gift. Circumcision of a male Hebrew baby, for example, was to be done on the eighth day, a signal of the child's membership in the covenant family of God. Additionally, the food offerings when offered had to be consumed on the same day of their offering, so as to prevent them from putrefying. Such organic deterioration of meat would have occurred rapidly.

That the animals were complete specimens, however, did not mean that they were effective in taking away the sins of the worshiper completely and permanently. If they had been, the writer to the Hebrews said, there would have been no need for continued offerings each day. The priests offered sacrifices every morning and evening, always keeping the altar fires burning. But in the perfect offering of Jesus, even his own body, as the unblemished sacrifice for our sins, the forgiveness he provided was perfect and complete (Hebrews 10:1–14). The cost of the death of our Lord Jesus was incomparable! Yet, he places a demand upon all of us who have received the forgiveness of sins. We too have a cross to bear, Jesus said (Matthew 10:38). Christian stewardship is costly, although it pales in comparison with the great reward of glory that we will receive at the Lord's coming (2 Corinthians 4:17). We are called upon to offer ourselves wholly to the service of the Lord, clergy and laity. "I appeal to you therefore, brothers, by the mercies of God, to present your bodies as a living sacrifice, holy and acceptable to God, which is your spiritual worship" (Romans 12:1).

# 18

# Holy Day or Holiday?

## LEVITICUS 23:1–3

IT MAY BE SURPRISING to our ears to think of *holy day* and *holiday* in the same way. But the origin of the word *holiday* was *holy* plus *day*. Originally *holiday* had the idea of a sacred religious feast or the meaning of a day of recreation. The idea of a day spent free from work came to dominate and is the general meaning we think of today. In Britain the expression *go on holiday* means that someone is, as we Americans say, going on vacation.

Which of these two words better describes our attitude toward Sunday? Is Sunday a holy day or a holiday? Some may remember the blue laws that were a common part of American and Canadian culture until the latter half of the twentieth century. A blue law was a legislative enactment that prohibited selling merchandise other than basic human necessities on Sundays. I remember as a youngster going into a local pharmacy that had covered aisles of restricted products that could not be purchased on Sundays. All or at least most of that tradition has disappeared from our cultural practices. The purpose of the blue laws was to encourage worship and rest on Sundays. Later in life when I moved from the South to the Midwest I was struck by how all the major shopping venues were open to customers on Sunday. There were no blue laws, and commerce flowed on Sunday as any other day, perhaps more so. A more striking cultural difference is Sundays in Middle Eastern countries in which the major day of worship is Friday or Saturday (i.e., the Sabbath). Sunday is just another typical work week day.

I am not leading up to a debate over the morality of the blue laws or calling for their reinstatement. What the trend tells me is that the traditional day set aside for worship is more and more treated as any other day. How does this trend impact the church's attitude toward Sunday? Your attitude toward Sunday worship? Sunday, of course, has hardly been tossed aside as the primary day for worship in America, since more people attend worship services on Sundays than sporting events on Sundays. The question for the church today is not what to do or what not to do on Sundays so much as it is to rediscover the significance of a gathered body of believers who set aside special times for worship. The Lord instructed the Israelites to observe special days and celebratory feasts as days of worship. The early church followed a similar pattern that recognized certain days for special times of worship.

Leviticus 23 offers a summary of the chief celebrations set aside for worship.[1] These are identified as "appointed feasts of the LORD" (vv. 2, 4, 37) and "holy convocations" (vv. 2, 4, 37) because they are days committed to meet with God, the Holy One of Israel. Five feasts are listed, each introduced by the same phrase that identifies the source of the instructions: "The LORD spoke to Moses" (vv. 1, 9, 23, 26, 33). But the mainstay of Israel's worship was the weekly Sabbath day, as stated near the beginning of the chapter. This day of worship was fundamental to the five calendrical feasts and for that matter to all of Israel's worship. The Sabbath was "the archetypal holy day."[2] For this reason we will now focus on the call to observe the Sabbath in verses 2–4 and will examine the remainder of the chapter in our next study.

### The Lord's Feasts (vv. 2, 4)

Verses 2 and 4 announce the sacred nature of the convocations. Three descriptions mark the feasts as especially given by God. They are identified as "the appointed feasts of the LORD," "holy convocations," and "my [that is, the Lord's] appointed feasts." The repetition shows us that the importance of the feasts was their relationship to God as their source and designer. This was true of the Sabbaths, too, since the Bible refers to them as "my [that is, the Lord's] Sabbaths." The Lord instructed Moses "above all" to observe "my Sabbaths" because they were "a sign between me and you . . . that you may know that I, the LORD, sanctify you" (Exodus 31:13; cf. Leviticus 19:3, 30; 26:2).

The Sabbaths and the feasts were not the property of the Israelites to do with as they wished. The Scriptures rarely speak of "your Sabbath(s)," referring to the people of Israel (Leviticus 23:32; 26:35). It is "my Sabbaths," referring to the Lord as the author of the times of worship. The convocations were focused on the worship of God—they are his special times. The convocations were not solely fastidious formalities for their own sake or pomp and ceremony for priestly self-interests. Since they belonged to the Lord and were given for the chief purpose of knowing God, they were deemed "holy." The convocations were called "holy" because they were consecrated to the Lord's service. They were not family or community potlucks with a bit of religion thrown into the mix. They were celebratory remembrances of their God that called for the people to consecrate themselves to the holy task of worshiping the Lord. Yes, worship was an assignment for God's people to obey, as it is for us as his Church. The community at worship, both during the regular cycle of gatherings and during special seasons of the sacred year, is a holy task that demands all that we are and the best of what we are. Hebrews 10:24, 25 exhorts us "to stir up one another to love and good works, *not neglecting to meet together.*"

## Sabbath Rest (v. 3)

The Sabbath convocation was the sign of the covenant between God and the people of Israel as his community of covenant people (Exodus 31:13, 17; Ezekiel 20:12, 20). The failure to observe the Sabbath was a frontal attack on the rule of God in a person's life. The importance of the Sabbath and the feast days in the sacred calendar can be more fully grasped when we recall the meaning of the word "appointed," occurring six times in this chapter (vv. 2 [2x], 4 [2x], 37, 44). The word translated "appointed" is related to the word for "congregation" with the understanding that the congregation came together at an appointed place and appointed time.[3] It is a gathering. Who made the appointment? These are sacred days for meetings prearranged by God. In other words, God established meetings with his people who were obligated to attend. We might liken this with our modern day planners. We record meetings that a family head or employer has called. Based on family kinships, community commitments, and employment we have explicitly or implicitly agreed to be a part of assigned gatherings. When a meeting time is announced at the church, business, or family occasion, we attend if we take seriously our participation in the group's identity. When we skip out on a business meeting, sales meeting, or civic meeting, we in effect send a message, saying, "I don't care enough to be a part." Since God calls his people to meet him, and they have agreed to attend by virtue of their covenant membership, their failing to do so can only be understood as a rebellious act.

The term "appointed" also refers to an appointed place. The place of meeting had also already been established. It was the Tent of Meeting, the sanctuary structure, where, the Lord says, "I will meet with you" (e.g., Exodus 29:42, 43). As the Tent of Meeting was the epicenter of their lives in terms of space, the Sabbath was the focal point of their lives in terms of time.[4] By epicenter we mean that the Tent of Meeting where the people encountered the

Lord through worship was the centerpiece of the tribal occupation of the land. Wherever the Tent of Meeting was erected, in the wilderness or in the land, it stood as the chief emblem of God's presence. When a person wanted to meet with God, the first place he or she thought of was the Lord's residence, the sanctuary. Here was his symbolic resting place where he was to be worshiped and served. The Sabbath was of equal importance in the consciousness of the people. It was vital because the people's routine lives were ordered by the recurring Sabbath each week of the year. As we think of our high noon and midnight hour as signals of the momentous and ominous times of our lives, every seventh day without exception reminded the people that they were the covenant people of God.

The most obvious indication of the distinctiveness of the Sabbath was the cessation of daily activities. Ordinary life came to a screeching halt. Life in its richest expression could be enjoyed without the distractions of daily labor. This feature of worship occurs also at special high festival seasons. "You shall not do any ordinary work" appears in five verses in our chapter (vv. 7, 8, 21, 25, 35). The idea of "rest" is emphasized in verse 3 by the phrase "*solemn rest.*" The language literally reads, "a sabbath of sabbath observance."[5] This expression emphasized the importance of the Sabbath. The particular language occurring here is rare. In addition to naming the weekly Sabbath rest (Exodus 31:15; 35:2), this phrase describes two other special times. It depicts the Day of Atonement, which occurs in the seventh month, that is, the Sabbath month (Leviticus 16:31; 23:32). It also describes the sabbatical year when cultivation of the land was prohibited each seventh year (25:4). And the number seven occurs in the calculation of the Year of Jubilee, the fiftieth year after seven Sabbaths of years, equaling forty-nine years (25:8–10). There is a link between the seventh day, the seventh month, and the seventh year,[6] giving the people a sense of symmetry and wholeness in their worship of God throughout their lives.

Why is the number seven and multiples of seven so key to calculating sacred periods of worship? The number seven in the Bible is the number of perfection and symbolizes perfection. This is the appropriate number for the worship of God who alone is complete in his perfections. This helps us understand why the instructions for worship required such exacting obligations in order to be acceptable worship in God's eyes. Deviation from the sacred times or from the ritual procedures compromised the holiness of the worship offered to the Lord. Sometimes severe penalties were called for in the case of flagrant transgressions. For example, the penalty in the Mosaic law for working on the Sabbath was death (Exodus 31:14–16; 35:2). There is an incident in the book of Numbers that reports that a man who broke Sabbath by gathering sticks was executed by stoning by the community (15:32–36).[7] The specifics of what constituted crimes against the Sabbath are not detailed in the Bible. The elaborate "do's and don'ts" that governed the Sabbath in later Judaism came from the Jewish rabbis who added to the laws to supply or explain what was not in the Biblical teaching.[8]

All attention was directed toward the Giver of the Sabbath. It was the day of focused worship when all members of the community devoted themselves to this one mind. The seventh day involved a Sabbath rest for the community, and all were to participate, including the livestock, which were given rest from their chores. The cessation of work was a blessing from God because the people could enjoy the abundance that God had given them and they could reconnect their daily lives with the Lord as their Covenant-Master. It stressed the sense of community that the covenant promises from God had created.

As a day of rest from their daily occupations—whether in the fields, the home, or the marketplace—the Sabbath was a benevolent relief from the toils of daily work. It was therefore a harbinger of the future rest that God had promised those who were members of the covenant community of faith. Sabbath was a present hope for a better future. The writer to the Hebrews recognized that the saints of the Old Testament had entered into the land of Canaan and had successfully controlled their enemies, but they never received the final, complete rest in the land.[9] The author of Hebrews concludes, "So then, there remains a Sabbath rest for the people of God, for whoever has entered God's rest has also rested from his works as God did from his" (Hebrews 4:9, 10). This rest is available to those today who place their faith in the Lord. It is received in its full measure at the resurrection when "the mortal [body] puts on immortality" (1 Corinthians 15:54).

We as human beings living in a sinful world face the realities of our decaying bodies as we age and the overwhelming pressures of a modern society that idolizes work's productivity. The internal anguish of the human soul is described by Ecclesiastes 2:22, 23: "What has a man from all the toil and striving of heart with which he toils beneath the sun? For all his days are full of sorrow, and his work is a vexation. Even in the night his heart does not rest. This also is vanity." The popularity of self-help books and the new trend in spirituality in modern conversation reflect this torture of the soul and the sought-after relief that the human spirit desires. The popular Chicken Soup for the Soul series was first published in 1993. "In 2008, Chicken Soup for the Soul became the best-selling trade paperback series in the history of publishing."[10] These heartwarming anecdotes for inspiration and motivation are the best remedy that human ingenuity and imagination can prescribe. But the final, satisfying peace that the human soul yearns for can be only found in the rest that Jesus offers: "Come to me, all who labor and are heavy laden, and I will give you rest. Take my yoke upon you, and learn from me, for I am gentle and lowly in heart, and you will find rest for your souls" (Matthew 11:28, 29).

## Sabbath Celebrations

The observance of Sabbath communicated the need for spiritual rest but also remembered two momentous events in the religious life of Israel. The first was the creation of the world when God ceased from his creation work on the seventh day. The second was the redemption of Israel when the Lord freed the Hebrews from their Egyptian overlords. The significance of the Lord as Creator and Redeemer was the foreshadowing of the new creation and eternal rest that the Lord Jesus has achieved in behalf of the church.

*Creation and redemption.* The seventh day of the creation week, that is, the Sabbath day, was the chief day of creation's days (Exodus 20:8–11, "Remember the Sabbath . . ."). It was the day of acclamation by God that the creation had been completed in all its perfections. It is the only day of the week that the creation account in Genesis says was "holy" (Genesis 2:1–3). The seventh day was holy because it was the day of the week set aside for the recognition of God as the Creator and Provider of all that exists and is enjoyed by his creatures. Repeatedly in the sacred calendar of Leviticus 23 with its set times of the year, month, and days, there is reference to the Sabbaths as the point of orientation for calculating the sacred times. For example, the timetable for the Feast of Weeks is determined by counting seven full weeks from the Sabbath that concludes the Feast of Firstfruits (v. 16). Sevens and multiples of seven characterize the timetable for the seasons of worship. Although the feast days were calculated by movements of the sun, moon, and stars (cf. Genesis 1:14), the Sabbath never was. The Sabbath day was counted every seven days without reference to astronomical movements. This showed that Israel's God was the Lord of time as well as of space. The psalmist could declare to the Lord, "My times are in your hand" (Psalm 31:15a).

The second event tied to the celebration of Sabbath was the great redemption at the Red Sea when Israel was liberated from Egyptian bondage (Deuteronomy 5:15). Together the Sabbath remembered these two features of God's grace as Creator and Redeemer. When the Israelites paused each week to remember the Lord, they were declaring his role and rights as Creator and Redeemer of his people. Moreover, the linkage with creation indicated that Sabbath rest was a gift for all creation, a universal gift enjoyed by all. This means that the Sabbath event in the life of Israel was not a mere cultural phenomenon, since it was tied to the universal setting of the cosmos. Sabbath was unique to Israel, not practiced by any other ancient people. It was a weekly renewal of Israel's identity as the people of God whose task was to worship the one true God and to declare his righteousness to the nations. Sabbath was a day of joyous celebration. It was not a private experience but a public proclamation. Verse 2 reads, "you [the people] shall proclaim . . ." Convocations on the Sabbath entailed proclamation. The convocations announced the reign of God as Creator and Redeemer, and by the people's attendance and triumphal praise they showed their recognition of his lordship over their lives.

*Eternal rest.* The expression "Sabbath of solemn rest" in verse 3 invites us to consider how this "solemn rest" might be entered. Those who were members of the covenant community and those who were aliens in the land enjoyed this time of refreshment by virtue of Israel's relationship to God as Creator and Redeemer (Exodus 23:12). The Sabbath as the chief sign of covenant loyalty to the Lord God of Israel was the magnet that would attract all nations to the house of the Lord.[11] As the Jewish people returned from their captivity to the holy hill of Jerusalem, the nations would join them in offering obeisance, including the keeping of the Sabbath. Then, as the prophet Isaiah forecasted, "[the Lord's] house shall be called a house of prayer for all peoples" (Isaiah 56:7c; cf. Matthew 21:13). But that solemn rest was never complete, for it was followed by six days of work. The pattern of work and rest was part of the covenant life of the people. The writer to the Hebrews recognized, however, that God had provided a permanent rest for those who were consecrated to his service. That eternal rest is a spiritual Sabbath that Jesus has achieved for those who are his people. This spiritual rest was made known from the moment of the seventh day's dawning at creation. The six days all conclude with the same refrain—"and there was evening and there was morning, the first day," "the second day," and so forth to "the sixth day." But this concluding refrain is absent at the conclusion of the seventh day. Obviously there was a conclusion to the seventh day since there was an eighth that followed, but there was a spiritual lesson to be learned from the creation chapter regarding the eternality of the seventh day. The writer to the Hebrews acknowledged that there is a Sabbath rest that continues uninterrupted (Hebrews 4:10). That rest is provided by the Lord Jesus Christ for those who will enter into it. God the Creator was in Christ reconciling this world unto himself through the incarnational life, death, and resurrection of the Lord Jesus (2 Corinthians 5:17–20).

The second image of eternal rest is painted by the promise of Canaan's land of rest. After the redemption of Israel, the Lord led his people to the land that would give them rest from their enemies (Joshua 21:44). But those who refused to enter the land died in the wilderness, short of the promise intended for them. The writer to the Hebrews remembered the failure of Israel and urged his Christian readers not to falter in their faith but rather to trust God to give them an eternal rest (Hebrews 4:6–9). This is the rest that God has for us now, an eternal rest that is ours through the cross of Jesus Christ. The Scriptures say, "For in [Christ] all the fullness of God was pleased to dwell, and through him to reconcile to himself all things, whether on earth or in heaven, making peace by the blood of his cross" (Colossians 1:19, 20).

## The Lord's Day

What does the Sabbath mean for us since we come together on Sunday, the Lord's Day? The difference between Saturday and Sunday is not a mere historical hiccup, in which the Jews have their special day and we Christians have ours. That we worship on Sunday trumpets a victorious declaration that the Sabbath could not. All four Gospels identify the first day of the week as the day of Jesus' resurrection. Each Gospel notes that it came after the Sabbath evening. By Jesus' resurrection on the "eight day," that is the day after the Sabbath, he inaugurated the eternal rest that is available to any person who will confess his sins and trust in him as the Lord of the new creation. This is the continuation of God's creation rest that has no end. The early church met on this day in the New Testament (Acts 20:7; 1 Corinthians 16:2), and the tradition has continued to this hour. This is why we refer to Sunday as "the Lord's day," a name given to Sunday by the early Christians as found in the book of Revelation (1:10). There was a necessary period of transition from the Jewish tradition to the new meaning of the sacred calendar. The earliest Christians were Jewish and continued their worship days. The pattern of special times continued in the church but was infused with new meaning in light of the gospel. Once the old had been filled up by the inauguration of the new covenant, the "symbolic importance"[12] of the holy days no longer continued. The shadows had been superseded by the reality of the reign of Jesus.

We may raise practical questions regarding observance of the Lord's Day and other important sacred seasons, such as Easter. What is required of the Christian today? Are we bound by obligation, as the ancient Israelites were, to attend Sunday services? If our attendance is irregular or absent, what does that say about our Christian profession? Is our claim to be Christians genuine? Is it voided by negligence of church services? Furthermore, how much attendance is enough? Where is the dividing line between success and failure? Also, what kinds of activities are permitted on Sundays? Are we prohibited from commercial activities, such as grocery shopping and visiting retail sites? How about recreation? Afternoon golf? Football on TV? Can "work" for one individual be "rest" for another person?

As in the case of the Sabbath in the Old Testament, there is little direct instruction regarding the specifics of the Lord's Day and how it was observed in the New Testament. We are dependent on inferences from the New Testament and from early church tradition.[13] This suggests that the observance of the Lord's Day will take on a number of different expressions, depending on the culture in which the local church operates. Although the specifics of the Lord's Day may vary from setting to setting, the one consistent factor is the requirement of believers to gather at appointed times for the purpose of worship and spiritual edification (Hebrews 10:24, 25). It was so common for the church to gather, it is assumed by the Apostle Paul in his instructions regarding the life of Christian believers individually and collectively (1 Corinthians 11:17–34; 14:26; Ephesians 5:18–21; Colossians 3:16). It was clearly the practice of the early church as shown by the references to gathered bodies in house churches (Acts 2:41, 42; Philemon 2).

Another consistent teaching on the Lord's Day in the New Testament is the limitation of the value of Sunday observance. Observance of holy days does not gain us saving merit in the eyes of God. By church attendance we do not add to or subtract from the absolute value of the death of Christ and the grace that flows from it (Galatians 4:9, 10; Colossians 2:16–19). The death of Christ and the regenerating work of the Spirit in the lives of believers are based on the righteousness of Christ, not on our religious performance. The Apostle Paul did not condemn the observance of Jewish food laws and of designated holy days, practices that he himself undertook as a Jew. But he did reject the false motivations or conclusions drawn from the keeping of religious rituals that were at odds with the gospel of grace and liberty that he had proclaimed.[14]

Although our salvation is not secured by our religious fastidiousness, our obedience to the Word of God testifies to authentic Christian commitment. Connection with the gathered church is a necessity for Christians for the verification of saving faith. If a person does not connect with a local body of believers, this is good reason for that person to pause and evaluate his faith (2 Corinthians 13:5). Such a connection is necessary for the believer's identity with the Church, signaling his or her bond with Christ and the salvation that he has won for him or her on the cross. It is a necessity for the believer's life in spiritual discipline and growth in spiritual character. To submit to the preaching of God's Word, to join the congregation of the righteous in praise of God, and to be accountable to church leaders and fellow pilgrims is part of the

Christian experience. It would have been unthinkable in the early church for a Christian to ignore the gathered body of believers without detriment to that believer's spiritual life. We might compare this to a man or woman who says wedding vows in a formal ceremony but soon thereafter behaves as a single person, not living in the same home and not attending to the commitments spoken at the covenant wedding ceremony. Whether one wears a wedding ring or not, a married person must act like a faithful companion in marriage or the actions of the person make the words of commitment drivel.

Although we have emphasized the importance of Sunday observance as a special day of worship, we do not think it advisable to draw up a detailed list of limitations or liberties on the conduct of Sunday behavior. Once specifics are legislated, there will be the splitting of hairs that create a complex grid of right and wrong behaviors that can be a false substitution for the authentic gospel. Such detailed requirements can prove to be a competitive righteousness that does not have its exclusive origin in the grace provided by the death and resurrection of the Lord Jesus. The operating principle should be what we hear from Paul regarding Christian behavior: ". . . whatever you do, do all to the glory of God" (1 Corinthians 10:31). The question we must ask ourselves each day, including each Lord's Day, is, am I honoring the Lord by my conduct today?

So, let us remember that when we come together as the Church of Jesus Christ we are declaring the new day, and we are witnesses that we have entered into the new creation—the eternal Sabbath rest—through faith in the resurrected Christ. The Christian hymn-writer Henry Ware penned these words that well prompt us to recall the purpose of our gathering on the Lord's Day: "Lift your glad voices in triumph on high, for Jesus hath risen, and man cannot die."[15]

# 19

# Worship for All Seasons

## LEVITICUS 23:4–44

OUR LIVES ARE FILLED with important seasons, the chief of which is Christmas in our American culture. We have several calendars that a typical family must live by—daily calendars, annual calendars, and, for religious people, sacred calendars. From billboard-sized digital clocks to the smallest timepiece, our daily experiences are saturated with and usually governed by the march of time. Today you can buy a projection clock that projects the time and temperature on the ceiling in your room or office, giving you a constant moment-by-moment display of the ebbing of your day or night. We especially memorialize the days that mark our lives, regularly acknowledging birthdays and anniversaries. I have too many grandchildren now to keep all their birthdays readily in mind. I read of one family, however, whose three children's birth dates were unforgettable. The two sons in the family were born three years apart, and their baby sister was one year younger—nevertheless, all were born on the *same* calendar date of October 2!

The calendar of special dates and seasons for ancient peoples was just as important, and probably more so than they are to us today. All peoples in the ancient world believed in the gods and goddesses of nature, understanding their days and seasons as sacred time. This was true of ancient Israel, too, which received from God a sacred calendar of religious worship. Yet, unlike the nations, the Hebrews rightly knew that the Lord God was Creator and that the astral signs of sun and moon were not deities to be worshiped. The purposes of the religious year for the Israelites included designating required convocations of community worship and using them to teach the faith of their ancestors to future generations (Exodus 12:25–27; 13:13–16). The Christian church continued the tradition of a sacred calendar, focusing on the two seasons of Christmas and Easter. Advent, Christmas, and the feast of Epiphany mark Christmastide, and Lent, Holy Week, and Easter distinguish the Easter season.

In the New Testament church the apostles understood that the Jewish calendar of holy days and seasons were pictures of the story of Christ and the coming of the Holy Spirit. In the letter to the Colossians, the Apostle Paul remarked that the religious festivals and sacred days of the Jews were "a shadow of the things to come, but the substance belongs to Christ" (Colossians 2:17). Jesus was the reality of what Israel's Sabbaths, Passover, Pentecost, and many other sacred days pointed to. The ancient Hebrews derived spiritual lessons from the remembrance of their religious days. The church also learned about Christ from looking at Israel's calendar in the full sunshine of the revelation of Christ and his church. We, too, as his church have much to glean spiritually from Israel's liturgical year.

Although many passages scattered throughout the Old Testament describe the special times of worship,[1] Leviticus 23 provides a convenient collection of the three pilgrim feasts and the two chief holy days. The latter half of the book of Leviticus defines the features of what holy living is—how the people were to conduct themselves in all matters of life in the presence of God. Instructions in the proper observance of public worship were recounted in chapters 21, 22, which address the priests in their roles. Now chapter 23 turns again to the primary audience of the book, the laypeople who came to the Tent of Meeting to worship the Lord God. This passage was not for ministers but for the rank and file who are the engine, so to speak, of the nation of God. The holy assemblies at the worship center were the chief occasions when the people collectively came before the Lord as his special people.

There were three pilgrim convocations, also called feasts, when the men of the household appeared before the Lord at his sanctuary (Exodus 23:14; 34:18–23; Deuteronomy 16:16). These included the Feast of Passover and Unleavened Bread, the Feast of Weeks (also known as Pentecost), and the Feast of Booths (also known as Tabernacles). These three were weeklong celebrations. Psalms 120—134, called the Songs of Ascents, were sung by the pilgrims on their journey to Jerusalem. Psalm 122:1, for example, reads, "I was glad when they said to me, 'Let us go to the house of the LORD!'"

The two holy days listed are daylong convocations—the Feast of Trumpets and the Day of Atonement. Attendance at the sanctuary for these two days was not required of the people, but they were to observe the days in their homes. The liturgical year was centered around two months, the first month and the seventh month of the year. We will look at each month's celebrations and see how each festival instructs us as the people of God who come together in convocation to worship the Lord. Before we do so, however, we will learn from the introduction to these seven feasts the proper orientation that we must have to appreciate each one's full significance.

### The Lord's Feasts (vv. 2, 4)

The opening verses (2, 4) announce the sacred nature of the convocations.[2] Three descriptions mark them out as especially given by God. They are identified as "the appointed feasts of the LORD," "holy convocations," and "my [that is, the Lord's] appointed feasts." The repetition shows us that the importance of the feasts was their relationship to God as their source and designer. The feasts were not the property of the Israelites to do with as they wished. They were distinguished as "appointed feasts," meaning these meetings were scheduled by God for the people to attend for worship. The convocations had to be focused on the worship of God—they were his. They were not solely fastidious formalities for their own sake or pomp and ceremony for priestly self-interests. Worship is not established by preachers for preachers to perform while the congregation watches from afar. Since the meeting times belonged to the Lord and were given for the chief purpose of knowing God, they were deemed "holy." The feasts were "holy" because they were consecrated to the Lord's service. As noted earlier, they were not family or community potlucks with a bit of religion thrown into the mix.

Worship was also not the property of pew-sitters who were entertained by the proceedings. They were celebratory remembrances of their God, calling for the people to consecrate themselves to the holy task of worshiping the Lord. The community at worship, both during the regular cycle of gatherings and during special seasons of the sacred year, had a holy task that demanded all they were and the best of what they were. The same is true today. Our attention must be focused on the Lord God, and we must prepare our hearts and design our services so that we are centered on him. Psalm 33:1 reminds us of this: "Shout for joy in the LORD, O you righteous! Praise befits the upright."

### The First Month (vv. 5–22)

The first month's celebrations recounted the redemption of God's people and the provision for God's people.

*The Passover redemption (vv. 5–8).* The Passover celebration was on the fourteenth day of the first month, and the Feast of Unleavened Bread followed immediately on the fifteenth day and lasted for a full week.[3] Together these feasts hearkened back to the glorious day of liberation that the nation experienced at their exodus from Egyptian bondage (Exodus 12—14). The story of Israel may begin with Father Abraham, but the birth of the nation had its roots in the redemption that God achieved for them at the Red Sea. In our own national history, we recall that thirteen colonies preceded the founding of the nation, prior to the Revolutionary War, but our identity as a nation began with the Declaration of Independence on July 4, 1776. So it was with the nation Israel as they looked back to the formative events of Passover. The Passover festival remembered the smearing of blood on the doorposts of the Hebrews' homes, providing deliverance from the angel of death who took the life of the firstborn in those houses not marked by the shed blood. Hence, death "passed over" the Hebrew domiciles but visited those of the Egyptians.

That event was the announcement of the liberation of the people, but preparations were also needed for their departure. Among them was the baking of unleavened bread, which accompanied the eating of the roasted lamb of the Passover meal. Unleavened bread was to be eaten all the week of the feast so as to reflect the haste that marked the departure of the slaves from Egyptian rule (Exodus 12:20, 33, 34, 39). That the Passover and Feast of Unleavened Bread were viewed together would be like our tendency to link Christmas Eve with Christmas Day or New Year's Eve with New Year's Day. Each event had its distinctive role, but they worked together to convey the message of God's deliverance.

Christian readers are not surprised that the Passover was held in such high regard in the early church. The early Christians whose roots were in Jewish life immediately saw the deeper meaning of the Passover deliverance. It pointed to the ultimate deliverance provided by Jesus who was the Passover lamb for the forgiveness of sins and the liberation of those who were destined for death in sinful servitude (1 Corinthians 5:6–8). Our Lord's last week was in Jerusalem on the occasion of the Passover meal. The night of his arrest occurred after the celebration of the Passover meal with his disciples (John 13:1). It was in the midst of the Passover memorial that Jesus transformed the meaning of the Passover to the Lord's Supper. The bread and the wine indicated the broken body and shed blood of Jesus who was the Passover Lamb of God (Matthew 26:17–29). The Apostle Paul was specific when he instructed the Corinthians, saying, "For Christ, our Passover lamb, has been sacrificed" (1 Corinthians 5:7b).

*The provision of firstfruits (vv. 9–22).* Two ritual events in the liturgical calendar announced the beginning of the harvest season. The first was the ceremony of firstfruits (vv. 9–14), and the second was the Feast of Weeks (or Pentecost) (vv. 15–22). After the redemption of Israel from Egyptian servitude, the Lord led his people into the desert where he demonstrated his provision and care for them, even when they were rebellious. The most important provision was the land that he led them to possess—the land of Canaan, where he had chosen their fathers and promised to give them this land. Upon arriving in the land, the people were to recognize God's grace by taking the first produce of the land's harvests and offering a portion to the Lord as a symbolic gesture of worship to the God of their provision. The day of firstfruits was embedded in the week's celebration of the Feast of Unleavened Bread, which stretched from the fifteenth to the twenty-second of the first month. It was offered up on the second day of that feast, that is, the sixteenth day of the first month. This would fall in the months of March/April. The ritual of firstfruits entailed presenting the first sheaf of the barley harvest to the priest at the sanctuary, who on behalf of the worshiper lifted it up before the Lord, indicating that the worshiper offered thanksgiving to God as the source of his livelihood. It was the first evidence of the coming months of spring harvest. The memorial included animal sacrifice and grain offerings. The people were not to indulge in the grain of the land until God had received his due first (v. 14). This was God's harvest; he was the owner of the land, and its produce was his to do with as he pleased. He graciously shared the land and its harvests with the people to farm as tenants. By their offering of firstfruits the people acknowledged that theirs was a bounty that had come from the Lord. The benefit of the land remained theirs as long as they lived as good tenants, keeping the agreements made with the divine Landowner (26:3–13).

The second harvest celebration, known as the Feast of Weeks, followed seven weeks after the Feast of Unleavened Bread. This was the second pilgrim feast in the liturgical calendar. The date for the Feast of Weeks was determined by counting fifty days from the day after the Sabbath of the Feast of Unleavened Bread.[4] Although this celebration was in the third month of the year, our May/June months, we can tie it to the first month by virtue of its association with the Feast of Unleavened Bread (v. 15). It was the celebration of the harvest of grain. The celebration was an elaborate one, involving a full week of special activities. The people were forbidden to work at their ordinary duties, setting the week aside for special recognition of the Lord. This festival focused on the grain crops. Special loaves of bread were baked and waved before the Lord at the sanctuary. Unlike the Feast of Unleavened Bread, these loaves were made with leaven, indicating the season of joyful gladness at God's provision. Additional animal offerings accompanied the bread, making a full meal, so to speak, in which the Lord partook.

That the ritual was not a superficial show for the bystanders to enjoy is shown by the instructions regarding the responsibility of the people in sharing their produce. The Lord compassionately shared the land with his people, and in turn they were to provide for the poor (v. 22).[5] That the Lord instructed the Hebrews to share with others reflects again that ultimately the harvest belonged to God. The Hebrew landowners were prohibited from reaping every row of grain, taking it all for themselves and their workers. There were members of the community who could not benefit materially from God's blessing since they had no land to work or were unable to work as day laborers. By leaving gleanings in the fields, the poor could make bread from the grain, which was the main staple for their daily diet. The succession of the gift was important theologically as well as practically. God gave the land to his people, and by enriching them the people could assist others. At the people's faithful obedience to the Lord, he supplied more than enough for their needs, which meant that the landowner shared his wealth with others too. The Apostle Paul recognized this principle and instructed the church, "You will be enriched in every way *to be generous in every way*, which through us will produce thanksgiving to God" (2 Corinthians 9:11). God gives to us liberally so we can be generous to others.

Many peoples yesterday and today formally commemorate seasons of harvest. But there was an important difference in the practice of Israel compared to their neighbors. Whereas the nations focused on the earth as the source of their wealth, the Israelites remembered that the harvest season was tied to a great historical act of divine promise. It was not merely a celebration of the cycle of nature but a remembrance of the Lord's gift of the land.[6] By miraculous deeds, the Lord fought the battles of Israel and brought them safely into the land of plenty. There is a similarity in our celebration at Thanksgiving, or at least should be. Thanksgiving is not an annual celebration that is focused on the bounty of American life but has its roots in a gracious historical act on behalf of God toward the first pilgrims to this land. It was a historical event that we remember each Thanksgiving Day—the harvest of 1621 was a bountiful one that sustained the fledgling colonists who had arrived the year earlier on the *Mayflower*. The native Indians who were instrumental in the Plymouth colonists' survival joined in the celebration.

Christian readers will know the Feast of Weeks better under the name Pentecost, meaning "the fiftieth day." The Jewish celebration of Pentecost was the background for the epic event of the coming of the Holy Spirit upon the disciples gathered in Jerusalem. This event, recorded in Acts 2, launched the inception of the church and enabled its worldwide impact upon the nations.

Our Lord had instructed the disciples at his ascent ten days earlier to await the coming of the Spirit before dispersing to spread the news of the kingdom's arrival (John 16:7–14; Acts 1:4, 5, 8).[7] In the liturgical calendar of the Christian Church, Pentecost is on the Sunday fifty days after Easter Sunday (counting Easter). Pentecost celebrates the theology of giving. God gave, and the people rejoiced at his generosity. This is what God has done for us as Christians. He has given us the Holy Spirit who resides in the life of the gathered church and in the hearts of each person who has received Christ as Savior (1 Corinthians 3:16; 6:19). When we gather as the church in worship, we are acknowledging the present reality of the kingdom of God. We are proclaiming the Day of the Lord and testifying to the transforming power of the gospel by the Holy Spirit.

## The Seventh Month (vv. 23–44)

The most important month of the Hebrews' liturgical year was the seventh month, and our passage gives special attention to it. The importance of the seventh month was due to the commemoration of three major events—the Feast of Trumpets, the Day of Atonement, and the Feast of Booths, also known as the Feast of Tabernacles. The seventh Hebrew month occurred in the autumn months of September/October.

*Trumpeting spiritual preparation (vv. 23–25).* The Feast of Trumpets inaugurated the call to worship.[8] Although trumpets were sounded at the beginning of each month, this month was special, and the trumpets sounded a summons to a sacred convocation. The people turned aside from their work and gathered for a full day of sacrifice and worship (Numbers 29:1–6 gives the details). The point of this day of rest and sacrifice was to prepare the people for the momentous events to follow.[9] Similarly, the Advent season in the Christian liturgical year prepares the church for the celebration of Christmas. "Advent" means "coming," and the Advent season occurs in the four weeks leading up to Christmas. The key idea for us when considering the Feast of Trumpets is the importance of spiritual preparation for worship. Spiritual preparation must accompany worship. We convene to lift up the Savior in prayer, praise, and proclamation. We must take this meeting seriously if we are to properly enter into the presence of the assembly of the righteous. I can tell the difference in my own attitude toward the hour of worship when I have prepared my heart for worship. When I have the right focus on God, the things pertaining to worship are not as important, such as the choice of music, worship style, and the preacher's message. All of these features may encourage or detract from worship, but they are not as likely to distract when I am yielding my mind and spirit to the voice of God. The fundamental problem in a person's worship is the failure to anticipate hearing from God. If we really believe that God has a word for us, we will have ears to hear and eyes to see.

Not only do we prepare for worship, but our weekly Christian worship itself prepares us for the future. Worship readies us for the Second Advent, the *parousia* of our Lord, who will come again at the blast of a trumpet. First Thessalonians 4:16 describes this dramatic conclusion: "For the Lord himself will descend from heaven with a cry of command, with the voice of an archangel, and with the sound of the trumpet of God. And the dead in Christ will rise first." The triumphant words of an old hymn capture this: "When the trumpet of the Lord shall sound, and time shall be no more."[10] Have we prepared for the coming of Christ when he shall judge the heavens and earth? Or will we be caught unprepared, remaining in our sins because we did not repent and confess Christ as our Savior?

*The fast of atonement (vv. 26–32).* Since the Feast of Trumpets called the people to reevaluate their commitment to the Lord, it is proper that the people began the month of worship with fasting, not feasting. The Day of Atonement was the only day in the calendar of worship that entailed fasting and contrition because it was a day of sorrow, a day of repentance for sin. The Day of Atonement was a special holy day that occurred on the tenth day of the seventh month. On this one day a year the high priest was permitted to enter into the most sacred place in the tabernacle, before the ark of the covenant, where he bore the blood of a slaughtered animal and sprinkled the blood on the seat of atonement (Leviticus 16:1–34; Hebrews 9:7). The ark of the covenant symbolically represented the presence of God among his people, Israel. The word *atonement* means a reconciliation of a relationship that has been broken. Reconciliation is achieved through removing an offense suffered between two parties. The people had offended God by their sin throughout the year, and this was the means for settling the issue of the nation's sins with God.

Three times in this passage (vv. 27, 29, 32) the text insists that the people must "afflict" (*innah*) themselves on this day. The Hebrew term translated "afflict" does not mean self-inflicted asceticism in order to reach a higher state of spiritual enlightenment. Rather, it is a humbling of oneself before God through refraining from the common pleasures of daily life and the ordinary work of daily life. It is an inner turmoil that is self-inflicted, a day of remorse. Our passage terms the day "a Sabbath of solemn rest" (v. 32). The whole day is set aside to consider the sins of the nation for which they seek forgiveness, lest they suffer the wrath of their disobedience. The Day of Atonement, known in Jewish tradition as Yom Kippur, is described in detail in chapter 16 of Leviticus.[11] Although it is a day of mourning, there is ample grace shown on this day.

The day provided sacrifice for sin, the purging of the tabernacle and people, and a scapegoat that took away the sins of the community.

Yet, each year the Day of Atonement had to be repeated because the sins of the people were not fully and finally absolved on the Day of Atonement. The perpetuity of the event was a sobering reminder to the people that their acts of contrition, the giving of animal sacrifices, and the ritual purging of the sanctuary were not sufficient to remedy *permanently* the people's mounting sins. The writer to the Hebrews remarks on this recurring necessity for annual repentance, observing the incompleteness of the atonement that the animals provided. There remained, however, a permanent solution to their sins, a purging so thorough, so effective that never again would the people need to experience a year of jeopardy by living in their sins. That sacrifice was the once-for-all offering of Jesus Christ, the eternal Son of God, whose life was without sin and whose shed blood won perfect and complete atonement for sins. By entering into the heavenly throne room of God the Father, he presented the only satisfying solution to the gravity of human sin. "[Christ] entered once for all into the holy places, not by means of the blood of goats and calves but by means of his own blood, thus securing an eternal redemption" (Hebrews 9:12). As Christians we have been spared the nagging doubts of unresolved sins, for Christ has secured for us a place in the heavenlies (Ephesians 2:6). Our security, however, came at the costly price of the death of Jesus. His cross was our Day of Atonement. Now we must take up that cross of sacrifice, living a life consecrated to God. Our lives must also be ones of humble contrition, seeking God's forgiveness in the name of Jesus and knowing that the forgiveness we seek has already been secured for us. "If we confess our sins, [God] is faithful and just to forgive us our sins and to cleanse us from all unrighteousness" (1 John 1:9). An essential part of genuine worship is the confession of our sins before God, a genuine remorse over our sins, and renewed zeal to live a life of uprightness (Romans 6:13).

*The Feast of Booths (vv. 33–44).* The fast of atonement is answered by a weeklong festive celebration, the Feast of Booths, also known as the Feast of Tabernacles. On the fifteenth day of the month, five days after the Day of Atonement, the festival begins with a sacred assembly, and it closes after a week on the eighth day in the same fashion. There was to be no ordinary work on those two days of assembly. What distinguished this celebration from others was the building of temporary huts or booths, which the people constructed out of fruit and branches of palms, willows, and other leafy trees on the first day of the festival (v. 40; Nehemiah 8:14–17). The people lived in these booths during the seven days of the festival. Today Israeli Jews build colorful dwellings with ceilings made of green and yellow vegetation. The fragile walls are made of interlocking panels dazzlingly painted with fruits and vegetables and scenes of temple celebrations.[12] The fall festival today in Jerusalem includes pageantry, music, a carnival, and art fairs.

The Feast of Booths brought together two reasons for Israel to remember the Lord. The reason cited in our text is, "when [the people] have gathered in the produce of the land" (v. 39).[13] This ingathering was a joyous occasion, a blessing that urged the people to thank God for the autumn month's harvest of fruit (Deuteronomy 16:13–15). It concluded the agricultural year, rounding out the provision that God had given for the year. The second reason for the Feast of Booths explains why the festival was called "Feast of *Booths*." During the wilderness period after their liberation from Egypt, the people lived in temporary huts (v. 43). God provided for the people's needs during the travail of this time, including miraculous provisions of food, water, and shelter.

The feast not only looked back but also was a portent of the future when the Lord would bring his people back from their exile among the nations. Zechariah spoke of this future age, describing how the nations would join with the returning Jews in the land to worship God in his temple (14:16, 17). One of the signs of the nations' repentance and assent to the God of Israel as their own God would be their celebration of the Feast of Booths. The message of the feast spoke of this inclusiveness, for the Jews and foreigners both benefited from the harvest and could join their voices in joyful celebration at the Lord's goodness.

That there was an eschatological dimension depicted by the feast is also shown in the interpretation given to it by our Lord. John's Gospel describes the appearance of Jesus at the feast and recounts the teaching he presented in the temple on that occasion (John 7:14). On the final day of the feast, he declared, "If anyone thirsts, let him come to me and drink. Whoever believes in me, as the Scripture has said, 'Out of his heart will flow rivers of living water'" (vv. 37, 38). The offer of the spiritual water that satisfies the thirsty soul drew on the imagery of the Feast of Booths as it was celebrated in Jesus' day. According to rabbinic tradition, although not found in the Biblical text, the ritual included a pouring out of water by the priest at the temple's altar.[14] In Jesus' interpretation, this outpouring of water symbolized the gift of the Holy Spirit. Jesus presented himself as the source of that water and called upon all to drink of it by faith in him as Savior.

The concluding verses of Leviticus 23 call upon the people of God to worship during all seasons of the year. Worship was the core of their identity as God's people and the core of their experience. It can be no different for us as the people of God. We too are called upon to worship the Lord, coming to him in repentance and receiving his forgiveness as secured for us through the death of our Lord Jesus Christ. Then we as a redeemed community can revel in the bounty of God's spiritual provisions—the gift of the Holy Spirit and the fellowship we have with God the Father, Son, and Spirit as well as with one another. When the Apostle Paul instructed his young protégé Timothy to be consistent in his witness despite hardships, he used the imagery of the seasons: "Preach the word; be ready in season and out of season" (2 Timothy 4:2a).

I would say the same for worship. Worship the Lord when it is convenient and when it is inconvenient. It is often costly to participate in the meetings that God has called us to attend. The early church recognized this and struggled with the temptations to abandon their loyalty to the people of God when persecution came or when pleasures beckoned. Let this never be said of us. Let us always persevere in our allegiance to Christ and to his church by loving him and his church, always participating in the life of the congregation of the redeemed.

# 20

# God's Sacred Presence

## LEVITICUS 24:1–23

SOME PEOPLE COMMAND ATTENTION from others just by their presence in a room. Most speak of this magnetic personality as a person's charisma. Others have a striking presence by virtue of their position of authority. Sports figures, politicians, and celebrities often garner that kind of enthrallment by the public. Billy Graham's authorized biographer John Pollock spoke of interviewing Dr. Graham at one of his evangelistic crusades in the mobile home parked backstage in the stadium. The biographer commented that when he entered the mobile home, there was a presence about Graham that made the room seem too small. I haven't forgotten that story because I too have known people who fill up rooms just by their presence.

If this is true of mere mortals, how much more stirring it is when we come into the presence of God. The Bible depicts the presence of God in dramatic, unforgettable ways. When he first appeared in the Tent of Meeting (Exodus 40:34, 35) and later in the Jerusalem temple (2 Chronicles 5:14; 7:2), the glory of the Lord so filled the sanctuary that the people were driven out of the building. God's presence translates into God's power and blessing. Moses acknowledged the necessity of God's presence if the people were to survive the desert and enter the land of promise: "And [Moses] said to [the Lord], 'If your presence [lit., "your face"] will not go with me, do not bring us up from here'" (Exodus 33:15). We sing about it and read about it, but what does the presence of the Lord mean to us in our Christian lives and in our worship? The famed author Pearl S. Buck commented, "One faces the future with one's past." When we look at the instructions in our passage from the past, it will also instruct us in living in God's presence today.

Our passage brings together two images derived from the Tent of Meeting and a narrative that depicts a disturbing incident of blasphemy against the sacred name of God. These three speak to the character and importance of God's presence for us. After the instructions in the previous chapter regarding the festivals in the liturgical calendar of the Hebrews, it was appropriate for Moses to receive instructions from the Lord regarding the sacredness of God's home, the Tent of Meeting. The Feast of Weeks (or Pentecost) and the Feast of Booths recognized God's provision of the seasonal harvests, the grain harvest in the spring and the fruit and olive harvest in the autumn months. The golden lampstand and gold table of the bread of the Presence were fixtures in God's home. The olive oil derived from the autumn olive ingathering was necessary for the fueling of the lampstand in the Tent of Meeting and for the anointing oil for the priests and the holy sanctuary. The bread of the Presence consisted of baked loaves of grain that was derived from the wheat harvest and was remembered during the weeklong celebration of the Feast of Weeks. These two images, the light and the bread, tell us about the sanctity of God's presence.

## God Is Our Light (vv. 1–4)

The first set of instructions regards supplying the oil for the lamps of the golden lampstand that stood in the Holy Place of the Tent of Meeting. The core message of the sanctuary's lampstand was that God provides light for his people. The instructions, however, were not for the priests but for the laypeople. Although the priests alone were permitted to enter the tent to perform religious duties, the people also had a critical part to play. They were required to bring to the priest the items necessary for carrying out the various rituals of the Tent of Meeting (Exodus 25:1–9; 35:4–29). For the lampstand, the Lord exhorted the people to bring olive oil to fuel the lamps. This lampstand was a seven-branch golden candlestick that was one of three pieces of furniture in the Holy Place.[1] In the Tent of Meeting was the tent shrine enclosing two rooms partitioned by a veil. In the outer room, called the Holy Place, were the lampstand, the table on which the bread of the Presence was placed, and the altar of incense. The Most Holy Place, the inner room, contained the ark of the covenant (26:33). The lampstand had a striking appearance, being made of pure gold hammered and shaped into one piece that resembled an olive tree.[2] The lampstand was about five to six feet in height, standing on the floor of the room. On each side of the main trunk of the lampstand were three offshoots that each possessed at its top cups that contained oil lamps. The cups were sculpted so as to appear as almond blossoms, and in each cup the oil lamp rested. The lamps were filled with olive oil in which the wicks floated for burning (25:34).

The shape of the candlestick in the form of a budding tree symbolized life and with its lamps communicated that God is the source of both life and light. The lamp was, however, not for the Lord. He has no need of light since he is the embodiment of light. The lamps were positioned to shine in front of the candlestick into the Holy Place where the priests functioned (Numbers 8:2). The priests needed the light as they ministered inside the tent. The lamps were lit each evening and burned until morning, when they were extinguished (v. 3). The responsibility of Aaron as high priest was to ensure that the lamps had sufficient oil each evening to burn through the night hours.[3] Three times in our short passage of four verses, the text's instructions insist that the lighting of the lamps was to be done "regularly" (vv. 2, 3, 4; cf. v. 8).[4] The importance of this practice was its teaching value for the Israelites. It conveyed that the Lord was ever-present in the Tent of Meeting. In other words, the Lord kept the lights burning in his home. It communicated that he was the constant overseer of the welfare of his people.

We can look to the message conveyed to the people of God in the past and learn from it for us as Christians today. The lampstand recalled two important events in the life of Israel. First, the lampstand recalled the creation account when God said, "Let there be light" (Genesis 1:3). By God's word the darkness that enveloped the universe was dispelled, contributing to a world that could sustain human and animal life. Second, the lampstand commemorated the redemption of the nation when it was liberated from Egyptian bondage and was led through the wilderness to the promised land of Canaan. When the Israelites constructed the Tent of Meeting, it represented the residence of God among his people. Hovering above the tabernacle was a pillar of cloud by day and a pillar of fire by night (Exodus 40:38; Numbers 9:15, 16). The message of the lampstand was that the Lord God is sovereign Creator and benevolent Redeemer. He is the source of all light and life in the world and also the source of light and life of his people.

The lampstand also prefigured our Lord Jesus Christ. Jesus claimed in John 8:12, "I am the light of the world." When Jesus declared this, he was in Jerusalem at the time of the Feast of Booths. During that commemorative week, the Jews remembered the booths or huts that their ancestors lived in as they journeyed through the desert to Canaan. During the times of Jesus, according to Jewish tradition, the Jews set up four tall candlesticks on which were golden bowls in the Court of the Women. They were lit each night of the festival.[5] This was the background imagery of Jesus' declaration. He was making a remarkable claim because only God was said, according to the Old Testament Scriptures, to be the light of the world, and God was the One who brought light into the world (e.g., Psalm 104:2; 139:12; Isaiah 60:19, 20). When Jesus came into the world at his incarnation, he embodied the light of God that dispels the darkness: "The true light, which gives light to everyone, was coming into the world" (John 1:9).

DeathBut more fundamental to the light was the life that it represented. John's Gospel says of Jesus, "In him was life, and the life was the light of men" (1:4). Jesus is our light *and* our life. Without light there is no life. Those who reject the light of Jesus are held captive by spiritual darkness, and without the true light there is no life. The Apostle Paul likened the gospel to the glory of God's light at creation and as depicted in the Tent of Meeting (2 Corinthians 4:4–6). All on earth have been blinded by Satan: "[T]he god of this world has blinded the minds of the unbelievers, to keep them from seeing the light of the gospel of the glory of Christ, who is the image of God" (v. 4). I remember an embarrassing moment when I was touring Israel in my younger years. The tour group was walking through an underground tunnel that led from within the walls of an ancient city to a spring of water outside the city. As we traversed the darkened tunnel, we had only small candles provided by the tour guide to help us navigate the rock-hewn tunnel. I noticed that I was stumbling inordinately compared to others. Even the seniors hiked more easily and more quickly than I could. The whole matter came into sharp clarity for me when at last I emerged from the tunnel into the bright sunshine of the day. The tour guide who sat at the end of the trek greeted me with the comment, "Wasn't the tunnel dark enough without wearing your sunglasses, Ken?" I had compounded my problem of walking in the dark by absentmindedly wearing my sunglasses. This is the predicament faced by the unbeliever today. He lives in darkness *and* he is blinded by the devil. But the gospel of Jesus can transform our blindness into sight. The psalmist declared, "[T]he LORD my God lightens my darkness" (Psalm 18:28b).

## God Is Our Provider (vv. 5–9)

The second testimony to God's presence among his people was the loaves of bread that were displayed in the Tent of Meeting. This bread was called "the bread of the Presence" (Exodus 25:30), referring to the presence of God among his people. In the Holy Place stood a table measuring thirty-six inches long, eighteen inches wide, and twenty-seven inches tall that was overlaid with pure gold (Exodus 25:23–30). On the table were placed twelve loaves of baked bread sprinkled with fragrant frankincense. With the bread were placed the typical accoutrements for dining, such as plates, dishes, pitchers, and bowls. This symbolized a meal that the people had prepared for the Lord in his home.[6] Our passage explicitly says that the bread of the Presence came "from the people of Israel as a covenant forever" (v. 8). This then was a symbolic gesture that was carried out in perpetuity to show the people's thanksgiving to God and their commitment to him as their Covenant Lord. Regardless of the fortunes of the land and their concomitant prosperity or poverty, the people were to carry out this ritual acknowledgment of God as Lord. The same can be said of us when we as Christians make our gifts to the Lord. We are in effect saying that come rain or shine, the Lord Jesus is our Lord, and we will honor him with our tithes and offerings. To neglect setting our offerings before the Lord is tantamount to saying that we have no part in the covenant of blood provided by the Savior. A covenant member gives to the Lord and to the Lord's people. There is no way around this dictum.

That there were "twelve loaves" also symbolized an important message. The twelve loaves were arranged into two groups of six each, symbolizing the twelve tribes of Israel. The twelve loaves indicated that *all* Israel had given to the Lord. All the people in covenant with God could claim a share in the blessing of God as loyal covenant members. They collectively as a community were the recipients of God's redemption and provision. The priest placed pure frankincense on the bread, which was also a common feature for the regular daily grain offerings (Leviticus 2:1, 2, 15, 16). The bread of the Presence was replaced every Sabbath day on a weekly basis by freshly baked bread. Similarly, modern rituals of our day such as the changing of the military guard at the Tomb of the Unknown Soldier or the daily raising of the American flag communicate a message that is visual and memorable. These symbols and actions in our culture indicate a respect for and a reminder of what the rituals stand for—such as liberty, honor, and sacrifice.

The ritual of setting out the bread was a weekly ceremony that honored God and reminded the people that the Lord was their covenant provider. Unlike these modern rituals, however, the placement of the bread was accomplished within the enclosure of the tent. The laypeople could not have seen the replacement process, but they may have had some view of the priests who would eat the bread in the open courtyard, perhaps near the altar of burnt offering. By witnessing this weekly service, the laypeople would be reassured that the Lord had accepted their worship. When we witness in our worship services the ordinances of baptism and the Lord's Supper, we are encouraged in our faith and faithfulness.

The aromatic quality of frankincense was a desired effect for the burning of incense (Exodus 30:34) and for the secular use of perfuming the body (Song 3:6). It was an indication of joyful blessing (Isaiah 60:6). Whereas grain for the baking of bread was a regular feature in the daily diet of the people, the frankincense added to the grain offerings or in this case to the twelve loaves was a costly addition and therefore required a considerable personal sacrifice. To accommodate the poor, for example, frankincense was not expected of them (Leviticus 5:11). A regular grain offering involved the priest burning up a "memorial portion" on the altar as the share of the offering devoted to God. The memorial portion included a representative portion of the grain and oil but always the full measure of frankincense. This indicated that the memorial portion, the most costly portion, was reserved for God. The priest who received the remainder of the grain for his daily stipend could not benefit from the frankincense since it was the prized portion that the Lord alone received.

Unlike the regular offerings, however, a memorial portion of the bread of the Presence was not burned on the altar. Rather, the priests who served the Lord in his house were commanded to eat the bread (v. 9). As "a most holy portion," the priests were required to eat it in the sanctuary precinct since the sanctuary was holy ground. By eating the bread, not only did the bread benefit the priests as their weekly stipend, but it also indicated that the offering had been shared by God with his people. The priests represented the people before the Lord. The gift of the bread to the priests showed that the Lord and his people enjoyed a communal meal together. It symbolized their fellowship. It further indicated that the Lord was the provider of the bread that the people had received from the goodness of God who had enabled them to derive their sustenance from the fertile land. Although there is no reference in our passage to the wilderness episode when Israel traversed the wilds of the desert, the bread of the Presence may have brought to the nation's consciousness a reminder of the manna that God gave their fathers. Manna was bread provided by the Lord that gave the people their daily diet during the forty-year sojourn. Without it they would not have survived. Each morning the people awakened to find the bread awaiting them on the ground. They only needed to pick up what food would be used that day (Exodus 16:4, 35). Each morning they could count on the Lord's faithful provision, but the bread would spoil if not eaten and therefore could not be stored up on a long-term basis (16:20). This tested their faith in the Lord's promise for the coming day's food.

The manna and the bread of the Presence pointed forward to the time when God would be present among his people in a way that was not symbolic but actual. This occurred at the incarnation of our Lord Jesus Christ. As Jesus claimed to be the light of the world, he also claimed to be the bread of the world. "I am the living bread," Jesus said, "that came down from heaven. If anyone eats of this bread, he will live forever. And the bread that I will give for the life of the world is my flesh" (John 6:51). The bread that Moses provided could spoil; it was not a permanent solution to the people's hunger.[7] The audience that Jesus addressed was made up of common persons whose lives were dependent on daily bread. We say this in the recitation of the Lord's Prayer: "Give us this day our daily bread" (Matthew 6:11).[8] We today in the Western world rarely face a daily deprivation of food, but ordinary people in ancient times had a daily grind to obtain the food to sustain their families. Jesus, however, spoke more profoundly of their deepest spiritual need—a heavenly bread that would satisfy their souls. Jesus urged the people to receive him as their satisfying bread of life: "Do not work for the food that perishes, but for the food that endures to eternal life, which the Son of Man will give to you. For on him God the Father has set his seal" (John 6:27). This is what God would have us know from the bread of the Presence and from the manna of long ago: Jesus is the bread from God that satisfies and is permanent. This bread does not spoil and does not need replacement. Partake of the Lord Jesus, and our hungry souls will be satisfied with the dynamic, living presence of the Lord. The Lord taught his disciples, "Blessed are you who are hungry now, for you shall be satisfied" (Luke 6:21).

## God Is Our Honored Judge (vv. 10–23)

After instructing the congregation in the proper symbols of God's presence among the congregation, the third reminder is the exhortation to honor the Lord by honoring his "Name." The passage makes an unexpected change in the means of conveying its message. Instead of legislation alone, the text provides a specific example of dishonoring the holy name of God and then follows with the giving of the legislative principle to be obeyed. Once before the book of Leviticus gave such a narrative account followed by legislation. The sons of Aaron offered "unauthorized [margin, strange] fire" at the altar, and the Lord's wrath destroyed the two priests suddenly inside the Tent of Meeting (10:1, 2). This startling event forewarned the priests to manage the holy fires of God responsibly. The Lord then spoke to Aaron directly, instructing him in the proper conduct of the priestly service. At this point in the book of Leviticus, the author gives a matching account, but this time referring to the conduct of the laity. The principle learned was the necessity of the people showing proper honor concerning the Lord's presence in their everyday activities.

The text describes two men who were tangled up in a scuffle, and in the midst of the struggle one of the men "blasphemed the Name, and cursed"

(v. 11). That the one who offended the Lord was of mixed ethnic heritage (v. 10) is probably important for us to take into account. Although he was an Israelite on his mother's side, his father was Egyptian. Perhaps the implication is that he did not have the same respect for the Lord as the average Israelite person. But it did not matter whether the culprit was a full Israelite by birth or a resident alien. There was no exception and no excuse for either group, whether native or alien (v. 16). The person who committed this crime must "bear [the consequences of] his sin" (v. 15). We are not told in the text precisely what the man said, and perhaps this was omitted because the exact words he used were not as important as the principle. What was the "Name" that the man "blasphemed"? "The name of the LORD" (v. 16) was a sacred name and was employed only in the most cautious manner. In later times, the Jewish people refused even to pronounce the Hebrew name, choosing a substitute name instead.[9]

To "curse" meant to treat disrespectfully or show contempt. It is the same word used to "curse" a parent (Exodus 21:17; Leviticus 20:9), thus breaking one of the Ten Commandments that calls for children to "honor" their parents (Exodus 20:12; Deuteronomy 5:16). This word for "curse" meant "revile" or "blaspheme" when used of cursing God (Exodus 22:28). This transgressed the third commandment: "You shall not take the name of the LORD your God in vain, for the LORD will not hold him guiltless who takes his name in vain" (20:7). This is not a matter of profanity alone but any use of the name of the Lord in a presumptuous way, either taking the name falsely in an oath or showing contempt for the Lord God.

Why, we might ask, was cursing the name of God so troubling that the man had to "be put to death" (v. 16)? The importance of God's "Name" is not a mere word, and the blasphemy was not a matter of a ghastly four-letter word. Rather, in the Bible the existence of the Lord's "Name" constituted the personhood and presence of the Lord (cf. Deuteronomy 12:5).[10] "The name of the LORD" (v. 16) was also indicative of his authority. For a prophet or priest to speak or minister in the name of the Lord meant that the person was claiming the approval and authority of God (Deuteronomy 18:15–22). This is why the church baptizes "in the *name* of the Father and of the Son and of the Holy Spirit" (Matthew 28:19). The authority that the church possesses is derived from the Lord God himself, and the actions we take must be in accord with the will of the Lord. By cursing "the Name," the man was dishonoring the person and presence of the Lord as the Covenant Lord.

That the dishonoring of the Lord had life and death consequences is emphasized in this passage. First, the community held the man "in custody" until they learned from the Lord directly what was to be done with him (v. 12). They dared not act independently of the Lord's instructions, lest they too act presumptuously. What the offender had failed to do, the people chose to do—to honor God as Covenant Lord by seeking his guidance. Second, the gravity of the penalty was not lightly considered by the community. There had to be witnesses who had overheard the scurrilous offense (v. 14; cf. Numbers 35:30). And the witnesses were the ones who played a critical role in carrying out the penalty. It is one thing to call for the death penalty, but quite another to have the responsibility to pull the switch. They placed their hands on the head of the criminal, and then twice we are told that "all" of the congregation carried out the death penalty by stoning (vv. 14, 16). The purpose of laying hands on the criminal was to show that the community's guilt was now on the head of the offender. If the community had failed to deal with the blasphemer, the whole community would have incurred guilt. Third, the passage states that the death penalty was merited for this grave offense (v. 16), not giving opportunity for the community to avoid their responsibility. The matter was just as grave for the community as it was for the offender.

This incident precipitated an explicit condemnation and a specific directive as to what the community was to do with the person, after which the passage broadened the discussion to comment on the severity of the death penalty in general and who was deserving of the sentence. Verses 17–22 establish two important principles governing the community's policy of capital punishment. First, there was a difference between the murder of a human being and the killing of an animal. Although the killing of an animal was important, the killing of a human being was far more egregious. To penalize for killing an animal, the offender compensated the animal's owner monetarily. A work animal was vital for tilling and harvesting crops as well as for selling off newborns from the owner's herds. But the killing of a person could not be remedied by a payment. In other cultures in the ancient Near East this could be done but not in Biblical legislation. This is because human life in God's eyes is special—the only creatures made "in the image of God" (Genesis 1:26, 27)—and deserves the utmost protection.[11]

The second principle to be followed regarding the death sentence was just as important. It must be practiced with evenhanded justice by matching the severity of the punishment with the severity of the crime. When the Bible calls for "fracture for fracture, eye for eye, tooth for tooth" (v. 20; cf. Exodus 21:23–27), the passage is not to be taken literally. It is not calling for the maiming of a person. Rather, it removes personal vendettas (Leviticus 19:18), which inevitably escalate into excessive acts of revenge. The Law was actually designed to restrict the extent and severity of the penalty. "'Vengeance is mine, I will repay, says the Lord'" (Romans 12:19; cf. Deuteronomy 32:35). It was calling for impartial judges to render an equitable penalty that fit the crime, the principle of law known as *lex talionis*, a Latin phrase meaning "law of retaliation." Thus, from this strange incident in the book of Leviticus we take away an important lesson: We honor our Lord when we acknowledge him as the Sovereign Judge who demands an accounting of every person's behavior. He is the "judge of the living and the dead" (Acts 10:42; 2 Timothy 4:1; 1 Peter 4:5).

Moreover, we honor him as our Judge and Lord when we who live as members of the Christian community live justly and honestly. If we live in a way that brings disrepute on the Lord Jesus and the Father of Heaven who sent him, we cause others to blaspheme "the Name" (cf. 1 Timothy 6:1; Titus 2:5).[12] The Apostle James warned his readers, "Do not grumble against one another, brothers, so that you may not be judged; behold, the Judge is standing at the door" (James 5:9). But Jesus tells us to go beyond the Old Testament's prescription for just compensation. "You have heard that it was said, 'An eye for an eye and a tooth for a tooth.' But I say to you, Do not resist the one who is evil. But if anyone slaps you on the right cheek, turn to him the other also" (Matthew 5:38, 39). Jesus is telling his disciples that we are not to demand just compensation in a court of law.[13] The life of a Christian must rise above individual claims and put in practice the law of love. We must treat those who would oppose and injure us with love. Love—loving one's enemies—doing what's best for our enemies—that is the measure by which we respond to others.

In our Lord Jesus, we receive the source of our light and life. He also is our heavenly bread that finally and fully satisfies our souls. And he is our Judge who commands us as faithful covenant members of his church to honor him as our Lord and Master.

# 21

# Free at Last!

## LEVITICUS 25:1-55

AN OLD NEGRO SPIRITUAL proclaimed with jubilation:

> Free at last, free at last
> I thank God I'm free at last
> Free at last, free at last
> I thank God I'm free at last
> Way down yonder in the graveyard walk
> I thank God I'm free at last
> Me and my Jesus going to meet and talk
> I thank God I'm free at last
> On my knees when the light pass'd by
> I thank God I'm free at last
> Tho't my soul would rise and fly
> I thank God I'm free at last
> Some of these mornings, bright and fair
> I thank God I'm free at last
> Goin' meet King Jesus in the air
> I thank God I'm free at last

This song declares every Christian's expectation of meeting Jesus in the life to come. It was adapted by Dr. Martin Luther King Jr. to meet the circumstances of the Civil Rights Movement in his famed historic speech at the Lincoln Memorial in Washington, DC on August 28, 1963. His "I Have a Dream" speech ended in these rousing final words:

> . . . when we allow freedom ring, when we let it ring from every village and every hamlet, from every state and every city, we will be able to speed up that day when all of God's children, black men and white men, Jews and

Gentiles, Protestants and Catholics, will be able to join hands and sing in
the words of the old Negro spiritual, "Free at last! Free at last! Thank God
Almighty, we are free at last!"

From Biblical passages to enshrined hymns that the church has historically
sung, there has been a constant in the proclamation of the gospel—namely, men
and women are freed from the bondage of sin and the finality of death. Romans
6:22 declares, "But now that you have been set free from sin and have become
slaves of God, the fruit you get leads to sanctification and its end, eternal life."
All of creation will be set free from its decaying inevitability: "[T]he creation
itself will be set free from its bondage to corruption and obtain the freedom of
the glory of the children of God" (Romans 8:21). We sometimes sing the chorus
of "Victory in Jesus": "O victory in Jesus, my Savior, forever. He sought me and
bought me with His redeeming blood. . . ." Although we speak of the spiritual
release that we have received in the Lord, there is also a victory that concerns our
earthly pilgrimage. The Christian church must declare that the kingdom of God
includes promoting peace and justice as far as possible in this present world.
We do not naively think the world will be perfectly transformed by us. This can
only come to pass by future salvation through Christ at his second coming. But
we must strive toward these goals as much as we can, influencing our culture as
the salt and light of the world. The Scriptures teach the dignity of all men and
women because we are created "in the image of God" (Genesis 1:26, 27; 9:6;
Acts 10:34; James 3:9). Also, the gospel establishes human equality in Christ:
"There is neither Jew nor Greek, there is neither slave nor free, there is no male
and female, for you are all one in Christ Jesus" (Galatians 3:28; cf. Philemon).

The same two aspects of emancipation from slavery are found in our Leviticus passage: (1) social liberation and (2) spiritual liberation. The Leviticus
passage focuses on the release that the sabbatical year and the Year of Jubilee provided Old Testament Israel at the social level. The second level is the
spiritual emancipation that the sabbatical year and the Year of Jubilee foreshadowed—the hope of a final liberty from sin and death through the perfect
Liberator, Jesus Christ, God's Son. We will look at what the sabbatical year
and the Jubilee meant for ancient Israel, and we will learn what we can gain
from them as Christians today. Finally, we will see how the sabbatical year and
the Jubilee pointed ahead to the proclamation of the gospel.

## The Sabbath Rest (vv. 1–7)

The sabbatical year designated a full year's suspension of all normal agricultural activities. The basis for this institution was theological. Its practice

assumed that the land was a gift from God and that he, as the Lord of creation, provided a "rest" for his creation. During this year the work animals and human laborers in the fields and vineyards enjoyed a respite from the daily grind of toil.

*The gift of the land (vv. 1, 2).* The instruction for observing the sabbatical year was directed toward the laypeople, "the people of Israel," not to the clergy. The sabbatical year was for the benefit of the whole community. It could not be put into practice as God wanted if the laypeople—such as landowners, merchants, and community leaders—refused to observe its demands. There were benefits but also costs in carrying out the Lord's instructions. The instructions for the sabbatical year relied on an important expectation: The people would receive from God's hand the land of promise and settle in peace and prosperity. The Lord's instructions regarding the land reflected more, however, than promise. He asserted the divine ownership of the land and showed his generosity by sharing the land with his people. The land was for human use but certainly not abuse. This was not an ecological or economical measure for its own sake, however. Although the practice may have had those effects, the sabbatical year taught a higher spiritual dimension. There is no room in Biblical revelation for deifying Mother Earth or for setting the concerns of "green politics" above the welfare of human beings.

What was the primary lesson that the sabbatical rest taught the people? The land itself is said to "keep a Sabbath to the LORD" (vv. 2, 4). The land was expected, as were the people who inhabited it, to acknowledge the Lordship of God.[1] As the community set aside a weekly Sabbath (Exodus 31:13–17), the people had to permit the land to recognize its divine Owner. The people were the servants of the Lord; the land too was subservient to the Lord (v. 23). By this connection of people and land, there was an inextricable linkage between them. They were to work in concert to benefit mutually under the sovereign rule of God. The people were to respect the land as God's possession and work it in a responsible way. God had created the land and had promised the land to his people for their benefit but never for wanton pillage. The land in turn, by God's enablement, produced for the needs of the community.[2]

*A respite for the land (vv. 3–7).* The pattern of six years followed by the exceptional seventh year indicated a pattern in the life of the people and in the life of the land. This pattern of work followed by rest was inaugurated at creation for creation. Six years of productivity reflected God's merciful provision for his people. There was no interruption in the six agricultural years. The passage assumes that the Lord would bless his people with crops and vineyards. The people would enjoy the peace and bounty that God had promised. The seventh year in which the normal agricultural activity was prohibited showed that the year was reserved by the Lord for the Lord. It is identified twice as "a Sabbath *to* the LORD" (vv. 2, 4) and distinguished as "a Sabbath of solemn rest" (v. 4).³ Although the people were not to participate in the typical activities of sowing, pruning, harvesting, and gathering, they were free to eat the produce that the land produced on its own (v. 6).⁴ Animals too were free to roam about, eating as they pleased. The Sabbath year enabled the varying members of society, whether rich or poor, to enjoy the produce of the land on equal standing (Exodus 23:10, 11).⁵ The plan enabled the land to have its Sabbath, but at the same time the land's yield supplied the needs of the people. The food would be plentiful enough to sustain all members of the community regardless of native or alien status.

### The Jubilee Renewal (vv. 8–55)

The sabbatical year described above is foundational to understanding the importance of the Year of Jubilee, which is the focus of our passage. The passage gives far more attention to its observance because of its greater implications for the life of the community. The word "jubilee" is a transliteration of the Hebrew word *yobel*, not a translation. The word either refers to the trumpet horn sounded at the initiation of the Year of Jubilee (v. 9) or refers to the act of the land bringing forth its produce. The essential principle underlying the Year of Jubilee is spelled out in verse 23, where God says, "The land is mine." This is a striking statement because the land was divinely distributed to the tribes upon their entrance into the land of Canaan. Its distribution among the people was decided by the casting of lots (perhaps like stones or dice) for each tribe, clan, and family (Joshua 19:51). Casting lots was one way that the will of God was made known to the people (cf. Acts 1:26). Although the original allotment of territory was handed down from generation to generation within the family, this was actually a lease because ownership was retained by God. The people were only tenants on the land, and they enjoyed the benefits at the pleasure of the divine Owner (v. 23).

As in our modern rental agreements, there are obligations and restrictions accepted by the lessee when entering into contract for rental, such as a payment schedule and a general regard for the upkeep of the structure. There are usually penalties that kick in if there is failure to comply. If the Israelites defaulted in their obligations as good tenants, they were subject to eviction. The colorful language "vomit" describes their exile: "You shall therefore keep all my statutes and all my rules and do them, that the land where I am bringing you to live may not vomit you out" (Leviticus 20:22). Disobedience to God's word merited eviction. Faithfulness, on the other hand, reaped longevity in the land (vv. 18, 19). The Lord used Israel to expel the Canaanite inhabitants because of the Canaanites' blatant wickedness. The Scriptures say, "Not because of your [Israel's] righteousness or the uprightness of your heart are you going in to possess their land, but because of the wickedness of these nations the LORD your God is driving them out from before you, and that he may confirm the word that the LORD swore to your fathers, to Abraham, to Isaac, and to Jacob" (Deuteronomy 9:5). This shows us that the gift of the land was not a special privilege based on Hebrew ethnicity. It was not that the Lord loved the Israelites more than he loved other people. God held Israel to the same moral standard as he did the nations who had preceded them in the land (Leviticus 20:23).

What is most important for us to remember when considering this passage in Leviticus is the role of tenants and owners. The tenants do not have the authority to dispose of rental property permanently. Today renters sometimes sublease housing to another person, but only on a temporary basis. This is a common practice by college students who sublease an apartment to another person over the summer months until they return to the campus in the fall semester. The practice of subleasing a property must be agreed upon by the owner in the original rental contract. The same was true of Israel's land. The land was a gift, but only provisionally, and therefore the people had limitations in the buying and selling of the divine Owner's property. They could not sell it to another family in perpetuity (v. 23). Concessions were made for the temporary transference of property, but safeguards were put in place to ensure that the allotment returned to the family that had first received the inheritance from the Lord. The land thus held a critical place in the psyche and self-identity of the people. It was concrete evidence that they were counted as members of God's covenant people. To this day we see this same affection for Eretz-Israel, "the land of Israel," by Jews the world over. Although most Jewish people have never seen the land of their ancestors, they are quick to defend it and invest in it. It is part of who they are as a distinct people. The same can be said of families today in our Western world who farm family land or families that own businesses. It is the family's legacy reaching back generations to ancestors who possessed and worked the land.

The loss of land was every bit as devastating for the Israelites as any eviction of a person today from his family homestead. My mother, a child during the deepest period of the economic Depression in the 1930s, recalls the hard times her mother faced as she tried to provide for her two children on her own. Although it has been eighty years since that time, my mother painfully and vividly recalls the day she came home from school to find all their belongings on the front lawn and the sheriff serving eviction papers. Fortunately, her uncle was willing and able to take them in until they could find another place to rent.

God provided a stop-gap measure to render aid to the dispossessed families of Israel. From the instructions God gave the people in the way they were to treat his property, we can learn about the God of grace who has reserved an inheritance for his people and ensured that theirs will be a plentiful future of bounty and blessing. We are reminded of this teaching in the New Testament, which declares that Christians have received an inheritance not of land and temporal riches but, far greater, eternal life and spiritual blessings that God has made sure through Christ our Lord (1 Peter 1:3–5). Our inheritance, unlike the land that Israel possessed, is an eternal blessing that cannot be spoiled or stolen. It is ours to enjoy in part now but is placed in reserve for us in Heaven, awaiting our full inheritance. Jesus promised his disciples on the night of his arrest, "In my Father's house are many rooms. If it were not so, would I have told you that I go to prepare a place for you?" (John 14:2).

*The Jubilee return (vv. 8–34).* The stop-gap measure that God put in place was the Year of the Jubilee. This year was every fiftieth year, the year following seven sabbatical years, yielding forty-nine years. It was announced in the seventh month of the calendar, the most important month for the Hebrews. The tenth day of the month was the momentous Day of Atonement. It was on that day of the Jubilee Year that the trumpet was sounded to announce the year, meaning properties were to be released to the original families as their rightful inheritance from the Lord. How appropriate that it should be on the Day of Atonement, the most important day of repentance and forgiveness! The day when the people acknowledged their sins and their need for God's grace announced liberty. The Day of Atonement meant the liberation of the nation from their sin and guilt, assuring them that their national sins would not stand in the way of another year of blessing in the land. For the Christian we can appreciate this correlation between jubilee and atonement in its fullest sense: "For the Lord himself will descend from heaven with a cry of command, with the voice of an archangel, and with the sound of the trumpet of God. And the dead in Christ will rise first" (1 Thessalonians 4:16).

The Jubilee presupposed that many families had sold off their land to others outside the family because of troubling circumstances, such as crop failures or death in the family. A widow, for example, without adult sons would not be able to care for family land and would sell it off for her own economic viability. This is similar to the case of Naomi and Ruth whose husbands perished, leaving them to themselves to draw daily rations from working the field of the landowner Boaz. The return of the property to the original family at Jubilee, however, could not be settled without equitable payment to the purchaser. The selling and buying of land must be figured according to the number of years before the next Jubilee. The essence of this principle was that the buyer sub-leased the land for a specific number of harvests and therefore was owed for that original investment since he would not obtain the remaining harvests. The proper handling of fair payment was rooted in the people's relationship with God. They were to treat their neighbors justly because of the "fear [of their] God" (v. 17). This is important for us to remember. Our just dealings with others are a reflection of our faithfulness to God. The Lord God demands that we treat our neighbor with love and justice because we love God. These are the two great commandments noted by Jesus—to love God and to love others (Matthew 22:36–40).

In the text a number of specific cases follow, including disposal of tracts of land (vv. 25–28) and special considerations for houses in cities (vv. 29–34). The disposition of the land was most important because it was the most common circumstance since rural life dominated. If a person became poor and sold a portion of his land, there were two possible resolutions (vv. 25–28). First, a relative could step up and purchase the land so as to retain it in the family. The role of the relative was called "nearest redeemer" in verse 25. Other translations may have the phrase "nearest kinsman" or a similar term emphasizing the family connection of the relatives.[6] The Bible describes the Lord as Israel's kinsman-redeemer who delivers Israel from her servitude to sin and to the nations (e.g., Isaiah 41:14). God is qualified as a kinsman because of the covenant relationship that he formed with the nation. The human institution of redemption has its parallel in the Divine Redeemer who saves his people. The second possibility is a farmer who sold his property but at a later time recovers financially. He has the right to purchase back the property for himself. If he does not financially recover or has no family member willing and capable of buying the land, the territory will revert to the first owner in the Year of Jubilee.

*Generosity for the poor and for the slave (vv. 35–55).* But what if the poor landowner, even after selling a portion of this harvest, cannot make a go of his farming? In this case the farmer will call upon a relative to float him a loan and provide his family with food until he can get on his feet financially (vv. 35–38). Since God's people belong to him alone (v. 38) and are not slaves to any other, the relative must treat his unfortunate kinsman well, not further adding to his burden by ostracizing him.[7] A relative who falls on hard times can be an embarrassment to family members. The book of Proverbs acknowledged this likelihood: "The poor is disliked even by his neighbor, but the rich has many friends" (Proverbs 14:20). Moreover, the Leviticus passage says that the relative who lends must not gain interest on the loan or profit on the food supplied to the kinsman (v. 37). This means that the wealthy relative gives the destitute kinsman every opportunity to get ahead without any additional encumbrance. Greed, especially at the expense of a fellow Hebrew, was condemned.[8] Generosity, not greed, was God's expectation of the Israelites since the Lord had given so freely to them. They were in a financial position that enabled them to share freely with others only by God's grace toward them. The goal was for all members of God's covenant to enjoy the fruit of the land because it was each family's inheritance from God. The land's produce was plenteous and unending as long as the people acknowledged the lordship of God by practicing his commandments.

But what if the farmer *still* fails to produce a living based on the loan? The only means left to him was paying his debt by selling himself as an indentured servant to his wealthy relative. An indentured servant was a person who bound himself in a contractual relationship to an employer in order to settle a debt. Crop failure for two or three years in a row spelled disaster for any family of modest means. Drought, pestilence, or raiding marauders threatened the rural Israelites. If this happened to a farmer, his wealthy relative again was forewarned against taking advantage of the impoverished kinsman (vv. 39–44). He was not to treat him as a common debt slave. Debt slavery was a common practice in the ancient world. An Israelite still had protections despite his indebtedness because he was a member of the covenant community and was ultimately a "servant" *only* to God. This is how the chapter concludes in verse 55: "For it is to me that the people of Israel are servants. They are my servants whom I brought out of the land of Egypt: I am the LORD your God." Thus he was to be treated as a hired laborer, not as a slave (v. 40). Our passage shows that humane treatment of the poor is a divine mandate. Consideration for the needy is a mark of a godly person. "A righteous man knows the rights of the poor; a wicked man does not understand such knowledge" (Proverbs 29:7; cf. Deuteronomy 15:7; James 2:1–13).

Although the methods of assisting the disadvantaged today are different from Biblical times, the message is the same. Both individually and collectively, we must set in place opportunities for the poor to succeed financially. We must never be a roadblock or support any roadblocks to a deprived person's escape from poverty. It is presumptuous for us to think that what we have gained in this world's goods came by our own doing. A good God gave us the advantages of intellectual capability, health, and marketable skills that enable us to provide for our families. Christian communities have taken this seriously in our times. They are more involved than ever in providing low- or no-interest loans to the poor in Third World countries where capital for small business entrepreneurship is unavailable. By economic development in poverty-stricken communities, many social ills can be alleviated, such as disease, homelessness, education, and the selling of family members for slave trade. There are many innovative ways that we can be involved; there is no shortage of opportunities. The only shortage is a Christian's *will* to do it.[9]

One more potential situation is addressed in this passage. This is the case of the most destitute farmer who has gone through the preceding steps without recovery. He may be so destitute that he must sell himself to a foreigner (vv. 44–54). This would be on the face of it an embarrassment and the opposite of what God had in mind for his people. Foreigners in God's economy were not to rule over the covenant people. Foreigners were welcomed and well treated by the Hebrews, but they were to be under the social orbit of the native Israelites. Israelites were permitted to purchase slaves who were foreigners but never fellow covenant members (vv. 44–46). In this case the Year of Jubilee ensured that the servant would be released.

We may be troubled by the Bible's apparent acceptance of slavery as an institution. Our proper response is always to condemn institutional slavery. How do we explain the Bible's apparent acceptance of slavery since it is the Word of God? Slavery *as an institution* is not condemned outright in the Scriptures, but those same Scriptures teach that all men and women are created "in the image of God" and so are to be treated with equity and integrity (Genesis 1:26, 27). There have been times when Christians justified the institution of slavery by selectively appealing to Scriptures that regulate slavery.[10] The best way to understand the passages that accept slavery is the teaching that Jesus gave regarding divorce. He clarified that divorce was not the plan of God, but he permitted it, even regulated it (Deuteronomy 24:1–4), because of human "hardness of heart" (Matthew 19:8). Because men and women are sinners and live in a fallen world, such things as divorce, and we can add for our purposes slavery, occur. It is sadly a part of the human experience, and the Bible sets out to first *regulate*[11] treatment of slaves and then to set the grounds for slavery's elimination. The Bible makes it clear that slaves were not mere chattel but had God-given protections and certain rights (e.g., Exodus 21:7–11). For example, a runaway slave *from a foreign country* was not to be returned to his master (Deuteronomy 23:15, 16). The motivation for gentler treatment of slaves was theological: The Israelites had once been slaves in Egypt whom God had delivered. The cruelty that they experienced in Egypt was not tolerated in Israel.

But having said that, we still may not be satisfied that the Bible says enough to condemn slavery or racial bigotry. When we turn to the New Testament we see that Jesus did not specifically outlaw slavery, and the Apostle Paul assumed it when he directed slaves to obey their masters as their Christian duty (Ephesians 6:5–8; 1 Timothy 6:1). Yet we discover that Jesus and Paul also set in motion values that when applied to slavery inevitably broke the back of slavery as an institution. Jesus instructed his disciples that servants, not rulers, epitomized the nature of the kingdom of God: "The Gentiles lord it over" others, he said, but it should not be so among them (Matthew 20:25–28; cf. "Blessed are the poor in spirit, for theirs is the kingdom of heaven," Matthew 5:3). Paul, too, showed that slavery was inconsistent with the gospel. The gospel makes all who believe equal partners in the kingdom of God. Thus, masters and slaves are now spiritual brothers, members of the same body: "There is neither Jew nor Greek, there is neither slave nor free, there is no male and female, for you are all one in Christ Jesus" (Galatians 3:28; cf. 1 Corinthians 7:22). And more importantly, Paul's instructions to his partner in the gospel, the slave-owner Philemon, made it impossible for Philemon to continue in the practice of slavery if he were to take seriously the implications of his new relationship to the returning slave Onesimus. Paul wrote Philemon, "So if you consider me your partner, receive [Onesimus] as you would receive me" (Philemon 17). Philemon and Onesimus were brothers in Christ.

Of course, after the abolition of slavery in England and the United States Christians contended for racial segregation on the basis of the Bible's prohibition of integration with the nations, such as proscribing interracial marriage (Deuteronomy 7:1–4). But the reason for this prohibition was not due to ethnic bias; rather, the religious plurality that resulted from intermarriage with the nations was the threat that gave rise to this prohibition. Such marriages typically meant the corruption of godly life by assimilating pagan idolatry and immorality. There was no inherent difference between people groups, making one group superior to another. The prohibition for religious reasons is akin to the exhortation in Paul's letter to the Corinthians prohibiting marriage between Christians and unbelievers (1 Corinthians 7:39; 2 Corinthians 6:14).

In all the cases of our passage, the motivation for obedience was the Israelite's "fear" of God (vv. 17, 36, 43). Obedience to God's Word was the reason why Israel would agree.[12] The Bible presents a theology of economics, and our passage contributes to our understanding of the proper role of money in the context of our obligations to our fellow humans in and outside our family community. As Christians we do not observe the sabbatical year or Year of Jubilee, but they set forth the proper attitude that we must have toward our financial resources. The money that God has bestowed on us is but a tool to carry out the kingdom mandate of the gospel. The overarching teaching that should guide our attitude is best stated by the Lord Jesus himself: "It is more blessed to give than to receive" (Acts 20:35). Our devotion to Christ who himself gave up his heavenly riches to be poor in spirit in our behalf is the motivation for our Christian charity (2 Corinthians 8:9).

The Year of Jubilee also shows us that only God can provide our release from slavery, debt, and the burdens of this life. The ultimate Year of Jubilee is our release from the cares of this world and the possession of the eternal inheritance promised by the Lord (Matthew 25:34; Ephesians 1:11–14; 1 Peter 1:4, 5). This complete, perfect Year of Jubilee is possible because of Jesus whose death initiated our spiritual and eventual physical jubilee. When Jesus taught in the synagogue of his hometown, Nazareth, he announced the purpose of his teaching by quoting a Jubilee passage from the prophets: "The Spirit of the Lord is upon me, because he has anointed me to proclaim good news to the poor. He has sent me to proclaim liberty to the captives and recovering of sight to the blind, to set at liberty those who are oppressed, to proclaim the year of the Lord's favor" (Luke 4:18–20; Isaiah 61:1, 2). Now is the time to respond to the Year of Jubilee in Jesus that God has announced to us. The trumpet has sounded, debts are canceled, and rest is at hand. Answer the trumpet. Enter by faith into the Jubilee.

# 22

# Grace Has the Last Word

## LEVITICUS 26:1–46

THERE IS ALWAYS AN ADVANTAGE for the speaker who has the last word in a discussion or debate. The last words in any conversation are typically the ones best remembered. Also, the expression *the last word* can refer to ultimate authority, such as, "The doctor has the last word on my physical therapy." That chapter 26 presents the Lord's "last word" on worship and holy living in Leviticus makes this chapter especially important for our Christian lives. The final verse of the chapter reads, "These are the statutes and rules and laws that the LORD made between himself and the people of Israel through Moses on Mount Sinai" (v. 46). This verse implies all of the instructions found in the whole book, not just chapter 26. The verse echoes the very first verse of the book: "The LORD called Moses and spoke to him from the tent of meeting, saying . . ." (1:1). After that the Lord gave Moses the message of the book to the people. So chapter 26 wraps up the revelation made at the Tent of Meeting.

In chapter 26 the Lord sets before the people the choice between obedience and disobedience and describes the consequences that will ensue in each case. If the people choose to obey, the consequences are wonderful blessings. If they choose to disobey, the consequences will be calamitous. But the Lord reveals that the people in the days to come will choose disobedience, and their persistent recalcitrance will result in eventual exile from the land. The history of Israel proved that God was right. Although deserving final annihilation, the Lord promised that in their exile the people would come to their senses and repent. They would be restored to their land, and the blessings of God would flow once again. Why did the Lord relent on his judgment? we may ask ourselves. The passage ends on the Lord's last word on the matter: God's faithfulness to his promises incites him to show grace to the repentant. God himself will change the hearts of the people, and he will restore them.

The chapter conveniently falls into four units. The first unit is verses 1, 2, which refer to two crucial commandments that call for loyalty to God. The final unit is verses 40–46, in which the Lord promises his loyalty to the Israelites. These two units border and encircle the two middle units that dominate the chapter. Verses 3–13 describe the blessings of God, and verses 14–39 describe the curses of God.

## The Gold Standard for Worship (vv. 1, 2)

In a word the gold standard for measuring the loyalty of the people to the Lord is their sole worship and obedience to him. By gold standard I mean the highest example of faithfulness. The passage expresses this by listing two commandments found in the Ten Commandments. The Ten Commandments were the centerpiece of the covenant agreement that God and the Israelites entered into on Mount Sinai (Exodus 20). The covenant included promised blessings but also forewarnings of covenant curses depending on the response of the people to the stipulations of the covenant agreement (cf. Exodus 23:25–33; Deuteronomy 27, 28). The two commandments are connected because they both concern the worship of God.

*False worship (v. 1).* The second commandment in the covenant prohibited the making and worship of idols (Exodus 20:4–6; 34:17; 1 Corinthians 10:7; 1 John 5:21). The worship of idols was universal in ancient religions. Typically, ancient religions boasted of a pantheon of gods and goddesses. Theirs was an inclusive system in assimilating the various gods of the nations into religious syncretism. It was the Israelites who were the "odd" ones, for they worshiped a God who could not be represented by any physical object. God is Spirit and must be worshiped in spirit (John 4:23, 24). The idea that any deity could be captured in a stone or metal idol is the height of spiritual darkness, utter foolishness (Psalm 14:1; 53:1; Isaiah 41:29; 44:9–20; 1 Corinthians 8:4). Christian worship today is also countercultural, not in step with the prevailing notion that the worship of God can be legitimate as long as it is moral and sincere. The Christian claim that only through Christ can a person come to God is an unthinkable tenet today. This, it is said by our popular culture, reflects the West's intolerance and prejudice. Christian orthodoxy that teaches there is but one Savior and Mediator, the Lord Jesus Christ who is the Son of God, has been denigrated as nothing more than religious dogma used for subjugating others by the ruling powers of Western culture.

If we give in to the pressures of the popular voices today, we fail to worship God in the only means whereby we can authentically know God and serve him. The clearest statement of this is Jesus' own words, "I am the way, and the truth, and the life. No one comes to the Father except through me" (John 14:6). But elsewhere the New Testament continues to make this abundantly clear: "For there is one God, and there is one mediator between God and men, the man Christ Jesus" (1 Timothy 2:5).

*True worship (v. 2).* The positive call to true worship is the faithful observance of God's "Sabbaths" and "reverence [for God's] sanctuary" (also Leviticus 19:30). "Reverence" means "to stand in awe" of God.[1] The word occurs only three times in the book of Leviticus, and each time it is tied to the observance of Sabbath. The point is to honor God by showing obedience, as in the exhortation, "Every one of you shall revere his mother and his father" (19:3). In particular God says "*my* Sabbaths" and "*my* sanctuary." These are distinctive of their God. They are his and must be honored by following his instructions. Chapter 25 called for the people to honor the Sabbath year and the Year of Jubilee. Our passage builds on this. Here the Lord calls for the people to observe his Sabbaths, which would include the two just mentioned and the weekly Sabbath. The Sabbath day was the sign of God's covenant with the Israelites (Exodus 31:13, 17). By keeping Sabbath the Israelites were expressing in a tangible way their surrender to the rule of God. It was their visible weekly claim on God's promises.

The mention of "sanctuary" refers to the former instructions of Leviticus that pertain to the central place of worship in the life of the community. The Tent of Meeting was in the middle of the wilderness camp. This symbolized that God was the center of Israel's identity. He and he alone was the One who united them into a nation and who had redeemed them from Egyptian bondage. The purity of the sanctuary was essential in the worship of the people. It was at the various sanctuaries of the ancient peoples that their gods and goddesses were known by their clay, wooden, and metal idols. But Israel's sanctuary had no such images. The image of God was the people themselves. Keeping the instructions regarding the sanctuary, properly carrying out the sacrifices by the priest and people, and the holy living of the people exhibited the people's reverence for God in his sanctuary. The prophet Habakkuk said it well: "But the Lord is in his holy temple; let all the earth keep silence before him" (Habakkuk 2:20). We as Christians know that the temple of the Lord is not of the same sort as found in the Old Testament. Now the presence of God in Christ, the incarnational tabernacle of God (John 1:14), has made worship centered in a person, not a place. We come to the Lord only through the incarnational Jesus, whose body is the way into the presence of the Father (John 2:19–21; Hebrews 9).

### Blessings for His People (vv. 3–13)

*Blessing with obedience (v. 3).* God promised his people blessings. But the continuation of the blessings was coupled with the obedient behavior of the Israelites. It was common in ancient covenants to list benefits for the faithful observance of the covenant's stipulations. When nations entered into treaties, the Great King promised benefits to vassal kings who entered into the treaty. The most important requirement of a vassal king was loyalty to the Great King who received tribute from the vassal.[2] In the setting of Biblical theology the Great King is the Lord God, and his vassals are the twelve tribes of Israel. The Lord is Protector and Provider of Israel, and the Israelites are loyal subjects who bring offerings of worship.

*What is a blessing? (vv. 4–13).* The blessings that the passage lists were appropriate ones for Israel as a nation. These were national promises and were not necessarily applicable in every case to an individual Israelite. The word "blessing" (*barak*) is common in the Old Testament Scriptures. The blessings that God promised Abraham and his descendants were chiefly expressed as material blessings, especially prosperity and protection. The reason for national promises of blessing was the purpose of the blessings. God's plan was to deliver all nations from their sins and to form a living relationship with the nations. He did this by creating a special nation that would be his vehicle of grace and salvation. Abraham and his descendants were blessed by God so they could found a nation that prospered and enjoyed security, enabling them to survive and be a witness to the nations (Genesis 12:1–3). But the promise of blessing was not solely material in nature: "And I will walk among you and will be your God, and you shall be my people" (v. 12).[3] Blessing included the presence of God among his people and the spiritual benefits of knowing the one true, living God (Psalm 103:2; 116:12). He will love and care for his people (Deuteronomy 7:13).

The blessings listed are four. First, the Lord promises the seasonal rains that will produce dependable harvests. Second, the Lord will grant the people peace in the land. This peace is achieved by driving out harmful beasts that otherwise would prowl the land, mauling people and robbing animal herds. Also, this peace is secured by the Lord's granting Israel victory over her national enemies. The third blessing is the promise of population increase, which was evidence of God's covenant commitment to Israel (cf. Genesis 1:28; 9:1; 17:20; Deuteronomy 28:11). The last blessing is the promise of God's enduring presence among his people. "I will walk among you," he says (v. 12), indicating the continuance of the covenant. In summary the blessings regard security and prosperity.

*Blessings for Christians.* After naming the blessings promised to the people of Israel so long ago, we are challenged to think about how God's character of blessing his people applies to Christians today. We typically think of our God as a good God who provides for his people. There is recognition in the New Testament that there are material blessings as well as spiritual ones (Romans 15:27). Jesus taught in his Sermon on the Mount, "Therefore do not be anxious, saying, 'What shall we eat?' or 'What shall we drink?' or 'What shall we wear?' For the Gentiles seek after all these things, and your heavenly Father knows that you need them all" (Matthew 6:31, 32). Or consider Jesus' comforting words in Luke 11:9–12: "And I tell you, ask, and it will be given to you; seek, and you will find; knock, and it will be opened to you. For everyone who asks receives, and the one who seeks finds, and to the one who knocks it will be opened. What father among you, if his son asks for a fish, will instead of a fish give him a serpent; or if he asks for an egg, will give him a scorpion?"

We usually think of blessings as those answers that meet an immediate crisis, such as healing for sickness, resources for indebtedness, or reconciliation for troubled marriages. Wherever the need is most acute at the moment, we reckon the fillings of those needs as blessings. And indeed they are blessings for which we give thanks to God. When we consider, however, the idea and language of "bless" in the New Testament, it usually refers to the spiritual benefits that God has secured for us through Christ. The Beatitudes especially point us to the spiritual promises that are received by those who are kingdom citizens (Matthew 5:3–12). The two passages that we quoted above that address the material needs of believers clarify that the intention of answering our physical needs is so we can focus on the spiritual inheritance God has for us in Christ. In the Sermon on the Mount, Jesus adds to the passage already quoted, "But seek first the kingdom of God and his righteousness, and all these things will be added to you" (Matthew 6:33). And in speaking of the Father's love for his children, Jesus concluded with, "If you then, who are evil, know how to give good gifts to your children, how much more will the heavenly Father give the Holy Spirit to those who ask him!" (Luke 11:13). The truly prized blessing that God has for us is the gift of the Holy Spirit in the life of believers. Our blessings are said to be "every spiritual blessing in the heavenly places" (Ephesians 1:3). The blessings we have are those of the saving grace of the gospel (Acts 3:26; 1 Corinthians 9:23; Galatians 3:14), the crown of eternal life (James 1:12), spiritual understanding and knowledge (Colossians 1:9), prayer (2 Corinthians 1:11), spiritual gifts and love (1 Corinthians 12—14), spiritual peace, hope, and assurance (Philippians 4:7–9; Titus 2:13), and spiritual fruit (Galatians 5:22, 23).

God's blessing for his people is at its heart the *relationship* with God that he has made possible through his Son, Jesus. For most Christians in the world today and across the centuries, the idea that the blessedness of Christian living is the result of bartering with God over accrued wealth and emotional happiness is totally foreign. In fact, in many places in the world today becoming Christian means the loss of financial security, the fracturing of family ties, and the sadness of personal trials. We must think in terms of a vibrant meaningful relationship with God as the blessedness of Christian living. We sing the hymn's refrain, "I am satisfied with Jesus, But the question comes to me, As I think of Calvary, Is my Master satisfied with me?" When B. B. McKinney penned these words, he also explained in the lyrics of the hymn the meaning of his satisfaction with Jesus: "[Jesus] has done so much for me: He has suffered to redeem me, He has died to set me free."[4] The blessedness of belonging to Jesus and Jesus belonging to us is the greatest benefit of all. We may compare this to our relationship with a spouse or family members. What makes our lives rich in our relationships with others is to know, love, and trust one another. Yes, my spouse meets material and physical needs, too, but it is not that feature of our relationship that makes marriage a marriage. One could hire a nurse or servant to do the same tasks of domestic living. What makes a relationship rich beyond measure is sharing in one another's lives, making memories and growing old together.

## Curses for God's People (vv. 14–39)

*Curses for disobedience (vv. 14, 15).* God's covenant with Israel also included curses for disobedience (e.g., Deuteronomy 11:26, 29; 30:1, 19; Joshua 8:34). In this Leviticus text the word *curse* does not occur, but the catalog of punishments named in the text match those of the curses enumerated in Deuteronomy 28 and other passages. (1) We first notice that much more is said about the penalties than the blessings. This corresponds to ancient covenants. The forewarnings are more detailed than the benefits because the force of the forewarning was the likelihood of its necessity. Disobedience was the predisposition of Israel (Exodus 32:9). (2) Yet we see that the passage emphasizes the conditional nature of the penalties by the recurring use of the preposition "if" in verses 14, 15. The people have the responsibility of right behavior. If the penalties rain upon Israel, it is the people's own fault, not fickleness on God's part. (3) Another indication of God's standpoint toward Israel's disobedience is reflected by the growing intensity of the penalties as they are listed. God showed mercy toward Israel's disobedience. The Lord never enjoyed penalizing the Israelites. The recurring "if" in verses 18 and following show the stepping up of the penalties because of the continued resistance of the Israelites. Verse 18 reads, "And if in spite of this you will not listen to me . . ." Repeatedly the Lord warned that failure to respond to each judgment meant a greater judgment "sevenfold" (vv. 18, 21, 24, 28). God gave measured responses to the sins of Israel with the goal of reclaiming them. Repentance would mean the end of their trials, if they would only repent.

*What is a curse?* Modern conceptions of curses should not be the way we understand the Biblical idea of *curse*. Curses today are usually considered magical incantations, specially worded formulas that set in motion evil penalties, often in the setting of a vendetta against someone. They are akin to hexes, which presuppose that there is power in the words spoken that affect the curse of the magical words. The victim believes himself doomed by the curse and can only appeal to another spoken formulation that will reverse the curse. The Biblical view of curse is not magical at all. The words spoken are not inherently powerful, able to bring about curse or blessing. There is no repertoire of magical chants that cause irreversible suffering. Moreover, Biblical curses are *not* based on ritual performance, that is, a sequence of special rites that call upon mystical cosmic powers to override the wishes and behaviors of people, be they good or evil. Blessings and curses are the result of God's moral order in the universe. By his autonomous will, God governs by his sovereign power. His judgments are rooted in his moral character and his right to sovereign rule. God's words are effective because he is supreme ruler of creation and history.

Superstitious incantations or sorceries are strongly condemned in the Bible because they are beliefs that in effect rival the rightful rule of God. The means whereby people know the will of God is the revelation of God's word through his appointed prophets and apostles. And true worshipers of God submit to God's will in faithful obedience. To resort to magical arts to learn of or to circumvent God's will is cast in the Bible as open rebellion against the rule of God (Deuteronomy 18:9–22; Galatians 5:20). Also, Biblical curses do not set in motion inevitable outcomes because they are conditional in nature. They are conditioned by human behavior, which permits genuine repentance and so God can choose to reverse the judgment he has cast.

The word for "curse" (*'arar*) in the Old Testament (for example, Deuteronomy 27:15; 28:16) means simply the opposite consequences of blessings. In our passage, however, we read the specific judgments that are the curses forewarned by God. These include disease, pestilence, famine, drought, wild beasts, foreign enemies, and finally national exile. It is God who brings these increasingly severe calamities. The pronoun "I" refers repeatedly to God's initiation of the various judgments, including the most severe—the dissolution of the nation. Verse 33 reads, "*I* will scatter you among the nations." God does not hesitate to take responsibility for the judgments that occur. He does not leave any room for a rival power or authority or some all-powerful principle of justice that cannot bend. He determines the outcome according to his will. But this does not mean he disregards the accountability of the people themselves. On the contrary, the passage assumes that the choices made by the people are real and have real outcomes related to those choices. The Lord's judgments evidence a correspondence of mercy and severity in relation to the egregious character of the crimes committed by the people. His judgment does not exceed the nature of the crime. Thus, the most awful judgment of deportation comes only at the end of a series of trials designed to avert the final cataclysm.

*Discipline for Christians.* As in the case of the blessings, we must ask if Christians live under the threat of the judgments listed in the covenant made with Israel. Do we find in the New Testament Scriptures a list of the curses that can befall a disobedient Christian? The quick answer is no. The New Testament nowhere lists penalties against Christians in the same sense as our Leviticus passage.[5] Rather, the New Testament describes the response of God to Christian disobedience as "discipline." The words for "punishment" and "penalty" in the Greek New Testament describe retribution that inflicts suffering. The term "discipline" (*paideuo*) means to chasten or correct with the view of teaching right behavior.[6] The writer to the Hebrews in 12:5–11 compares Christian discipline to the discipline that children receive from their parents. He concludes: "[God] disciplines us for our good, that we may share his holiness. For the moment all discipline seems painful rather than pleasant, but later it yields the peaceful fruit of righteousness to those who have been trained by it" (vv. 10b, 11). The discipline that we receive shows that we are valued by God because he cares for us. A basketball coach invests time and energy in those players who have potential for success, whereas he neglects others who don't show promise of making the team. God does not condemn us, but he also does not neglect our spiritual training. Punishment is for those who stubbornly reject the gospel and die in their sins, but discipline is for those who are part of the family of God and who grow up into good behavior.

Why is it that Christians do not suffer God's eternal wrath? Why are Christians not accursed by God? Jesus took upon himself the curse of disobedience and suffered death on the cross for us. The Apostle Paul shows this in Galatians 3:10–14:

For all who rely on works of the law are under a curse; for it is written, "Cursed be everyone who does not abide by all things written in the Book of the Law, and do them." Now it is evident that no one is justified before God by the law, for "The righteous shall live by faith." But the law is not of faith, rather "The one who does them shall live by them." Christ redeemed us from the curse of the law by becoming a curse for us—for it is written, "Cursed is everyone who is hanged on a tree"—so that in Christ Jesus the blessing of Abraham might come to the Gentiles, so that we might receive the promised Spirit through faith.[7]

We were not exempted from the wrath of God because of our sorrow over our sins, and not because God sympathetically understood our shortcomings, choosing to let us off scot-free. Rather, God showed his mercy toward us as sinners because Jesus on the cross bore the wrath of God against human sin (Romans 5:10). This is indeed good news!

### Repentance and Restoration of God's People (vv. 40–46)

Despite the obstinacy of the people of Israel, the Lord God was not through with his people altogether. Grace is his last word in this chapter. After purging the people of their sins, he promised to restore them to their land and prosperity. Historically, we know that the people went into exile, but the story of Israel continued (e.g., Ezra 1—6). God brought them back from their exile, establishing them once again in their land. The covenant always held out hope because the Lord committed himself to fulfill his promises to their fathers by saving his people from their sins (Exodus 6:1–8; Deuteronomy 7:7, 8; 30:1–10). It was due to their sins, not God's disregard, that the people would experience national devastation. Restoration was promised, but only after repentance and confession of their sins. Yet, how could they change their "uncircumcised" hearts (v. 41) toward God since they were so spiritually incorrigible? The description "uncircumcised" meant that the people were not in right relationship with God, for the covenant required the people to commit themselves to God by *spiritually* circumcising their hearts (Deuteronomy 10:16). Only God could regenerate their hearts. Verse 41 reflects this spiritual regeneration of the human heart: "if then their uncircumcised heart is humbled." The text does not read, "if the people humble their hearts"; rather, the passive construction occurs in the passage, "is humbled."[8] God humbles them; he is the one who spiritually circumcises his people (Deuteronomy 30:16). Christian regeneration of the heart can only be achieved through Christ who circumcises our hearts: "In him also you were circumcised with a circumcision made without hands, by putting off the body of the flesh, by the circumcision of Christ"

(Colossians 2:11; cf. Philippians 3:3). It is incumbent upon all people today to repent of their sins and place their trust in the Lord Jesus Christ as the Savior who has taken away our sins by his death on the cross (e.g., Acts 17:30b; Colossians 2:14). In the future New Jerusalem there will be no "accursed" thing, only the blessing of the Lamb: "No longer will there be anything accursed, but the throne of God and of the Lamb will be in it, and his servants will worship him" (Revelation 22:3).

# 23

# Promises

LEVITICUS 27:1–34

THERE IS ONLY ONE PROBLEM with making a promise—keeping it! This is especially true in our day since fulfilling a pledge does not have the same importance now as it once did. We live in a fast-paced world in which being first is more valued in many cases than being right. Since the mind-set is to "get out in front," it is not surprising that this fosters hasty and regrettable decisions. Some call this "buyer's remorse." At one time this expression referred to buying a home, but now the phrase can refer to almost anything. The popularity of skin tattoos in the last few years has produced a trail of tears by those who regret indulging in the fad. "Think before you ink" is the now-popular cautionary word of advice to potential customers.

The final chapter in the book of Leviticus concerns making vows. A vow is simply a pledge a person makes. We pledge allegiance to the United States or we say our wedding vows. Sometimes people make commitments to God. These can be formal, such as monastic vows taken in a Roman Catholic Church order, or they may be informal promises whispered only in our souls when trouble hits home. The book of Leviticus unexpectedly ends on the subject of fulfilling vows to the Lord. The chapter's instructions regulate the procedures for vows. The chapter seems anticlimactic. The previous chapter offered what might seem a more compelling conclusion to the book. It listed the blessings and curses that pertain to Israel's covenant with God based on the behavior of the people. But that is the answer to our surprise. The book closes on the subject of vows because the whole book of Leviticus has concerned the promises that God made to his people. He had committed through a covenant agreement to dwell among his people if they would live up to the obligations they had sworn to keep. Since God was faithful in all instances to his vow, the question naturally arises, how are you doing in fulfilling your pledge to God? The chapter presupposes that the Israelites would make vows. Previously in the book there were instructions regarding animal sacrifices that fulfilled vow offerings (chapters 7, 22). Vow offerings were gifts to the Lord at completion of a vow made to the Lord, often given in thanksgiving to God for deliverance (e.g., Psalm 56:12).

Although there are many details in this chapter that do not correspond to Christian living today, it contains a message that still holds true for us. The message is one that we particularly need to hear because of the ready temptation today to renegotiate, so to speak, our commitments to God. The chapter's topics include the dedication of persons and the dedication of possessions to the service of the Lord.

## Promises and More Promises

Before we read the passage, however, we must set the stage for our understanding. The instructions concerning vows assume four important Biblical teachings.

*God is generous.* First, a whole chapter given to the regulations of vows assumes that vows made to the Lord were sufficiently commonplace to merit such focused attention. And why not? Vows were offered out of a heart that was thankful to God for his goodness and mercy. God was worshiped because he was the Divine Caretaker of Israel who had redeemed it, provided for it, and protected it. The Israelites individually and collectively owed their existence and liberation from slavery to the kindness of God. He enabled all that they were and all that they had. Their relationship with God defined who they were. Apart from the Lord the people had no purpose. God established expectations of them since they belonged to him.

*God is true.* God's promises are always reliable because he is faithful (e.g., 2 Samuel 7:28; Psalm 18:30). The certainty of the gospel in the New Testament depends on the truthfulness of God's promises realized in Christ. "For all the promises of God find their Yes in [Jesus Christ]. That is why it is through him that we utter our Amen to God for his glory" (2 Corinthians 1:20). That God is true is essential to the exhortation in Leviticus 27 that Israel too must be true to her vows.

*God's people must be true.* If God is true, then his people too must be true. The faithfulness of God made it incumbent upon the Israelites to respond in kind, faithfully carrying out their vows to God and to others. The psalmist declared, "Make your vows to the LORD your God and perform them; let all around him bring gifts to him who is to be feared" (Psalm 76:11). Jesus taught in the Sermon on the Mount, "Let what you say be simply 'Yes' or 'No'; anything more than this comes from evil" (Matthew 5:37). Being honest in our response to God and in our dealings with others is Jesus' expectation of a kingdom citizen.

*God's people are sinners.* The flip side to this commitment, however, was the reality that the Israelites were no more than sinful human beings. They retained all the human failings that people have despite what God had been to them and what he had done for them. When it came to making vows, sometimes they had made them based on momentary enthusiasm without much thought given to the consequences of their actions. Also, they sinned at times by neglecting their vows, refusing to fulfill their intentions. They talked a good game but failed to play it out. The Bible warns against rash decisions. "It is a snare to say rashly, 'It is holy,' and to reflect only after making vows" (Proverbs 20:25). What this means is that if a person makes a dedication to the service of God, it must be a seriously considered decision, not entered into quickly.

Now we can turn to the text and learn what the Israelites could devote to the Lord. The chapter offers two broad categories of vows—vows that concern dedicated persons (vv. 1–8) and vows concerning dedicated possessions (vv. 9–25).

## A Promised Life (vv. 1–8)

The opening paragraph considers the most important commitment that a person can make to the service of God—the dedication of a human life. We make commitments at important points in our lives that involve our whole person. Marriage and parenting are the most common commitments. We as Christians also make the most deep-seated commitment of all when we entrust ourselves to Jesus Christ for salvation. The Apostle Paul says in Romans 12:1, "I appeal to you therefore, brothers, by the mercies of God, to present your bodies as a living sacrifice, holy and acceptable to God, which is your spiritual worship." For Christians, marriage vows and parenting rest on our decision to invest our lives in Jesus wholeheartedly. We are more faithful spouses and parents because we are Christian spouses and parents. Our business practices exhibit more integrity than otherwise because we are Christian businessmen and women. When we compromise our Christian allegiance, it inevitably shows itself in our human relationships too.

*The value of a committed life (vv. 1–7).* Leviticus recognizes the value of persons dedicated to the service of the Lord. Monetary values were assigned to persons dedicated to the Lord based on their capacity to do manual labor. Ask any employer and he will tell you that the persons most committed to the success of a company are also the persons most heavily invested in that goal, working tirelessly and honestly. Committed employees are a special asset that may not specifically show up on a balance sheet or inventory. Teachers will tell you the same. A devoted student makes a significant difference in the attitude and learning achievements of the whole class. These persons are, in a word, invaluable. The Israelites could dedicate members of their family, slaves, or themselves to the Lord's service. Hannah, the mother of Samuel, for example, devoted her son to the service of the holy tabernacle (1 Samuel 1:11). But the service of the Lord had its natural limitations since not all could help in the precincts of the Tent of Meeting. Only the priests and Levites could actually carry out the work of the Lord. Moreover, the tabernacle service in most circumstances required financial resources more than people. Therefore, it was possible for the Israelites to make a monetary contribution to meet the obligation by paying a sum based on the evaluation of the priest. The exchange of a monetary figure is called redeeming, meaning buying back the person.

Two factors contributed to the values placed on the persons dedicated— gender and age. The difference in the values corresponded to the reality that people in the prime of their lives make a better contribution, and generally speaking, males are more physically able for labor. The valuations do not reflect the inherent value of any person. All persons are valued by God. The Lord welcomes all who wish to dedicate themselves to his service. The Nazirite vow, for instance, was open to men and women (Numbers 6:2). That the issue was not a matter of gender alone is seen in the fact that a woman of older age was naturally more useful than a male who was a child or elderly. A woman at her peak health merited thirty shekels, whereas an elderly man was valued at only fifteen shekels (vv. 4, 7).

*The value of a common life (v. 8).* The valuations were significantly costly. Some commentators have suggested that the typical income of a person was one shekel per month.[1] People of modest means rarely could afford to make this kind of contribution to the service of the Lord. But the Lord did not shut them out. It didn't matter if they were not prosperous. What mattered was if the person making the vow had a heart for God. Whatever his financial station, a person devoted to God donated a portion of his income to the Lord. The instructions included a concession for the poor, who were held to a standard that took into account their meager wages. The procedure called for the poor person to appear before the priest, who made an evaluation according to the person's financial ability. That God would have a special accommodation for the poor is consistent with the benevolent attitude that God takes toward the poor in the Bible. They are especially dear to the heart of God. Jesus said, "Blessed are the poor in spirit, for theirs is the kingdom of heaven" (Matthew 5:3). Leviticus makes special concessions to the poor in the various sacrificial and purity laws (e.g., 5:7, 11; 12:8; 23:22).

What this passage tells us is what we know from the New Testament Scriptures. When it comes to dedicating our gifts to the Lord, the first thing we must do is give ourselves. In commending the Christians in Macedonia for sharing out of their means with the ministry of the church in Jerusalem, the Apostle Paul said of them, "[T]hey gave themselves *first* to the Lord and then by the will of God to us" (2 Corinthians 8:5). The greatest gift is a committed life to the Lord. Once we have given ourselves to the kingdom's work, then the release of our possessions more easily follows. The decision to give is already determined by our prior personal commitment to Christ. An example of the interrelationship of commitment to Christ and the yielding of our possessions is the case of Christian parents who accept the decision of adult children to surrender to foreign missions. This is a true test of a mother and father's commitment to the gospel. A genuine sacrifice is made. Aging parents may never see their children and grandchildren again. This is the depth of commitment that we as Christian parents teach our children to have. Do we make good on such pledges when God calls us or our loved ones to his service?

Another feature of the passage that is familiar to readers of the New Testament is the teaching on voluntary, proportional giving. Second Corinthians praises the Macedonian Christians who "gave according to their means . . . and beyond their means, of their own accord" (2 Corinthians 8:3). The Israelites gave according to their ability to serve, both in terms of their physical capability and their financial ability. It was not a matter of whether one person was more devoted because he could give more; the valuations were set according to a person's capacity. Jesus pointed out to his disciples the sacrificial giving of a widow who devoted her meager two coins to the temple's treasury, yet it was all she had. Others gave more money but less of themselves than she to the Lord, for she gave all (Mark 12:41–44). God does not ask of us more than he has enabled us to give. The issue for us, however, is really not our ability to give. It is a matter of our desire to give. If we desire to give ourselves to the Lord, then we will prioritize our expenditures, ensuring that we give of our possessions freely. By giving to the service of the Lord we are expressing our recognition of Christ's love for us. It is our act of devotion to God.

## A Promised Possession (vv. 9–25)

Since the Lord delivered and abundantly blessed them, individuals expressed vows of thanksgiving by dedicating their material assets. This meant giving animals, houses, and tracts of land. The patriarch Jacob made such a vow to the Lord, swearing to return a tenth part of all that he might acquire if the Lord returned him to his homeland safely (Genesis 28:20–22). Today people will sometimes bequeath to charitable organizations cars, houses, furniture, and properties. We call this "giving in kind." These items are liquidated, and the monies are used for operating the charity or the church. Regulations in Leviticus 27 set the practice in the framework of Israel's covenant commitment to God.

*Animals "holy" to the Lord (vv. 9–13).* Animals pledged to the Lord might be of two kinds—clean or unclean animals. Chapter 11 detailed what was a "clean" animal; these species were fitting for an offering since they could be presented at the altar to the Lord. "Unclean" animals were animals that did not qualify for an offering presented on the altar. Clean animals were deemed "holy" in our text because they were consecrated to the worship of God. Once a person had vowed a clean animal, he was prohibited from substituting an animal of less value. If he tried to do so, both the original and substitute animals would be deemed "holy," and therefore both would belong to the sanctuary. The animals could not be redeemed. In the case of an "unclean" animal, the priest evaluated it and set a redemption price. The Israelite could redeem it by paying the valuation plus a 20 percent surcharge. What we see from this example is that making vows to the Lord was a costly business and required the careful decision of the worshiper. Israelites viewed their pledges far more seriously than people seem to think of them today. The Bible encourages and expects Christians to give of their resources, but the Bible also expects us to be thoughtful and loyal in our giving. We only trivialize God when we make empty promises or half-baked ones.

*Houses and land are "holy gift[s]" to the Lord (vv. 14–29).* A person might choose to "dedicate" his house or land to the service of God, making such donations "a holy gift" (vv. 14, 21, 23). The word "dedicates" is the translation of a word meaning "to consecrate," that is, to contribute something or someone to the sacred work of the Lord (e.g., vv. 14, 16).[2] In the case of a house, the same rules applied to it as for unclean animals. The priest appraised the worth of the house, and the owner could redeem it by adding 20 percent of the assessment.

The dedication of land, however, was a more complicated matter and required further explanation. Without going into too many details, we can summarize by observing that the rules of depositing land were influenced by three factors. First, the rules were adjusted based on the custody of the property—whether the land belonged to the donor presently or if it had been sold or purchased (v. 22)—in other words, the custody of the land. Second, the custom of Jubilee took precedence in evaluating the worth of the land. In the Year of Jubilee, land reverted to the original family ownership (25:8–55). This meant that the priest's evaluation included calculating the number of harvests that remained until the Year of Jubilee. And third, the monetary measure of the assessed value was consistently the same, specifically here called "the shekel of the sanctuary" (v. 25).[3]

The dedication of such costly items showed the enthusiasm that a person had for the worship and ministry of the sanctuary. Making and faithfully keeping one's vows was a sign of a person's spiritual condition. Vows were considered holy gifts to the Lord that were to be given out of a holy motivation and for a holy purpose.[4] The psalmist declared, "So will I ever sing praises to your name, as I perform my vows day after day" (Psalm 61:8). A vow offering that celebrated the fulfillment of a vow usually was an animal sacrifice and bread offerings (Leviticus 7:11–36). The vow offering was one of three kinds of peace offerings, in addition to thanksgiving offerings and freewill gifts. Portions of the animal not burned up on the altar were eaten by the priests and the worshiper.[5] A fellowship meal concluded the peace offering, and family, friends, and the poor were invited (Deuteronomy 12:7, 12, 18; 26:12–15; Psalm 22:25, 26). This symbolized fellowship with God and with the community, for the peace offering was a "food" gift to the Lord (Leviticus 3:11, 16).

## A Promise with Integrity (vv. 26–34)

Because of the human temptation to renege on promises or manipulate the system, the regulations closed potential loopholes and encouraged godly behavior. The importance of integrity in our promises is strikingly illustrated by the frightening deaths of a husband and wife in the early days of the church. Acts 5:1–11 recounts the lies of Ananias and Sapphira who gave to the church proceeds from the sale of land—all to their credit—but lied to the Holy Spirit by falsely claiming that they gave *all* of the proceeds although they had kept some back for themselves. Their crime was not that they held some back but that they made false pretenses. Our Leviticus passage addresses three ways that a person may have attempted to dodge his responsibility.

*Dedicating the firstborn (vv. 26, 27).* The Law already required that all firstborn children and animals belonged to the Lord (Exodus 13:2). These firstborn could not be dedicated to the Lord a second time as a fulfillment of a special pledge. This would be akin to offering up a tithe to the Lord as both your regular gift to the church and also as a special offering to the service of the church. The firstborn of unclean animals were redeemable, however, since they could not be offered to the Lord on the altar.

*Devoted things (vv. 28, 29).* The same principle applied to land, animals, and persons devoted to the Lord. "Devoted" items were totally restricted to the Lord's service as shown by their identity in the text as "most holy" gifts. "Devoted" items or persons could not be redeemed. The word "devoted" in the text is the same word used for "putting something or someone under the ban." This was true of cities, persons, and things committed to total destruction because they were an offense to the Lord.[6] Such were the cities that made war against the Israelites (Joshua 6:17; cf. Achan's sin, 7:12, 13). Persons "devoted" to the Lord were probably slaves who were committed to service in the sanctuary by their owners (v. 28). Those who were "put to death" were persons who had been assigned to destruction, such as criminals and prisoners of war (v. 29). We must assume that this fatal decision was in the hands of an appropriate tribunal as the Mosaic law called for (Numbers 35:30–32).[7] Since these persons were already given over to the Lord, they could not be redeemed. This was true of murderers, whose lives could not be spared by paying a monetary penalty.

*Tithes (vv. 30–33).* The third loophole was the use of a tithe. The people were commanded to offer up a tithe of all their land's produce and of all their herds as the portion belonging to the service of the Lord's sanctuary (Numbers 18:21–29; Deuteronomy 14:22–29). Since tithes were already set aside as holy, they could not be offered again in the case of a vow. An exception permitted here is the tithe of agricultural products that could be translated into money. In this case the Israelite must add a fifth to the valuation as in the ordinary vows. Animals, however, destined for the sanctuary could not be redeemed.

## Promises We Offer

In many ways the New Testament teaching on giving to the Lord parallels what we have discovered for the conduct of vows and peace offerings. Hebrews 13 exhorts us, "Do not neglect to do good and to share what you have, for such sacrifices are pleasing to God" (Hebrews 13:16). The giving practices of the church included giving liberally, faithfully, and proportionally. It was a yardstick measuring the spiritual condition of a Christian and of a church. Giving to the service of the Lord reflects the sacrificial giving of Christ who set aside his personal prerogatives to provide the riches of glory for us who

were impoverished by our sin. For a Christian, material wealth and their acquisitions are subject to spiritual goals. We don't have a choice. Each master
demands a complete commitment, either to wealth or to the kingdom of God.
Jesus forewarned, "You cannot serve God and money" (Matthew 6:24b).

We want both because we are children of the consumer age, and our prosperity in the West has lifted us to unparalleled affluence but also unparalleled
avarice. It is striking that as Christians we have sworn allegiance to the cause
of Christ by dedicating our souls, our families' futures, and our hopes and
ambitions to the gospel, but we sometimes stumble at devoting our material
goods or ourselves to the work of the Savior. This is a tell-tale sign that demands that we look at ourselves. In our culture of affluence there is a reticence
in some circles to reveal what we earn financially because it has a direct bearing on our status in society. Yet, at the same time the persons who hide their
financial worth do not flinch at telling about the intimate matters of their lives.
This incongruity shows how "holy" money has become for us in the West. As
Christians we can give a strong witness to our heavenly priorities when we
manage our money in a godly manner.

One of the hindrances to our giving to the church today is the confusion
that some Christians have regarding to whom we give our resources. Is it to the
Lord? To the church as an institution? To the pastor? The gifts we bring to the
work of the church for the spreading of the gospel are devoted to the Savior,
not to the church leadership. Our offerings are in the safekeeping of leaders
for sure, but ones who under God must act with integrity by realizing that they
handle holy things (2 Corinthians 8:18–22). Again, if we are willing to subject
our souls to the preaching and example of a pastor and church leaders, yet we
cannot support their financial leadership in our church, we must reconsider
the priorities we have in our handing over money for the Lord's work. If we
cannot support the work of the Lord in our church in good conscience, we
should consider placing our lives in a church where we can enthusiastically
support the mission of the church. We must not be guilty of neglect or holding
the church hostage because of our personal dissatisfaction.

The chief lesson to take from this chapter in Leviticus is the costly discipleship that worship and ministry require. We stand on the shoulders of those
who have preceded us, making sacrificial gifts for the Christian gospel. These
sacrifices are not only the giving of money but also the offering of themselves
in time, energy, and career. It was the Asia Minor (modern-day Turkey) church
of Philippi that supported the missionary travels of the Apostle Paul in Macedonia where the gospel came to Europe for the first time (Acts 16:9, 10). The
evangelization of Europe initiated by the apostle resulted in the shift of the

epicenter of the gospel from the Middle East to Europe. Europe was in turn the seedbed for the rise of the church in colonial America and the modern missions movement.[8] We are the beneficiaries of the saints who came before us. The forefathers of our churches gave themselves and their resources to make the gospel known to us and to our loved ones.

Perhaps a word is in order regarding the practical aspects of making pledges and the outworking of developing budgets for ministry. Some may find such things too secular, even unspiritual. But the Bible shows that planning and strategizing are taken into account when the Spirit works through human instruments.[9] The Apostle Paul advised the Corinthian church to establish a plan for gathering money for their gift to the poor in Jerusalem (1 Corinthians 16:1–4). Moreover, the Spirit is not bound by our human plans, and he moves to change our directions to coincide with his mission for us (e.g., Acts 16:6; Romans 15:20–23). Careful planning is characteristic of good stewardship and does not necessarily oppose the work of the Spirit. We are not to be wishy-washy in our pledges, lest we be charged with irresponsibility, for integrity in our decision-making should describe our Christian character.[10] The book of Proverbs often refers to planning as a necessary part of human existence and commends it in 21:5: "The plans of the diligent lead surely to abundance, but everyone who is hasty comes only to poverty." The Bible only forewarns against being presumptuous in our planning as though we know God's will with certainty (1 Corinthians 4:19; James 4:15). Rather, in matters of dispute and uncertainty we should humbly pray, "Let the will of the Lord be done" (Acts 21:14b).

The Scriptures teach us that Christian duty is a part of the outflow of receiving the gospel. When we come to know Christ as our Savior, we make a decision to give *all* that we are and *all* that we have to him for his service. The chief idea here is surrender, meaning that we "obey the gospel of our Lord Jesus," as Paul wrote (2 Thessalonians 1:8). "The obedience of faith" (Romans 1:5) calls us to serve the Lord without reservation and with full-hearted integrity in worship to God and in service to others. We can capture the message of this chapter and for that matter the whole book of Leviticus in this one sentence: "The robust gospel calls for a robust response of a robust person."[11]

*Soli Deo Gloria!*

# Notes

## Preface and Acknowledgments

1. Malcolm Falloon, warden of Latimer Fellowship.
2. Thomas Schreiner, "Preaching and Biblical Theology," *Southern Baptist Theological Journal* 10 (2006): 20.

## Chapter One: Hearing from God before Seeing God

1. *The Columbia World of Quotations* (New York: Columbia University Press, 1996); http://www.bartleby.com/66/24/2324.html.
2. "The tent of meeting" refers here to the tabernacle (referred to as the Tent of Meeting in this volume) that was located in the midst of the Israelite camp; it was the place of Israelite sacrifice and worship. Also there was a "tent of meeting" outside the camp that was a temporary tent where Moses met with God for revelations (Exodus 33:7–11; Numbers 11:16–30).
3. Allen P. Ross, *Holiness to the LORD* (Grand Rapids, MI: Baker, 2002), 62.
4. For this phrase and its variations, see 4:1; 5:14; 6:1; 7:22, 28; 8:1; 10:11; 11:1; 12:1; 13:1; 14:1, 33; 15:1; 16:1, 2; 17:1; 18:1; 19:1; 20:1; 21:1, 16; 22:1, 17, 26; 23:1, 9, 23, 26, 33; 24:1, 13; 25:1; 27:1; cf. "commanded Moses" and its variations in 7:38; 8:4, 9, 13, 17, 21, 29, 36; 9:5, 10, 21; 10:5; 16:34; 24:23; 27:34.
5. Jacob Milgrom, *Leviticus 1–16*, Anchor Bible (New York: Doubleday, 1991), 142, 143.
6. G. Auld, "Leviticus: After Exodus and Before Numbers," *The Book of Leviticus: Composition and Reception*, eds. R. Rendtorff and R. Kugler (Leiden: Brill, 2003), 41–54, esp. 43.
7. Gerald Borchert, *John 1–11*, New American Commentary (Nashville: B&H, 1996), 121.

## Chapter Two: Commitment

1. "Thus the main point appears to be that God measures the gifts of his people not on the basis of their size but on the basis of how much remains." Robert Stein, *Luke*, New American Commentary (Nashville: B&H, 1992), 509.
2. The word *tamim* indicates what is whole, complete, and physically sound.
3. The same term *tamim* describes the moral character of the patriarchs Noah (Genesis 6:9), Abraham (Genesis 17:1), and Job (Job 12:4).
4. The Hebrew word *mishkan* ("tabernacle," "dwelling-place") is different than "tent of meeting" (*'ohel mo'ed*).
5. The Hebrew cubit was eighteen inches.

6. Quoted in Jacob Milgrom, *Leviticus: A Book of Ritual and Ethics*, Continental Commentary (Minneapolis: Fortress, 2004), 21.

7. Ibid.

8. Jewish tradition identified it as the *Tamid* ("continual") offering, translated "regular" (Exodus 29:42).

9. F. F. Bruce, *The Epistle to the Hebrews*, New International Commentary on the New Testament (Grand Rapids, MI: Eerdmans, 1964), 397–400.

10. The one exception was the priest alone handling a bird offering due to its small size (Leviticus 1:14–17).

11. The high priest placed two hands on the animal in the Day of Atonement ritual (Leviticus 16:21), whereas the layman placed one hand.

12. Second Kings 10:7 may suggest that "kill" (*shachat*) meant cutting the throat, which in this case was in the extreme, beheading the victims.

13. Jacob Milgrom, *Leviticus 1–16*, Anchor Bible (New York: Doubleday, 1991), 154, 155 refers to an illicit technique and the correction of King Saul in 1 Samuel 14:32–34.

14. That the cattle have a different location for slaughter is inferred from 4:4, 15 with 4:24, 29, 33; 6:18; 7:2; and 14:13; animals of the flock have a designated "place" for slaughter for the burnt and sin offerings. See ibid., 164.

15. John Calvin, *Commentaries on the Last Four Books of Moses Arranged in the Form of a Harmony*, second volume (Grand Rapids, MI: Eerdmans, n.d.), 325.

16. The Hebrew *notsah*, often translated "with its contents," is unknown; it means "feathers, plumage" in Ezekiel 17:3, 7.

17. A second ash pile was outside the camp in a ceremonially "clean place" where the officiating priest deposited the powdery remains (4:12; 6:10, 11).

18. The mistaken notion that the Hebrew root *k-p-r* meant "to cover" resulted from the confusion of two different Hebrew words that are spelled the same (homonyms). The word *kpr* ("to cover") describes the pitch used to seal Noah's ark (Genesis 6:14), but *kpr* ("to make atonement") means appeasement as in Jacob's gift to angry Esau so as to "appease [*kpr*] him" (Genesis 32:20).

19. Allen P. Ross, *Holiness to the LORD* (Grand Rapids, MI: Baker, 2002), 94.

20. "Looking at the World Through the Word (Romans 15:4)," delivered at E. K. Bailey Ministries Preaching Conference, April, 26, 2005, at Beeson Divinity School Chapel, Birmingham, Alabama.

21. The Hebrew word translated "pleasing" (*nichoach*) is related to the word "to be at rest, be quiet" (*nuach*).

22. The ESV (1:9, 13, 17) has translated "a food offering" (*'ishsheh*) rather than the traditional expression "an offering made by fire." The Hebrew term is used of offerings that are not burned up (e.g., Leviticus 23:13; Numbers 15:10) and thus can be a general term for a food gift. Milgrom, *Leviticus 1–16*, 161, 162.

23. The Greek Old Testament translation, also known as the Septuagint, is *osme euodias*, which occurs in the New Testament.

## Chapter Three: Thank You, Lord!

1. *Whitefield's Sermons* (Grand Rapids, MI: Christian Classics Ethereal Library, n.d.); available at http://www.ccel.org/ccel/whitefield/sermons.ix.html.

2. One exception to this rule was the offering of firstfruits, but it could not be burned on the altar (v. 12).

3. Allen P. Ross, *Holiness to the LORD* (Grand Rapids, MI: Baker, 2002), 105.

4. See www.cyberhymnal.org/htm/b/b/bbtttb.htm.

5. The Greek word translated "fellowship" and "share" in 1 John and in Hebrews is *koinonia*, which describes communion among partners and the freewill gifts of financial support (Romans 15:26).

6. Literally, the Hebrew has "an offering [made] by fire"; this traditional translation, however, does not explain why this expression is used for offerings not burned on the altar by fire, such as drink libations (Numbers 15:10). Jacob Milgrom, *Leviticus 1–16*, Anchor Bible (New York: Doubleday, 1991), 161, therefore suggests the more accurate translation "a food gift."

7. "Fat" that "is the LORD's" (v. 16) refers to the fat removed from the altar in worship (Ezekiel 44:7), not to the fat of butchered animals destined for the common table; the blood, however, could never be consumed under any circumstances (Leviticus 7:22–27; 17:10–14; Deuteronomy 12:15, 16, 20–24; cf. 32:14).

## Chapter Four: Purging the Soul

1. Accidental killing of a person (manslaughter) was more serious and required a different regulation (see Numbers 35:9–29 on the death of the high priest).

2. Commentators observe that the four offenses are arranged in a chiasmus (ABBA).

3. As a resident of the town Nazareth, Jesus was a "Nazarene," not a Nazirite (Matthew 2:23).

4. From his book *The Mortification of Sin*, quoted in the editorial "Reviewing the Fundamentals," *Christianity Today* (January 2007): 27.

5. John E. Hartley discusses the two aspects of "guilt" in *Leviticus*, WBC (Dallas: Word, 1992), 62.

6. H. Ray Wood, *Some Indispensables* (not yet published, 2006).

7. The word *tsalach* ("to forgive") occurs first in Exodus 34:9; it appears in connection with the sin and guilt offerings in Leviticus (4:20, 26, 31, 35; 5:10, 13, 16, 18; 6:7; 19:22; also Numbers 15:25, 26, 28), which are the only two of the five regular offerings that are required for the commission of sins.

8. See Numbers 30:5, 8, 12 for an example. John W. Kleinig, *Leviticus*, Concordia Commentary (St. Louis: Concordia, 2003), 104, 105.

9. The only explicit connection of ritual and confession in Leviticus is 16:21 (also see Numbers 5:7; cf. Proverbs 28:13).

10. The only possible provision for intentional iniquities was the Day of Atonement in Leviticus 16, which uses the inclusive language "all" sins (vv. 21, 22, 30, 33, 34); nevertheless, the Day of Atonement was a recurring annual necessity and therefore offered only a temporary reprieve.

11. The Greek word *hilasterion* that occurs only in these two verses in the New Testament describes the means of atonement in Romans 3:25 and the place of atonement (= mercy seat cover on the ark of the covenant) in Hebrews 9:5. The Greek Old Testament's translation of the atonement cover (*kipporeth*) in the Day of Atonement ceremony was the same word *hilasterion* (Leviticus 16:13, 14, 15). The

term means to reconcile but also to appease the wrath of God, namely, "propitiation by his blood" (Romans 3:25).

12. The author of Hebrews has in mind the Day of Atonement, on which the high priest took the blood of the slain animal into the Most Holy Place (Leviticus 16). The sin offering, as we have seen, involved taking the blood into the Holy Place at the veil that separates the two rooms. The principle is the same; the blood was the purging agent that removed the stain of sin from the tent and from the altar of sacrifice.

## Chapter Five: Debt-Free

1. Associated Press report (January 7, 2007).

2. Jacob Milgrom, *Leviticus 1–16*, Anchor Bible (New York: Doubleday, 1991), 327.

3. The Hebrew word is the verb form of *chata*, "to miss, go wrong, sin." The English versions vary in their attempts to render the word in this context as a cultic offense (e.g., KJV, "harm"; NIV, "failed").

4. "Holy things" refers to the Tent of Meeting and its various furnishings, such as the ark of the covenant. John W. Kleinig, *Leviticus*, Concordia Commentary (St. Louis: Concordia, 2003), 131.

5. Consider, for example, the fraud by Ananias and Sapphira that resulted in their dramatic destruction (Acts 5:1–11).

6. First Corinthians 7:14 refers to the sanctifying effects of a Christian's faith in the home on an unbelieving spouse or on children.

7. Derek Tidball, *The Message of Leviticus: Free to be Holy*, The Bible Speaks Today: Old Testament Series, ed. J. A. Motyer (Downers Grove, IL: InterVarsity Press, 2005), 90.

8. Jesus denied the popular view of his day that suffering was always due to a person's sin (Luke 13:1–5; John 9:2, 3). Robert Stein, *Luke*, New American Commentary (Nashville: B&H, 1992), 370.

9. Milgrom, *Leviticus 1–16*, 343 prefers translating "feels guilty" for the term *asham* since initially the offender did not realize his guilt and could not have known of it apart from a guilty conscience. The word thus indicates the result of psychological suffering.

10. The KJV (as does NLT, NRSV) has "sin" for the Hebrew word rendered "guilt" (ESV, NIV, NASB), which is the same word for "guilt offering."

11. Peter O'Brien, *Colossians, Philemon*, Word Biblical Commentary (Waco, TX: Word, 1982), 125 comments that the Jews were under contractual obligation to the Mosaic law and that the Gentiles were under obligation to their conscience, which served as their legal contract (Romans 2:14, 15), making both Jew and Gentile guilty.

12. Eugene Carpenter and Michael Grisanti, "vjk," *New International Dictionary of Old Testament Theology and Exegesis*, ed. W. Van Gemeren (Grand Rapids, MI: Zondervan, 1997), 2:632–634.

## Chapter Six: Handling Holy Things

1. The text has also been translated, "Everyone who touches them must *be* holy" (NKJV). The argument is that uncleanness only, never holiness, is a contagion;

for someone to *become* holy there must be a rite that sanctifies the person involved (see Haggai 2:10–13), which is not here in verse 18; Baruch Levine, *Leviticus*, The JPS Torah Commentary (Philadelphia: Jewish Publication Society, 1989), 37, 38. But Mark Rooker, *Leviticus*, New American Commentary (Nashville: B&H, 2000), 130, n. 234 observes that the Haggai passage is not parallel to our passage since it does not concern the "most holy" portions.

2. Gordon Wenham, *The Book of Leviticus*, New International Commentary on the Old Testament (Grand Rapids, MI: Zondervan, 1979), 121 surmises from the example of the Nazirite vow (Numbers 6:13–20) that a "de-sanctification" ritual may have been employed in such cases.

3. Allen P. Ross, *Recalling the Hope of Glory* (Grand Rapids, MI: Kregel, 2006), 271, 272.

4. Jacob Milgrom, *Leviticus: A Book of Ritual and Ethics*, Continental Commentary (Minneapolis: Fortress, 2004), 28 references this rabbinic observation (*b. Ber.* 54b). Other examples of deliverance are Psalm 56:12; 69:30; 116:17. Jonah offered assurances of thank offerings at his deliverance from his watery grave (Jonah 2:9).

5. F. F. Bruce, *The Epistle to the Hebrews*, New International Commentary of the New Testament (Grand Rapids, MI: Eerdmans, 1964), 405, 406.

6. David Garland, *1 Corinthians*, Baker Exegetical Commentary on the New Testament (Grand Rapids, MI: Baker, 2003), 550, 551.

7. Ibid., 173–75.

8. The word for "portion" is *mishchah*; the same term also means "anointing oil" (8:2; 21:10). Both the words "portion" and "anointed" (*mashach*, v. 36) are related to the noun "anointed one" (*mashiach*, "messiah"), from the verb *mashach*, "to smear, anoint."

9. John W. Kleinig, *Leviticus*, Concordia Commentary (St. Louis: Concordia, 2003), 181.

## Chapter Seven: The Mediator

1. Of course, the priests settled disputes between individuals (Exodus 24:14; Deuteronomy 19:17; 21:5), but when we speak of offense against God we are speaking of the priest's role metaphorically. No human priest could literally arbitrate a dispute between the Lord and a man: "If someone sins against a man, God will mediate for him, but if someone sins against the Lord, who can intercede for him?" (1 Samuel 2:25a).

2. See www.gracedestin.com/Bulletins/20081221_bulletin.pdf.

3. The rank-and-file priests, so to speak, also wore coats of fine linen (Exodus 29:8; 39:27; 40:14). Yet, since the text specifically says that the high-priestly coat was "of checker work" (Exodus 28:4), the sons may have worn plain garments. For a useful summary discussion of the priestly vestments, see C. van Dam, "Priestly Clothing," *Dictionary of the Old Testament: Pentateuch*, eds. T. D. Alexander and D. W. Baker (Downers Grove, IL: InterVarsity Press, 2003), 643–46.

4. The regular priests, Aaron's sons, received coats, sashes (probably the same as the high priest, Exodus 39:29), and caps (Exodus 28:40). All priests wore a linen undergarment (fine twisted linen for the high priest, Exodus 39:29) covering waist to thigh so as to hide their private parts (e.g., Exodus 28:42; Leviticus 6:10). One

striking omission was the absence of footwear. By being barefoot the priests avoided the refuse that footwear inevitably gathered. Moreover, the priests washed their hands and feet before serving at the altar from the waters of the bronze basin, which was stationed between the tent and the altar in the courtyard (Exodus 30:19, 21).

5.  Regular priests also possessed sashes, but they were not embellished (Exodus 28:40).

6.  The Hebrew "Urim" may be derived from the Hebrew word for "curse," and "Thummim" can mean "perfect, complete," thus together expressing the opposite meanings "cursed" and "innocent." Another popular theory is that the Urim and Thummim gave off a radiant light that gave divine confirmation of a prophetic oracle uttered by the high priest.

7.  Priests wore caps (Exodus 28:40).

8.  The precise meaning of "plate" (*tsits*) is uncertain. Another word, "crown" (*nezer*), describes the headpiece (Exodus 29:6) and "the plate of the holy crown" (Exodus 39:30).

9.  The common practice of the burnt offering, however, provided for the skin of the animal to be kept for the officiating priest (Leviticus 7:8); as an ordination ritual the skin was completely burned up so that neither Moses nor anyone else could benefit from the sin of the priests.

10.  The priests did not wear sandals, making it convenient to apply the blood.

11.  Bread made with yeast was not burned up on the altar (Leviticus 2:12; 7:13; 23:17; Numbers 15:18–21). Since wine is fermented, the question arises as to the offering of wine libations. Jacob Milgrom, *Leviticus 1–16*, Anchor Bible (New York: Doubleday, 1991), 188, 189 answers that the wine was not burned on the altar but was poured out at the base of the altar.

## Chapter Eight: The Glory of the Lord

1.  There is no specific account of these instructions in Exodus as is found for the ordination service of Aaron in Leviticus 8 (Exodus 29), but Exodus 29:43, 45 may be taken as reflective of the time that God instructed Moses concerning the particulars of the first communal service performed in the Tent of Meeting.

2.  This rare chronological notice (9:1) in the book of Leviticus has been viewed as the major structural division of the book: chapters 1—8 and 9—27. See A. Ruwe, "The Structure of the Book of Leviticus in the Narrative Outline of the Priestly Sinai Story (Exod 19:1–Num 10:10)," *The Book of Leviticus: Composition and Reception* (Leiden: Brill, 2003), 55–78.

3.  Also see Leviticus 15:14, 29; 23:36, 39; Numbers 6:10; 29:35.

4.  Jacob Milgrom, *Leviticus 1–16*, Anchor Bible (New York: Doubleday, 1991), 572.

5.  Ibid., 574.

6.  The Hebrew term is *kabod*, and its basic underlying sense is "weight, heavy." Thus when applied to God, the essential meaning of "glory" is the significance or "weight" that he inherently possesses and that he dramatically displays (cf. Psalm 19:1, "the heavens declare the glory of God"). C. John Collins, "dbk," *New International Dictionary of Old Testament Theology and Exegesis*, ed. W. Van Gemeren (Grand Rapids, MI: Zondervan, 1977), 2:577.

7. The offering of the inaugural service differed from the typical offering by the animal's being completely burned up (as also for the ordination service, 8:17), although the blood was not taken into the tent (cf. 6:30). Also, the priests customarily ate the meat (6:26, 29), but here they did not since the priests could not benefit from an offering presented for their own sin. Milgrom, *Leviticus 1–16*, 581.

8. The Hebrew word is *barak* and occurs most frequently in the book of Genesis where it usually describes procreation and prosperity (e.g., 1:28; 24:35). The "blessing" of God also occurs when his people offer up praises to the Lord (Genesis 14:20; Ruth 4:14). The New Testament's word "to bless" (*eulogeō*) conveys the same dual meaning of invoking God's favor and of human praise addressed to the Lord. The emphasis, however, in the New Testament's understanding of blessing is spiritual prosperity provided by Christ, not material procreation and prosperity (e.g., Ephesians 1:3); however, material blessing is also possible (Romans 15:26, 27).

9. Milgrom, *Leviticus 1–16*, 588 compares the dedication of the temple that has the dedicatory prayer of Solomon between the two public blessings (1 Kings 8:14–61).

10. This did not mean that God's presence was automatic or that he was held captive in the tent. The fiery cloud was mobile as God ascended and descended at will (Exodus 40:38; Numbers 16:42; cf. 1 Kings 8:27).

11. Compare also Gideon's and Elijah's offerings (Judges 6:21; 1 Kings 18:38).

12. See also Judges 13:20; 1 Kings 18:39.

13. John R. W. Stott, *The Incomparable Christ* (Downers Grove, IL: InterVarsity Press, 2001), 235.

## Chapter Nine: The Priestly Mission

1. The Hebrew *qarob*, meaning "near, close by," is related to the root word *qarab* which is a technical term that describes the "presentation, offering" of a sacrifice by the priests to the Lord on behalf of a worshiper (e.g., 1:5, 13, 14).

2. The Hebrew verbal forms (known as the *niphal* stem) can be rendered either passively or reflexively; some English versions have the reflexive sense (e.g., NIV, NRSV).

3. The word *damam* often means silence in the face of tragedy but can also mean "to wait, be still, rest," as in waiting in prayer before the Lord (Psalm 4:4; 37:7).

4. Certain mourning rites that were prohibited for all Israelites included self-inflicted cutting and the shaving of frontal hair; the purpose of such prohibitions was to differentiate Israel from these practices of neighboring nations (Deuteronomy 14:1, 2). It was also inappropriate for the Israelite to enjoy the community meal dedicated to the Lord when in mourning (Deuteronomy 26:14).

5. The special ingredients for the oil and its exclusive use for sanctuary furniture and personnel are commanded in Exodus 30:22–25; 40:9–15.

6. John W. Kleinig lists additionally three things that made an officiating priest unfit for service and that were penalized by death: absence of holy garments (Exodus 28:43), failure to undergo the washing ritual (Exodus 30:20), and a physical defect (Leviticus 21:16–23). *Leviticus*, Concordia Commentary (St. Louis: Concordia, 2003), 225.

7. "Surviving" (*hannotarim*) and "is left" (*hannoteret*) sound alike in the original language.

8. The Hebrew *darosh darash* repeats the basic root word (*d-r-sh*) for emphasis; the grammatical forms are the infinitive absolute *darosh* and the perfect *darash*.

9. The word "approved" renders the same idiom: "would it have been good in the eyes of the LORD?" (v. 19b) and "and it was good in his [Moses'] eyes" (v. 20).

10. This is developed in Allen P. Ross, *Holiness to the Lord* (Grand Rapids, MI: Baker, 2002), 238.

## Chapter Ten: Dining with God

1. Jacob Milgrom, *Leviticus 1–16*, Anchor Bible (New York: Doubleday, 1991), 1650, 1651.

2. Roy Gane, *Leviticus, Numbers*, NIV Application Commentary (Grand Rapids, MI: Zondervan, 2004), 216.

3. The words "detestable" and "defiled" are two forms of the same root word (*shaqats*), "to detest, make abominable."

4. Deuteronomy 14:5, 6 names others that qualify and also leaves open the possibility of still others unnamed.

5. Technically the rock badger and hare do not chew the cud; they only appear to make the jaw movements of chewing the cud, which was sufficient to rule them out; these four are also named in Deuteronomy 14:7, 8. Jacob Milgrom, *Leviticus: A Book of Ritual and Ethics*, Continental Commentary (Minneapolis: Fortress, 2004), 116.

6. As to why a special remark regarding four-footed animals that walk on "paws," such as dogs and cats, occurs here is unclear.

7. The specific instruction for cooking fixtures was necessary since such fixtures were set in the ground and readers might have wrongly deemed them as exceptions. Milgrom, *Leviticus 1–16*, 678–80.

## Chapter Eleven: Born into the Family of Faith

1. The expulsion of the placenta membrane results in an issue of blood and cell debris (known as lochia).

2. This is why the text refers to a woman's menstruation (12:2; 15:33), since it too was not a daily occurrence; a seven-day period of isolation followed by offerings was required (15:19, 29).

3. The passage parallels birth emissions and "menstruation" (v. 2b); this term in our text translates an expression that is related to the word for "sickness, infirmity." The Hebrew *niddat dewotah* is literally "the menstruation of her infirmity"; *dewotah* is related to the verb *dawah*, meaning "to be sick, ill." The New JPS (Jewish Publication Society) translation shows this by its literal rendering, "menstrual infirmity."

4. Jacob Milgrom, *Leviticus 1–16*, Anchor Bible (New York: Doubleday, 1991), 752.

5. The foreskin (prepuce) is the loose fold of skin that covers the penis glans. Today's Jewish custom of *Brit Milah* ("covenant of circumcision") is performed in a ceremony, typically at home, by a specially trained rabbi, a Mohel, who after the procedure declares a blessing and announces the name of the baby boy (see Luke 2:21).

For medical or cultural purposes many non-Jewish babies are surgically circumcised in a hospital setting within twenty-four hours of the birth.

   6. Though I do not personally believe that baptism of infants is Biblical, infant baptism in the Reformed tradition was viewed as a substitute for the act of circumcision based on the identification of God's covenant with Israel and with the Church. Calvin's *Institutes* (4.16.4) reads, "For just as circumcision, which was a kind of badge to the Jews, assuring them that they were adopted as the people and family of God, was their first entrance into the Church, while they, in their turn, professed their allegiance to God, so now we are initiated by baptism, so as to be enrolled among his people, and at the same time swear unto his name. Hence it is incontrovertible, that baptism has been substituted for circumcision, and performs the same office." The baptism of infants of Christian believers is viewed as a sign of the new covenant (1 Corinthians 7:14), not as the impartation of saving grace. For the Reformed position, see William Hendriksen, *New Testament Commentary: Philippians, Colossians and Philemon* (Grand Rapids, MI: Baker, 1985), 116, 117, notes 85–87.

   7. Ibid., 760.

   8. His call to join his band of disciples included the vagabond life of a first-century rabbi who had no home of his own ("nowhere to lay his head," Matthew 8:20), but this does not mean he was "penniless but homeless." D. A. Carson, *Matthew Chapters 1 Through 12*, Expositor's Bible Commentary (Grand Rapids, MI: Zondervan, 1995), 208.

   9. Ralph P. Martin, *2 Corinthians*, Word Biblical Commentary (Waco, TX: Word, 1986), 266.

   10. F. F. Bruce, *The Epistle to the Galatians: A Commentary on the Greek Text*, New International Greek Testament Commentary (Grand Rapids, MI: Eerdmans, 1982), 194–96.

## Chapter Twelve: Holy to the Core

   1. The title is indebted to the article by Joel Scandrett, "Holy to the Core," *Christianity Today*, 51/5 (May 2007), 38–40, in which he explores the disparity between moralism and the encompassing nature of holy living.

   2. Allen P. Ross, *Holiness to the LORD* (Grand Rapids, MI: Baker, 2002) repeatedly observes that the common idea to the purity laws is the believer's life and worship in a fallen world.

   3. A helpful summarization of the symptoms and the priestly responses are found in Baruch Levine, *Leviticus*, The JPS Torah Commentary (Philadelphia: Jewish Publication Society, 1989), 76.

   4. The Greek translation of Leviticus 13, 14 has the word *lepra* (leprosy); the essence of the Greek word group is the idea of "scaly, rough, uneven" matter. The Greek term referred to various dermatological conditions. R. K. Harrison, "Leprosy," *New International Dictionary of New Testament Theology*, ed. C. Brown (Grand Rapids, MI: Zondervan, 1975), 463–66.

   5. The ESV translates *bohak*, the skin malady described in verses 38, 39, as "leukoderma" (also known as *vitiligo*), which is patches of pale skin resulting from loss of pigmentation.

   6. Jacob Milgrom, *Leviticus 1–16*, Anchor Bible (New York: Doubleday, 1991), 805, 806, 817, 818 argues that the scaly afflictions described in Leviticus 13, 14 are

not medically contagious. He points to the example of Naaman whose "leprosy" (*tsaraat*) did not prevent him from normal social contact (2 Kings 5). What was important was the ritual uncleanness the abnormality presented.

7. Ross, *Holiness to the LORD*, 283, note 8.

8. Milgrom, *Leviticus 1–16*, 818, 819.

9. Gordon Wenham, *Leviticus*, New International Commentary on the Old Testament (Grand Rapids, MI: Eerdmans, 1979), 212.

10. Levine, *Leviticus*, 94. As in our modern culture, spitting on a person was demeaning (Numbers 12:14; Deuteronomy 25:9; Isaiah 50:6; Mark 15:19).

11. In the list of sexual prohibitions regarding the time of her flow, the man becomes unclean too (18:19).

12. Derek Tidball, *The Message of Leviticus: Free to Be Holy*, The Bible Speaks Today: Old Testament Series, ed. J. A. Motyer (Downers Grove, IL: InterVarsity Press, 2005), 169.

## Chapter Thirteen: Day of Atonement

1. The precise expression of this idiom also occurs in other passages describing the Day of Atonement (Leviticus 23:27, 32; Numbers 29:7). The text does not specifically state that fasting is what was meant; however, Psalm 35:13 and Isaiah 58:3 use the idiom and define "affliction" as fasting. The rabbis in *Mishnah Yoma* 8:1 (*Yoma* is Aramaic, meaning "the day," i.e., the Day of Atonement) included refraining from bathing, perfuming the body, wearing shoes, and sexual relations. Baruch Levine, *Leviticus*, JPS Torah Commentary (Philadelphia: Jewish Publication Society, 1989), 109. Levine's commentary is helpful but must be used cautiously as he intentionally weaves together the Biblical text and the Jewish traditions reflected in the tractate *Mishnah Yoma*.

2. Gordon Wenham, *The Book of Leviticus*, New International Commentary on the Old Testament (Grand Rapids, MI: Eerdmans, 1979), 229, n. 2.

3. The Hebrew term is *kapporeth*, which is a noun etymologically related to the verb *kipper* ("to atone") and the noun *kippur* ("atonement"), as in *Yom Kippur* ("Day of Atonement"). John E. Hartley, "Atonement, Day of," *Dictionary of the Old Testament: Pentateuch*, eds. T. Alexander and D. Baker (Downers Grove, IL: InterVarsity Press, 2003), 55 names these three spiritual purposes for the rite: atonement for the sins of the priests and people, the removal of the pollution generated by those sins from the sanctuary, and the release of the goat that removed the guilt from the community.

4. Some form of lots was cast by the soldiers at the foot of Jesus' cross when his discarded clothes were the object of their gambling (Matthew 27:35).

5. The Day of Atonement ritual is similar to the sin offering (Leviticus 4), but one difference is that here the priest places two hands, not one, on the animal's head. For the significance of the symbolic act, see Leviticus 24:14 where the corruption incurred from hearing the man's blasphemy is transferred *back* to the guilty party.

6. The phrases "over it" (v. 10) and "on itself" (v. 22), referring to the scapegoat, do not mean that the atonement is in behalf of the scapegoat, as though atonement is made *for* the animal. Rather, they indicate that the scapegoat's role achieves the purging of Israel's impurities and achieves atonement for the sins of the people. Jacob Milgrom, *Leviticus 1–16*, Anchor Bible (New York: Doubleday, 1991), 1023.

7. *Mishnah Yoma*, 6:6. Milgrom, *Leviticus 1–16*, 1046.

8. For example, the burning of the animals' carcasses outside the camp on the Day of Atonement is paralleled by the crucifixion of Jesus' body outside the city (Hebrews 13:10–14). The author by this analogy shows that the Jewish altar inside the city had to be left behind because the altar outside the city was superior. Donald Guthrie, *Hebrews*, Tyndale New Testament Commentaries (Leicester, UK: Inter-Varsity/Grand Rapids, MI: Eerdmans, 1983), 372–75.

9. F. F. Bruce, *The Epistle to the Hebrews*, New International Commentary on the New Testament (Grand Rapids, MI: Eerdmans, 1964), 236, n. 50.

## Chapter Fourteen: Honoring God at Table

1. This was reported in an Associated Press story that was widely published in the print and broadcast media, April 4, 2006.

2. The word *shachat* occurs most often in the book of Leviticus (thirty-five times) and in the context of tabernacle worship.

3. Herbert Wolf and Robert Holmstedt, "pv," *New International Dictionary of Old Testament Theology and Exegesis*, ed. W. A. Van Gemeren (Grand Rapids, MI: Zondervan, 1997), 4:222.

4. John W. Kleinig, *Leviticus*, Concordia Commentary (St. Louis: Concordia, 2003), 367.

5. C. F. D. Moule, *The Epistles to the Colossians and to Philemon*, The Cambridge Greek Testament Commentary (Cambridge: Cambridge University Press, 1957), 117.

6. B. S. Rosner, "Idolatry," *New Dictionary of Biblical Theology*, eds. T. A. Alexander and B. S. Rosner (Downers Grove, IL: InterVarsity Press, 2000), 574, 575.

7. Peter T. O'Brien, *Colossians, Philemon*, Word Biblical Commentary (Waco, TX: Word, 1982), 185.

8. The arrangement of chapters 1—7 begins with the burnt offering and names the remaining sacrifices, giving five in all. The two terms "burnt offerings" and "sacrifice" are probably figures of speech (*merism*) intended to be inclusive of all the sacrifices. John E. Hartley, *Leviticus*, Word Biblical Commentary (Nashville: Nelson, 1992), 273 observed that the burnt offering was a common public offering, and the word "sacrifice" may have referred to private, individual offerings.

9. See Leviticus 16:29; Exodus 20:10. In the case of Passover, the alien must be circumcised to partake, but either way he could not have leaven in the house, Exodus 12:19, 48, 49; Numbers 9:14.

10. The key term we use here is "willful" in the sense of a lifestyle; we do not speak of those who are encumbered by health issues or experience temporary absence for good reason.

11. Derek Tidball, *The Message of Leviticus: Free to Be Holy*, The Bible Speaks Today: Old Testament Series, ed. J. A. Motyer (Downers Grove, IL: Inter-Varsity Press, 2005), 208.

12. Stephen K. Sherwood, *Leviticus, Numbers, Deuteronomy*, Berit Olam (Collegeville, MN: Michael Glazier/Liturgical Press, 2002), 30–33 provides a list of all the Leviticus passages that relate speeches by God in the first person.

13. The Hebrew construction is very common; the negative particle "no, not" (*lo'*) is followed by the form of the verb known by grammarians as the imperfect

tense. The same language describes the prohibition in the garden, "you shall not eat of the tree" (Genesis 2:17; cf. 3:17).

14. Hartley, *Studies in Cultic Terminology and Theology*, Studies in Judaism in Late Antiquity 36 (Leiden: Brill, 1983), p. 97.

15. C. H. Spurgeon, "Praise for the Gift of Gifts," preached July 27, 1890, at the Metropolitan Tabernacle, based on 2 Corinthians 9:15.

16. Our discussion relies on David E. Garland, *1 Corinthians*, Baker Exegetical Commentary on the New Testament (Grand Rapids, MI: Baker, 2003), 533–57.

17. That this was a constant threat to the unity of the fellowship can be seen by the stigmatizing of the poor by the churches addressed by James (2:1–13).

18. John B. Polhill, *Acts*, New American Commentary (Nashville: B&H, 1992), 335 presents a succinct but effective treatment of the problem and its resolution.

19. Deuteronomy 12:13–28 appears to contradict the Leviticus law, since Deuteronomy allows for the slaying of animals in one's town for meat, and Leviticus does not. The Deuteronomy law assumes that the prosperity of the Israelites will mean that some will live far from the sanctuary and therefore are given the exception of slaying and eating meat elsewhere. In no situation, however, can the Israelites (and foreigners) consume the blood, and when the slaughter is intended as worship it must be brought to the tent for butchering. J. G. McConville, *Deuteronomy*, Apollos Old Testament Commentary (Downers Grove, IL: InterVarsity Press, 2002), 225–28.

20. Walter C. Kaiser Jr., "Leviticus," *New Interpreter's Bible*, Vol. 1 (Nashville: Abingdon, 1994), 1120.

## Chapter Fifteen: The Sanctity of the Family

1. Jacob Milgrom, *Leviticus*, A Continental Commentary (Minneapolis: Fortress, 2004), 202.

2. Among social scientists this practice is called endogamy; marriage outside a person's kinship group is exogamy.

3. R. K. Harrison, *Leviticus*, Tyndale Old Testament Commentaries (Downers Grove, IL: InterVarsity Press, 1980), 188.

4. Timothy George, *Galatians*, New American Commentary (Nashville: B&H, 1994), 398.

5. Our discussion of the list's arrangement depends on Milgrom, *Leviticus*, 202.

6. In the United States, some states permit first-cousin marriage, sometimes with restrictions, and other states prohibit it.

7. Deuteronomy 25:5–10 provides an exception, known as levirate ("brother-in-law") marriage, in which a brother marries his sister-in-law. The exception was highly limited, however, to brothers who lived under the auspices of their father, one of whom died childless, leaving the deceased brother without an heir. Some scholars, although the text does not specifically say it, believe that the sexual cohabitation occurred only until the sister-in-law's pregnancy (cf. Genesis 38:26).

8. Child sacrifice specifically to "Molech" is also found in 2 Kings 23:10 and Jeremiah 32:35; child sacrifice as an Israelite apostasy often occurred (e.g., 2 Kings 17:17; Jeremiah 7:31). David P. Wright, "Molech," *Harper's Bible Dictionary*, ed. Paul Achtemeier (San Francisco: Harpercollins, 1985), 646.

9. Verses 20, 21 have the same Hebrew word *zera* (literally "seed"), which is translated "lie sexually with" ("lieth carnally with," kjv) in verse 20 and "children"

in verse 21. Mark Rooker, *Leviticus*, New American Commentary (Nashville: B&H, 2000), 245.

10. For a brief overview, see Guy Greenfield, "Homosexuality," *Holman Bible Dictionary*, ed. Trent C. Butler (Nashville: Holman Bible Publishers, 1991), 663, 664.

11. J. W. Meiklejohn, "Barrenness," *New Bible Dictionary*, ed. J. D. Douglas (Grand Rapids, MI: Eerdmans, 1962), 134.

12. The perennial problem of understanding the Apostle Paul's interpretation of the Law is addressed in Frank Thielman, *Paul and the Law: A Contextual Approach* (Downers Grove, IL: InterVarsity Press, 1994), 129, 208–10, 238–45.

## Chapter Sixteen: Daily Christian Living

1. Michael Green, *2 Peter and Jude*, Tyndale New Testament Commentaries, rev. ed. (Leicester, UK: Inter-Varsity Press/Grand Rapids, MI: Eerdmans, 1987), 79.

2. Samuel Balentine, *Leviticus*, Interpretation (Atlanta: John Knox, 2002), 161.

3. William Hendriksen, *Exposition of Ephesians*, New Testament Commentary (Grand Rapids, MI: Baker, 1967), 227, 228.

4. John E. Hartley, *Leviticus*, Word Biblical Commentary (Dallas: Word, 1992), 316.

5. An example is Abigail's advice to David not to retaliate against Nabal, leaving it to God (1 Samuel 25:23–35).

## Chapter Seventeen: Raising the "Holy" Bar

1. The word *chalal* occurs in 21:4, 6, 7, 9 (2x), 12, 14, 15, 23 and 22:2, 9, 15, 32.

2. D. F. O'Kennedy, "llj," *New International Dictionary of Old Testament Exegesis and Theology*, ed. W. Van Gemeren (Grand Rapids, MI: Zondervan, 1997), 2:145–50.

3. Robert Miller, "The Name of God," August 20, 2007, www.firstthings.com/onthesquare/?p=828.

4. Timothy George, *Is the Father of Jesus the God of Muhammad?* (Grand Rapids, MI: Zondervan, 2002), 129–31.

5. Also, no food from the tithe could be eaten in mourning (Deuteronomy 26:14), and physical contact with the dead required purification (Leviticus 11:31, 32; 21:1, 11; 22:4; Numbers 5:2; 19:11–22). For more on the cult of the dead, see K. A. Kitchen, "Burial and Mourning," *New Bible Dictionary*," ed. J. D. Douglas (Grand Rapids, MI: Eerdmans, 1962), 171, 172, and P. S. Johnston, "Burial and Mourning," *Dictionary of the Old Testament: Pentateuch*, eds. T. Alexander and D. Baker (Downers Grove, IL: InterVarsity Press, 2003), 104–106.

6. It was the same for the Nazirite who had taken a vow of separation unto the Lord (Numbers 6:6–12).

7. Leon Morris, *The First and Second Epistles to the Thessalonians*, New International Commentary on the New Testament (Grand Rapids, MI: Eerdmans, 1959), 137.

8. The Hebrew word is *mum*.

9. Thomas D. Lea, *1, 2 Timothy*, New American Commentary (Nashville: B&H, 1992), 158.

10. The only exception to the laity's prohibition was the fellowship offering, which involved a fellowship meal (Leviticus 3).

11. This instruction parallels the guilt offering, which required an offering plus a 20 percent added penalty (Leviticus 5:15; 6:5).

12. Verse 23 provides for an exception in the case of a freewill offering. This offering was given without obligation by the offerer purely from a joyful spirit.

13. The word is *tamim*; it is in the same word group that describes the "blameless" character of righteous Noah and Job (Genesis 6:9; Job 1:1).

14. Cf. Deuteronomy 14:21; 22:6, 7 also. Some believe such legislation is motivation for humanitarian regard for animals. Allen P. Ross, *Holiness to the Lord* (Grand Rapids, MI: Baker, 2002), 393 and others contend that these laws are a reaction to Canaanite worship practices—for example, Lloyd Bailey, *Leviticus–Numbers* (Macon, GA: Smyth & Helwys, 2005), 273.

## Chapter Eighteen: Holy Day or Holiday?

1. Numbers 28, 29 give the most extensive directions for honoring the holy days.

2. John W. Kleinig, *Leviticus*, Concordia Commentary (St. Louis: Concordia, 2003), 495.

3. The Hebrew words *ya'ad* ("to appoint"), *'edah* ("congregation"), and *mo'ed* ("appointed") are all in the same word group.

4. Kleinig, *Leviticus*, 487.

5. The alliteration of the Hebrew *shabbat shabbaton* exhibits the repetitious sound, producing an emphatic effect.

6. Kleinig, *Leviticus*, 334.

7. For other potential violations, see Exodus 16:23; 34:21; 35:3; Jeremiah 17:21–27; Amos 8:5; Nehemiah 13:15, 19–21. See John E. Hartley, *Leviticus*, Word Biblical Commentary (Dallas: Word, 1992), 375, 376.

8. These additional laws are believed by most to have been written down in the Jewish writings of the Mishnah and Talmud during the second to fifth centuries A.D.

9. F. F. Bruce, *The Epistle to the Hebrews*, New International Commentary in the New Testament (Grand Rapids, MI: Eerdmans, 1964), 77, 78.

10. See www.chickensoupforthesoul.com/newsroom.asp?cid=new.facts for this description.

11. Jacob Milgrom, *Leviticus*, Continental Commentary (Minneapolis: Augsburg, 2004), 275.

12. Allen P. Ross, *Recalling the Hope of Glory* (Grand Rapids, MI: Kregel, 2006), 415.

13. One of the earliest descriptions comes from a persecutor of the church, the Roman governor Pliny of Bithynia, who reported on the Christians to the Roman emperor Trajan in about 112. In his report he observed some of the worship practices of the Christians. They met before daylight for worship and took a binding oath by formal allegiance to Christ. Afterward they left and returned in the evening for a community meal, the *agape* feast. J. Stevenson, ed., *A New Eusebius* (London: SPCK, 1970, 5th repr.), 13–15.

14. Peter T. O'Brien, *Colossians, Philemon*, Word Biblical Commentary (Waco, TX: Word, 1992), 139.

15. Henry Ware Jr., "Lift Your Glad Voices in Triumph on High," in *Christian Disciple* (1817).

## Chapter Nineteen: Worship for All Seasons

1. These passages vary in the extent of the descriptions and in some of the details. See, for example, Exodus 23:14–17; 34:18–23; Numbers 28:16—29:40; Deuteronomy 16:1–16; and Ezekiel 45:21–25.

2. I am indebted to the discussion of the history of the feasts and their origin and development by John E. Hartley, *Leviticus*, Word Biblical Commentary (Dallas: Word, 1992), 376–83.

3. The Passover observance changed from a home celebration to a pilgrim celebration as long as the temple remained until its destruction in A.D. 70 (e.g., 2 Chronicles 30:1; Luke 2:41), at which time it reverted to family observance, as is the case today with the Jewish Passover Seder.

4. The day for beginning the count of fifty days is disputed in Jewish tradition. For the main proposals, see Hartley, *Leviticus*, 385, 386.

5. Also see Leviticus 19:9, 10; Deuteronomy 15:7–11; Ruth 2; and Jeremiah 49:9.

6. In later Judaism the feast was related to the revelation at Sinai, which also occurred in the third month (Exodus 19:1).

7. Paul mentions his attendance at this pilgrim feast in Acts 20:16; 1 Corinthians 16:8.

8. In later Jewish tradition the day was called Rosh Hashanah (lit., "head of the year," i.e., "New Year's Day").

9. Agreeing with the rabbinic teaching, Jacob Milgrom contends that the three convocations in the seventh month were focused on calling God to send the fall rains necessary for the ensuing agricultural year (*Leviticus*, Continental Commentary [Minneapolis: Augsburg, 2004], 280, 281).

10. James M. Black, "When the Roll Is Called Up Yonder," 1893.

11. It is considered the most important day in the Jewish liturgical year today.

12. Colorful pictures of booths (*Sukkoth*) can be seen in S. Riskin, "Huts or Tabernacles?" *The Jerusalem Post Christian Edition* (October 2007): 44, 45.

13. It is called the Feast of Ingathering in the book of Exodus (23:16; 34:22).

14. Jacob Milgrom, *Leviticus 23–27*, Anchor Bible (New York: Doubleday, 2000), 2043, 2044.

## Chapter Twenty: God's Sacred Presence

1. The Hebrew word for lampstand (or candelabra) is *menorah*, and that is the typical name used in Jewish literature today. The traditional Jewish *menorah* is a nine-branch lampstand that is lit for the commemoration of the Jewish holy days of Hanukkah.

2. Exodus 25:31–36 (and Numbers 8:1–4) describes the features of the lampstand. See the helpful explanation in Douglas Stuart, *Exodus*, New American Commentary (Nashville: B&H, 2007), 577–81.

3. Although the text (and Numbers 8:2, 3) has "Aaron" as the caretaker, Exodus 27:21 includes his sons. Aaron is named alone in our passage because he was the ultimate responsible agent of the tending of the lamps.

4. The Hebrew word *tamid* can be rendered "always, continually, perpetually" as in some English translations (e.g., KJV, NIV, NASB), but this does not mean the lamps remained afire during the day. Only the bronze altar possessed a constant fire (Leviticus 6:12, 13). The bread of the Presence was replaced "regularly" every Sabbath day (v. 8). See Jacob Milgrom, *Leviticus 23–27*, Anchor Bible (New York: Doubleday, 2000), 2088.

5. The Jewish source for this is the tractate *Sukkah* 5.2–4. See the discussion of this possible background to Jesus' words in C. K. Barrett, *The Gospel According to John* (London: SPCK, 1972 [reprint]), 277 and D. A. Carson, *The Gospel According to the Gospel of John* (Grand Rapids, MI: Eerdmans, 1991), 337, 338.

6. Stuart, *Exodus*, 574.

7. Carson, *The Gospel According to the Gospel of John*, 285, 286.

8. D. A. Carson, *Matthew, Chapters 1 Through 12*, Expositor's Bible Commentary (Grand Rapids, MI: Zondervan, 1995), 171, says of this verse, "The prayer is for our needs, not our greeds."

9. The Hebrew is *Yahweh* (pronounced *yah-way*), and the substitute is *Adonay* (pronounced *a-doh-nigh*), meaning "Lord." The traditional translation of the name *Yahweh* is "Lord." The meaning of the name *Yahweh* is uncertain but can be safely said to be related to the divine name revealed to Moses at Sinai, "I AM WHO I AM" (Exodus 3:14; cf. v. 15).

10. As an example of one's name standing for who he is, see, "They say, 'Come, let us wipe them out as a nation; let the name of Israel be remembered no more!'" (Psalm 83:4).

11. There are exceptions provided for in Biblical law, e.g., war (Deuteronomy 20) and accidental manslaughter (Numbers 35; Joshua 20).

12. H. Wälrisch and C. Brown, "Revile, Blaspheme, Slander," *New International Dictionary of New Testament Theology*, ed. C. Brown (Grand Rapids, MI: Zondervan, 1986), 3:343.

13. Carson, *Matthew, Chapters 1 Through 12*, 155.

## Chapter Twenty-One: Free at Last!

1. This figure of speech is personification, meaning that the inanimate land is conceived of as having the properties of a human being.

2. Also, not addressed in this discussion of the Sabbath year, liberation of Hebrew servants whose debts were canceled and who were released from slavery occurred in the Sabbath year (Exodus 21:2; Deuteronomy 15:1–18).

3. The Hebrew *shabbath shabbaton*, "a Sabbath of Sabbath observance," expresses a redundancy with the effect of emphasizing the idea of its importance.

4. John E. Hartley, *Leviticus*, Word Biblical Commentary (Dallas: Word, 1992), 433, 434 explains that the gathering of food could not be gathered for sale or storage but was available for the daily rations of the family.

5. Allen P. Ross, *Holiness to the LORD* (Grand Rapids, MI: Baker, 2002), 453.

6. The Hebrew term is *goel*, which refers to a relative who intervenes and delivers a relative who has fallen into poverty and/or debt slavery.

7. Gordon Wenham, *The Book of Leviticus*, New International Commentary on the Old Testament (Grand Rapids, MI: Eerdmans, 1979), 321.

8. Among the many passages that denounce the greedy, cf. Psalm 15:5; Proverbs 15:27; Nehemiah 5:7; 1 Corinthians 5:10; 6:10.

9. Among the many aid agencies is World Vision whose program of microenterprise development is explained at www.worldvision.org/worldvision/appeals.nsf/stable/med_home.

10. Some passages direct Israel to practice slavery in the context of war (e.g., Deuteronomy 20:10, 11).

11. For example, the prophet Amos condemned slave trade between nations (1:6) and the oppression of the poor by ruthless slave practices (2:6; 8:6).

12. In actuality there is little evidence that Israel regularly practiced the Sabbath year or Year of Jubilee; (cf. Leviticus 26:34, 35, 43; 2 Chronicles 36:21 with Jeremiah 25:11, 12; 29:10; Daniel 9:2; Zechariah 7:5); Nehemiah 10:31.

## Chapter Twenty-Two: Grace Has the Last Word

1. The Hebrew word is *yare'*, whose fundamental meaning is "to be afraid, to fear."

2. The closest parallel to the Biblical bilateral covenant is the Hittite Suzerain treaty from 1400–1200 B.C.

3. Allen P. Ross, *Holiness to the LORD* (Grand Rapids, MI: Baker, 2002), 471, 472.

4. "I Am Satisfied with Jesus." B. B. McKinney (1886–1952), Baptist hymnwriter and educator, penned this hymn in 1926.

5. There is the exception in 1 Corinthians 16:22 (*anathema*), which "delivers the offender to the punishment of God" in whatever way God determines appropriate. H. Aust and D. Müller say that even in this case the imprecation is designed to encourage the person to examine himself spiritually. See "Curse (*ajnayqema*)," *New International Dictionary of the New Testament Theology*, ed. C. Brown (Grand Rapids, MI: Zondervan, 1986), 1:414, 415. Gordon Fee, *The First Epistle to the Corinthians*, New International Commentary on the New Testament (Grand Rapids, MI: Eerdmans, 1987), however, contends that like the person in Galatians 1:8, 9 this is someone who opposes the gospel as preached by the Apostle Paul and thus places himself under the wrath of God.

6. E.g., 1 Corinthians 11:32. The word *paideuo* also means "to teach, educate, train" (e.g., Titus 2:12).

7. The word "curse" in this passage is the same word found in the Greek Septuagint for "curse" in Deuteronomy 27, 28, which lists the divine curses against disobedient Israel (*kataraomai*; cf. *kataras tekna*, "Accursed children!" which refers to the wicked, 2 Peter 2:14). W. Mundle, "Curse (*katara,somai*)," *New International Dictionary of the New Testament Theology*, ed. C. Brown (Grand Rapids, MI: Zondervan, 1986), 1:416.

8. The Hebrew verb is the passive voice, that is, "be humbled" (KJV) or "will be humbled" (NLT). The passive voice indicates that the subject is acted upon. For example, the active voice is "John throws the ball," whereas the passive voice is "The ball is thrown by John." Samuel Balentine, *Leviticus*, Interpretation (Louisville: John Knox Press, 2002), 201, 202 observes that the absence of animal sacrifice in this chapter affirms that animal sacrifice cannot be a substitute for authentic repentance.

Chapter Twenty-Three: Promises

1. Gordon Wenham, *Leviticus*, New International Commentary of the Old Testament (Grand Rapids, MI: Eerdmans, 1979), 338.

2. The Hebrew is a verbal form from the word group "(to be) holy" (*qadash*); "to consecrate" means to make holy what was ordinary.

3. The word "shekel" is the transliteration of the Hebrew word *shekel*, a weight or measure. The only Biblical definition is that it equaled twenty gerahs, also a transliteration (not a translation).

4. For this reason Deuteronomy 23:18 prohibits the monies derived from prostitution as redemption payments for vows.

5. W. H. Bellinger, *Leviticus, Numbers*, New International Biblical Commentary (Peabody, MA: Hendrickson, 2001), 33.

6. Leon Wood, "µr'j; (*ḥāram*) devoted thing, ban," *Theological Wordbook of the Old Testament*, eds. R. K. Harris, G. Archer, and B. W. Waltke (Chicago: Moody Publishers, 1980), 1:324, 325.

7. Jacob Milgrom, *Leviticus*, Continental Commentary (Minneapolis: Fortress, 2004), 332.

8. The bi-vocational pastor William Carey with some friends started the English Baptist Missionary Society that commissioned him in 1792 to bring the gospel to India.

9. Acts 1:8, for example, is the divine strategy that the Spirit implemented in the spread of the gospel. Cf. Ephesians 3:9.

10. Paul, for example, answered the charge that his change in plans was evidence of a carnal condition (2 Corinthians 1:17, 18).

11. Scot McKnight, "The Eight Marks of a Robust Gospel," *Christianity Today* 52/3 (March 2008), 39.

# Scripture Index

| | |
|---|---|
| 27:21 | 81 |
| 28, 29 | 270n1 |
| 28:14 | 101 |
| 29:1–6 | 209 |
| 29:7 | 266n1 |
| 29:35 | 262n3 |
| 30:5, 8, 12 | 259n8 |
| 35 | 178, 272n11 |
| 35:9–29 | 259n1 |
| 35:30 | 223 |
| 35:30–32 | 254 |

*Deuteronomy*

| | |
|---|---|
| 4:11 | 20 |
| 4:11, 12 | 19 |
| 5:15 | 198 |
| 5:16 | 222 |
| 5:24 | 90 |
| 6:3 | 167 |
| 7:1–4 | 234 |
| 7:7, 8 | 245 |
| 7:13 | 240 |
| 7:13, 14 | 164 |
| 7:26 | 110 |
| 9:5 | 229 |
| 10:8 | 93 |
| 10:16 | 121, 169, 245 |
| 10:17–19 | 180 |
| 11:26, 29 | 242 |
| 12:5 | 222 |
| 12:7, 12, 18 | 253 |
| 12:13–28 | 157, 268n19 |
| 12:15, 16, 20–24 | 259n7 |
| 12:23 | 74, 154 |
| 12:29–31 | 167 |
| 14:1, 2 | 263n4 |
| 14:5 | 157 |
| 14:5, 6 | 264n4 |
| 14:7, 8 | 264n5 |
| 14:21 | 157, 179, 270n14 |
| 14:22–29 | 254 |
| 15:1–18 | 272n2 |
| 15:4, 5, 11 | 177 |
| 15:7 | 232 |
| 16:13–15 | 212 |
| 16:16 | 204 |
| 17:2–5 | 152 |
| 17:8–13 | 102 |
| 18 | 166 |
| 18:9–22 | 243 |

| | |
|---|---|
| 18:10–12 | 40 |
| 18:15–22 | 222 |
| 19 | 178 |
| 19:17 | 261n1 |
| 20:10, 11 | 273n10 |
| 21:5 | 93, 261n1 |
| 22:1–4 | 62 |
| 22:6, 7 | 270n14 |
| 23:15, 16 | 233 |
| 23:18 | 274n4 |
| 24:1–4 | 233 |
| 25:5 | 98 |
| 25:5–10 | 268n7 |
| 25:9 | 266n10 |
| 26:1–11 | 38 |
| 26:12, 13 | 40 |
| 26:12–15 | 253 |
| 26:14 | 123, 263n4, 269n5 |
| 27 | 238 |
| 27, 28 | 273n7 |
| 27:15 | 243 |
| 28 | 165, 238, 242 |
| 28:1–14 | 93 |
| 28:11 | 240 |
| 28:16 | 243 |
| 29:18–22 | 153 |
| 30:1–10 | 245 |
| 30:1, 19 | 242 |
| 30:6 | 169 |
| 30:16 | 42, 245 |
| 32:4 | 28 |
| 32:5 | 188 |
| 32:14 | 259n7 |
| 32:16, 17 | 150 |
| 32:35 | 178, 224 |
| 34:10 | 22 |

*Joshua*

| | |
|---|---|
| 6:17 | 254 |
| 7:12, 13 | 254 |
| 8:29 | 114 |
| 8:34 | 242 |
| 19:51 | 228 |
| 20 | 272n11 |
| 21:44 | 200 |

*Judges*

| | |
|---|---|
| 3:5–7 | 161 |
| 6:21 | 263n11 |
| 13:20 | 263n12 |

# General Index

discharges/excretions, 133; female, 133–34
discipleship, cost of, 101, 255–56
disease, 128–29, 188; decisions of the priest
    concerning, 129–30; dermatological
    diseases, 129–31; diseases caused by
    abnormalities in clothing, 131; isolation
    of the diseased person, 130–31; leprosy
    (Hansen's disease), 129–30, 265–66n6;
    mercy of toward the sick, 135; purifica-
    tion ritual for houses, 132–33; purification
    ritual for skin diseases, 131–32
disobedience: curses for, 242–43; of God's
    commands, 59–61, 237; judgment against,
    98–100; of priests, 186
*Divine Design* (TV show), 67
Donne, John, 166

Eleazar, 103, 105
Esau, 49
Ezekiel, 110

Fawcett, John, 39
feasts. *See* convocations (the Lord's feasts)
Feigenbaum, John, 173
fellowship, 268n17; between God and his
    people, 97; spiritual, 120
fellowship offerings. *See* peace (fellowship)
    offerings
food and dietary laws, 107–9, 168; applica-
    tion of for contemporary Christians,
    112–13; basis of on the theology of God's
    holy character, 111; and the importance
    of holy nourishment, 109; as a means
    of distinguishing Israel from neighbor-
    ing nations, 108; as a means toward holy
    living, 113; persons or animals unfit
    for, 44, 74–75, 110, 113, 114, 131, 134,
    135, 263n6; tie of to the act of creation,
    108; why particular foods were chosen,
    111–12. *See also* food and dietary laws,
    specifics of
food and dietary laws, specifics of: carcasses
    forbidden for eating, 113–14; carcasses
    permitted for eating, 114; ground crea-
    tures, 110–11; land animals, 109; sea
    creatures, 109–10; sky creatures, 110;
    swarming ground creatures, 114
food offerings, 41, 67, 68, 69, 183, 188, 189,
    192, 258n22
forgiveness, 49–51, 168; and the shedding of
    blood, 49–50; through Jesus Christ, 60–61
freedom, from the bondage/slavery of sin and
    death, 225–26; and the gift of the land

of promise from God to Israel, 227; and
    God's merciful provision for the land of
    promise, 227–28; and the Sabbath rest,
    226–27, 228; and social liberation, 226;
    and spiritual liberation, 226; through gen-
    erosity for the poor and the slave, 231–35.
    *See also* Year of Jubilee
freewill offerings, 40, 71, 72–73, 104, 253,
    270n12

Gane, Roy, 108
George, Timothy, 184
"Get Me to the Church on Time" (Lerner and
    Loewe), 87
God, 45, 121, 140; benevolence of toward the
    poor, 251; completeness and perfection
    of, 188; concept of as asexual, 160–61;
    covenant relationship established by God
    with the Israelite slaves in Egypt, 18, 238;
    and creation (Creator God), 17, 111; dis-
    closure of to his people, 90; dishonoring
    of, 221–23; faithfulness of his promises,
    238, 247–48; generosity of, 248; grace
    of, 36, 53, 63, 66–67, 189, 198, 207,
    230, 232, 242; honoring of, 221; as the
    living God, 185; mercy of, 53; as the only
    true perfect One, 118; provision of the
    seasonal harvests by, 216; theophany of at
    Mount Sinai, 94; as the triune God, 184;
    wrath of, 130, 140–41, 153, 155, 165, 245,
    259–60n11, 273n5. *See also* God, gifts
    of; God, glory of; God, holiness of; God,
    message of to the people of Israel revealed
    to Moses; God, presence of
God, gifts of, 102–3; the gift of atonement,
    154; the gift of the Holy Spirit, 168, 173,
    212, 241; the gift of human life, 154; the
    gift of Jesus (the "Gift of gifts"), 154–55
God, glory of, 87, 90, 262n6; the glory of
    God's light at creation, 218; revelation
    of the "glory of the Lord," 18–19, 22–23,
    94, 95
God, holiness of, 127–28; the two senses of,
    172–73
God, message of to the people of Israel
    revealed to Moses, 17–21; message of
    from Mount Sinai, 19; message of from
    the tent, 19–21; Moses as the mediator of
    God's message, 21–22
God, presence of, 215–16, 263n10; as our
    light represented in the lampstand in
    the Holy Place of the Tent of Meeting,
    216–18; as our honored judge, 221–24;

# Index of Sermon Illustrations